D1285478

THE AUTHOR

FRANK S. MEAD is a recognized authority and an incisive and stimulating commentator on the contemporary church scene. Editor of *The Christian Herald* from 1942 to 1948, Dr. Mead has also served as consulting editor to a number of large religious publishing houses and institutions. For seven years he was a minister of the Newark Conference of The Methodist Church, holding pastorates in Newark and Kearny, New Jersey, and later he became editor of the *Homiletic Review*.

Dr. Mead's academic degrees include: B.A., University of Denver; B.D., Union Theological Seminary; Litt.D., Dickinson College. He is a member of Phi Beta Kappa.

In addition to his many articles in such magazines as *Christian Century, Christian Herald, The Reader's Digest, American Mercury*, and numerous other periodicals, Dr. Mead is author or editor of ten books.

Handbook of Denominations

IN THE UNITED STATES

Handbook of Denominations

IN THE UNITED STATES

Frank S. Mead

New York

Nashville

ABINGDON-COKESBURY PRESS

HANDBOOK OF DENOMINATIONS
in the United States

COPYRIGHT MCMLI
BY PIERCE AND SMITH

B

SET UP, PRINTED, AND BOUND BY THE
PARTHENON PRESS, AT NASHVILLE,
TENNESSEE, UNITED STATES OF AMERICA

To

THOSE IN THE CHURCH WHO SEE that the great truths we hold on common ground are of more importance to God and man than the little fences and barriers which divide us

This Book is dedicated

ACKNOWLEDGMENTS

$\mathcal{M}$any people, many books contribute to the building of such a book as this; to them I would immediately admit my debt. The account of each religious body represented in these pages has been prepared from the latest and most authentic data available, from historical records, statistical reports and the official statements of innumerable boards, commissions, and committees supplied quickly and gratis by innumerable and most co-operative denominational officials; without them the work would have been useless. Most sections of the book were read, corrected, and often amended by authorities within the churches; the critics, both friendly and furious, have had their say and, usually, their way, and out of it has come, I trust, a book both accurate and fair. To the critics—my unspeakable gratitude.

Hundreds of books have been consulted; it would be impossible to list a complete bibliography. I am most appreciative of the information made available in the report on the religious bodies of the nation in 1936, by the Bureau of Census of the U.S. Department of Commerce, especially in historical and doctrinal backgrounds. A dozen encyclopedias have been a very present help in time of need. In the field of American cults, minority religious movements, and the smaller sects, *The Small Sects in America*, by Elmer T. Clark (Abingdon-Cokesbury Press, 1949), and *These Also Believe*, by Charles S. Braden (The Macmillan Company, 1949), have been invaluable. Other important volumes include *How We Got Our Denominations*, by Stanley I. Stuber (Association Press, 1948); *Yearbook of American Churches* (Federal Council of the Churches of Christ in America, 1949); *The New Handbook of All Denominations*, by M. Phelan (Cokesbury Press, 1933); *The Story of Religions in America*, by William Warren Sweet (Harper & Bros., 1930); *Religion in America*, by Willard L. Sperry (The Macmillan Company, 1946); *Protestantism, a Symposium*, edited by William K. Anderson (Commission on Courses of Study, The Methodist Church, 1944); *The March of Faith*, by Winfred Ernest Garrison (Harper & Bros., 1933); *Primer for Protestants*, by James Hastings Nichols (Association Press, 1947), and *The American Churches*, by William Warren Sweet (Abingdon-Cokesbury Press, 1948).

Perhaps the reader should be warned: I have endeavored to produce, not a popular "digest," not a book of opinion, criticism, or value judgments, but a reference volume interested only in the factual truth and development of the religious bodies of the United States. If any body of importance has been slighted or omitted, if any aide or critic remains unmentioned or unsung, I offer my apologies. The book will be revised at intervals, probably biennially; in future issues I shall find opportunity to prove further that I write "with malice toward none," but in justice to all.

FRANK S. MEAD

CONTENTS

9

CONTENTS

CONTENTS

ADVENTISTS

$\mathcal{A}$dventism, generally, is a Chrisitan faith based upon the conviction that the world is evil and that it will be destroyed by way of divine intervention; the wicked are to perish in this cataclysm, but the righteous are to be saved. The heart of the doctrine is the belief that Jesus Christ will have his second advent at the time of the cataclysm or judgment, returning to reign in triumph through the thousand-year period, or millennium, mentioned in Revelation 20: 1-6. The whole Adventist structure rests heavily upon the prophetic and apocalyptic texts of Daniel and Revelation.

As a religious movement it began with an "awakening" on the advent question which developed spontaneously here and abroad in the early years of the nineteenth century. It became strongest and most clearly defined in the United States under the leadership of William Miller (1782-1849), a farmer of Low Hampton, New York, a veteran of the War of 1812 and a man respected as a diligent reader and a good student even though he had only a grade-school education. The movement under Miller was at first an interchurch movement with many Methodists, Christians, Baptists, and Congregationalists among its followers. It was a movement within existing churches, and in the days of its beginnings there was no intention or attempt to organize a separate denomination.

So influential was William Miller that for years his followers were known as Millerites. Miller himself became a Baptist in 1816; he began at once a careful study of the Scriptures, concentrating on the prophecies of Daniel and Revelation. Using only the Bible, its marginal references, and Cruden's *Concordance* as his sources, he came to the conclusion that the "day" of biblical prophecy really meant a year; he also concluded that the 2,300 days of Daniel 8:14 started concurrently with the 70 weeks of years of Daniel 9, or from 457 B.C., the year in which Ezra came to Jerusalem; these two periods would end coincidentally in or near the year 1843. Miller thought that the sanctuary mentioned in Daniel 8:14 was actually the earth, which would be cleansed by fire at the time of the Second Advent. He predicted specifically that all this would happen sometime between March 21, 1843, and March 21, 1844.

When the great event failed to materialize by the spring of 1844, many left the movement; Miller's associates set a second date, October 22, 1844, confident that "the day of the Lord is near, even at the door." By 1844 there were more than fifty thousand Adventists in this country; hundreds of them, perhaps even thousands, disposed of their property as the date approached, gave away their goods, settled all their accounts, and waited prayerfully for the fateful day to come. It came, and passed, with no Second Coming; now vast numbers lost all interest in Adventism and went back to their former churches. But there were enough left of the main group to form a loose Adventist organization at a conference in Albany in 1845. This group held generally to Miller's position and theology, emphasizing the personal and premillennial character of the second advent of Christ, the resurrection of the dead—the faithful to be raised at Christ's coming, the rest a thousand years later—and the renewal of the earth as the abode of the redeemed. Known at first as the American Millerite Association, a por-

15

tion of them later became known as the Evangelical Adventists, a church which has dwindled with the passing of the years to the point of almost complete obscurity. Another and larger group became the Advent Christian Church, in 1861.

Considering the nature of their doctrine and the opportunity for such wide divergence in the interpretation of the apocalyptic passages of the Bible upon which their conclusions are based, it was inevitable that the Adventists should divide into different groups maintaining different positions. Basically all Adventists were and still are agreed that the second advent of Christ will be premillennial—that is, that his return will *precede* the thousand-year period foretold in Revelation 20. Only the Life and Advent Union among present-day Adventist bodies is postmillennial. Beyond this their congregations were soon plagued with speculation and dissension on other questions. Just what is the state of the dead—conscious or unconscious—as they await the resurrection? Who are to arise—the righteous *and* the wicked, or only the righteous? Is there to be eternal punishment for the wicked or annihilation? What is the nature of immortality? Does the cleansing of the sanctuary of Daniel 8 refer to a sanctuary in heaven or on earth? When should the Sabbath be celebrated—on the first day or on the seventh, on Sunday or Saturday? Over these questions the Adventists have divided into the six separate groups in which we find them today.

Seventh-Day Adventists

Now THE largest single Adventist church in point of numbers in the United States, the Seventh-Day Adventists trace their beginnings back to the year 1844; they trace their ideas on the Sabbath back to a connection with the Seventh-Day Baptists of New England.

Their first real point of disagreement with other Adventist bodies, however, was not over the seventh day but over the question of the sanctuary in Daniel 8 and over the interpretation of that passage. A small group of Adventists in New England became convinced that this sanctuary was in heaven and not on earth, and that there would be a "work of investigative judgment" in this heavenly sanctuary immediately preceding the Second Advent. Other Adventists of the period held that the sanctuary was on earth.

Coupled with this dispute came another, concerning the date of the Second Advent. The Seventh-Day group claimed that the historical and prophetic evidence pointing to October 22, 1844, was correct, and that the error lay in a mistaken interpretation of Daniel 8:13-14 which placed the sanctuary and the judgment in the wrong place and at the wrong time. The group holding these dissenting views also advocated the observance of the seventh day.

As early as 1844 a small group of Adventists near Washington, New Hampshire, had begun celebrating the Sabbath on the seventh day. A pamphlet written by Joseph Bates in 1846 gave the question wide circulation and attention. Shortly after this Bates, together with James White, Ellen Harmon (later Mrs. James White), Hiram Edson, Frederick Wheeler, and S. W. Rhodes, set out definitely, with the aid of regular publications, to champion the seventh day. The growth of the group around these people was slow at first, owing to the general derision in which Adventists were held and to their economic and social handicaps, but by 1855 they were prosperous enough and numerically strong enough to set up headquarters near Battle Creek, Michigan, with a publishing house called the Review and Herald Publishing Association. In 1860 they officially adopted the name Seventh-Day Adventists; in 1903 they moved their headquarters to its present location in Washington, D.C.

Doctrinally the Seventh-Day Adventists are ultraconservative. Their standard statement of belief, appearing annually in their *Year Book*, reveals that they take the Bible as their rule of faith and practice; they believe in God as revealed in the Father, the Son, and the Holy Spirit, each equally and uniquely divine, personal, and eternal; they believe in creation by fiat of God, and in the fall of man. Man is not by nature immortal, but only mortal; he is saved solely by grace and redeemed only through the substitutionary death of Jesus Christ. They hold the Ten Commandments to be the standard of righteousness for men of all ages, and they base their observance of the seventh day as the Sabbath on the Fourth Commandment—"Six days shalt thou labour, . . . but the seventh day is the sabbath of the Lord thy God." They tithe their incomes; the support of the ministry in this church is entirely by the tithing system. Beyond the tithe they give toward current expenses and other church enterprises in unusually generous freewill offerings.

They believe in the gift of prophecy in the church, that the dead are awaiting the resurrection in an unconscious state, that the body will be resurrected in the last day with immortality for the righteous and extinction by fire for the wicked. They stand stanchly for religious liberty for all men and for the complete separation of church and state. They consider the body of man to be the temple of the Holy Spirit, and in consequence of that they rigidly abstain from the use of alcoholic beverages and tobacco. They believe in the premillennial personal, visible return of Christ "at a time unknown but close at hand," and in a new earth to be created out of the ruins of the old as the final abode of the redeemed. They practice immersion as the only true form of baptism, and they also practice foot washing.

The over-all administrative body of the church is the executive committee of the general conference, which is chosen by delegates from the various church groups in the quadrennial sessions of the General Conference of Seventh-Day Adventists. Working under this general conference are three lesser governmental units: the division organizations, administering affairs in different continents; union conferences and union missions, making up the divisional organizations; and local conferences and missions, the smallest executive units. Each unit has a large amount of autonomy; local congregations elect lay elders, deacons, and other officers; the local conference office supervises all pastoral and evangelistic work and relations and pays all pastors and other workers from a central fund. This is a highly representative form of government.

Evangelism, publishing, and health work are outstanding and highly successful among Seventh-Day Adventists. Regarding themselves not as just another church but as a movement established in fulfillment of Bible prophecy to prepare men for the Second Advent, and to restore the neglected truths of the Reformation and of the Apostolic Church, they conduct comprehensive evangelistic preaching in over 600 languages and dialects. They have established a total of 51 publishing houses all over the world, with four in the United States; literature is printed in 188 languages and dialects. In North America they have three junior colleges, nine liberal-arts colleges, and two graduate schools—a medical school and a theological seminary. In the United States and abroad they support 162 medical units, 290 colleges and secondary schools, and 3,341 elementary schools.

As they practice only adult immersion, there are no infants or children included in the Seventh-Day membership; that membership is also strictly limited to those who are faithful in abstaining from the use of liquor and tobacco, dancing, the theater, and card playing. There are 229,945 Seventh-Day Adventists in the United States, in 2,671 churches.

Advent Christian Church

DISAPPOINTMENT and confusion reigned in Adventist circles when the Second Advent failed to materialize in 1844 as prophesied; a number of them, led by Jonathan Cummings in New England, remained loyal to the main body but challenged it on the question of the heavenly sanctuary, the state of the dead, and the date of the Second Advent. This group held that William Miller and his associates had made an error of ten years in the date; it would come, they said, either in the autumn of 1853 or the spring of 1854. When they began the publication of a paper called the *World's Crisis* to publicize that opinion, a real split occurred.

The year 1854 passed with no Second Advent, and it was hoped that the rift might be healed; the old dispute over the state of the dead, however, prevented any reunion. The Cummings group held that man is by nature wholly mortal and unconscious in death, that mortality is not inherent in mankind but the gift of God. The older Adventists advocated a different doctrine, namely, that the dead are in a conscious state and that the wicked are doomed to suffer eternally. The gulf was too great to be bridged, and in 1861 Cummings and his followers organized the Advent Christian Association, later known as the Advent Christian Church.

This church believes that the Second Coming is imminent, but that it is not within the province of man to predict "the day nor the hour wherein the Son of man cometh." The dead, righteous and unrighteous alike, are unconscious, awaiting the resurrection at Christ's second coming, at which time the righteous will be raised to live forever and the unrighteous will be annihilated. The church has two sacraments, baptism by immersion and the Lord's Supper.

Congregational in government, each local church is completely independent. The churches are grouped in five districts and five annual conferences; over them is a national general conference, which meets biennially. There are three publishing houses, in Boston, Massachu-

setts, Oakland, California, and Live Oak, Florida; there are one college and one theological seminary, two homes for the aged, and one orphanage. Foreign missionary work is carried on in India, China, and Japan. There are 31,431 members and 470 churches.

Primitive Advent Christian Church

THIS is one of the smaller Adventist bodies, listing only 416 members in 15 churches, most of them in rural West Virginia. The sect is decreasing rapidly, and no statements on history, work, doctrine, or organization are available.

Church of God (Abrahamic Faith)

DIFFERING from other Adventist groups in their refusal to accept the prophecies or guidance of Mrs. Ellen Harmon White, members believe the name of their church to be divinely inspired, have no creed other than the Scriptures, and do not advocate observance of the seventh day. Doctrinally they stress the Second Advent and the establishment of Christ's kingdom on earth; they teach that man is mortal and will sleep in death until the resurrection and judgment, that the wicked will be destroyed and the righteous raised to live forever on earth.

Their first congregations were organized in the early 1800's; their present general conference was established in 1921. At the present they have about four thousand affiliated members and seventy-eight churches. General conference officers are incorporated under the name the National Bible Institution, through which they operate the Oregon Bible College, the Golden Rule Home, printing and publishing plants and departments, and missionary and evangelistic work.

Church of God (Oregon, Illinois)

THIS CHURCH grew out of the merger of a number of small independent Adventist bodies in the late years of the last century. Called at first the Churches of God in Christ Jesus, they later organized under their present name. The merging bodies, joined at Philadelphia in 1888, were the Church of the Blessed Hope, Brethren of the Abrahamic Faith, Restitutionists, Restitution Church, the Church to Come, and Age to Come Adventists.

Observing Sunday and accepting most of the Adventist doctrine, they differ in their idea of the Second Advent, teaching that Christ will return to set up his messianic-kingdom capital at Jerusalem and from there extend his rule over all peoples. The ancient favor of God will be restored to the Jews, they will again become the chosen people. The saints are to have special positions of honor, while the wicked suffer a second death.

Churches are grouped into state and district conferences; local churches are independent units, some having pastors and some working under elders or presidents. There is no formal ordination for ministers; those serving in a ministerial capacity are trained in a Bible training school located at Oregon, Illinois. There are also a publishing house, a home for the aged, and denominational headquarters at Oregon. There are 5,295 members in 79 churches.

Life and Advent Union

JOHN T. WALSH, as Adventist preacher and editor, created a sensation in 1848 with his preaching that there is no hope and no resurrection for the wicked. A group of Adventists sharing his views organized the Life and Advent Union at Wilbraham, Massachusetts, in 1863.

They are strictly Adventist in doctrine, but different in their thinking on the resurrection and the millennium. Indeed, they say that there is no such thing as a millennium; this is pure fable. Rather there are only the thousand years mentioned in Revelation 20:2, and these thousand years lie not in the future but in the past. Peace and happiness await the Second Coming, when the righteous will be lifted up to live forever on a purified earth, and the dead will go on sleeping, having no resurrection. Omens of the return are all about us in our loss of faith in an inspired Bible, in the unrest and confusion of the modern world. They refuse, however, to say when Christ will come. He is still, as he was to William Miller, "near, even at the doors."

The church has two annual summer camp meetings, in Maine and Connecticut. Home missions work is limited to Maine and North Carolina, foreign missions to the province of Anhwei, China. There are only 4 churches and 207 members.

African Orthodox Church

BELIEVING that Negro Episcopalians should have churches of their own, a Protestant Episcopal rector, the Rev. George Alexander McGuire, withdrew from that church in 1919 to establish independent Negro churches in the United States, Cuba, and Canada. He called them Independent Episcopal churches, but in 1921 the first general synod of the new body changed the name to the African Orthodox Church and elected McGuire as its first bishop. He was consecrated by Archbishop Vilatte, who took his episcopal orders from the West Syrian Church of Antioch; this put McGuire in the traditional apostolic succession, which he valued highly.

The church still lays strong emphasis upon the apostolic succession and upon the historic sacraments and rituals. It has the original seven sacraments of the Roman Catholic Church; in its worship we find a blending of Western and Eastern liturgy, creeds, and symbols. The liturgy is usually Western, a mingling of Anglican, Greek, and Roman patterns; three creeds—Apostles', Nicene, and Athanasian—are used.

The denomination maintains the adamant position of the Protestant Episcopal Church on marriage; no priest may remarry the guilty party to a divorce, and innocent parties are remarried only after special permission by a bishop. The government is of course episcopal; bishops are in charge of dioceses or jurisdictions, and groups of dioceses form a province, each led by an archbishop and a primate, who in turn presides over the provincial synod. At the head stands the patriarch, McGuire, who is general overseer of all the work of the church, which now extends over the United States, Canada, Latin America, and the Union of South Africa. Membership, as in the Roman Catholic Church, is counted not by communicants but by the number of persons baptized; in the United States there are 32 churches and 5,200 members.

African Orthodox Church of New York

A BRANCH of the African Orthodox Church, this church was organized by a Bishop Barrow, who was consecrated by McGuire. Barrow in his turn consecrated George S. A. Brooks, who established the Afro-American Catholic Church. Later Brooks took control of the African Orthodox Church of New York, which currently reports three churches and seven hundred members, all living in Brooklyn.

Amana Society

OFFICIALLY named the Amana (Faithfulness) Church Society but more popularly known as the Amana Society, this group stems from the Pietistic movement in eighteenth-century Germany. In 1714 a small company under the leadership of Johann Rock and Ludwig Gruber stirred the Germans with their preaching that the days of true and direct inspiration from God had not ended. Both these leaders were said to have the "gift of inspiration." Under persecution from the German government they came to America in 1842, settling near Buffalo, New York. There were eight hundred of them, organized then under the name Ebenezer Society.

Life was completely communistic in these first American settlements; each village had a common school, meetinghouse, and store. Local government was in the hands of a group of elected elders. They moved in 1855 to Iowa, where the villages of Amana, East, Middle, High, West, and South Amana, and Homestead were established. Here they became incorporated under their present name.

These Iowa villages still form an outstanding experiment in communal living; many of their early communistic practices have been abandoned, but there are still community efforts in farming, manufacture, and trade. They might properly be called co-operative rather than communistic.

Those in the society pool their property, accept no wages, receive board and housing and medical service and old age pensions. Marriage is permitted, but it involves temporary loss of standing. Amana members will not bear arms, and they refuse to take oaths. Any member may resign at will, in which case his property is restored. Men and women dress generally in the garb of the German peasant, but the younger generation is departing from this tradition. Amusements, formerly frowned upon, are now tolerated more generally.

The purpose of the society is purely religious; it is based upon "the salvation of souls, the service of God." They believe that "God can now as well as of old inspire men," but none seem to have been inspired in the old historic sense since the death of two early American leaders, Christian Metz and Barbara Heinemann. They accept the teachings of a holy universal church, the remission of sins and the communion of the saints, the resurrection of the body, the punishment of the wicked, and the life everlasting. There is no ordained ministry; services consist of prayer, testimony, and readings from the writings of Metz and Heinemann.

They acknowledge no baptism with water but only baptism "by fire and the Spirit." Members are confirmed and admitted at fifteen. All children from five to fourteen are required to attend society schools. Membership, which is declining, was reported at 794 for 1949; there are 7 congregations.

American Ethical Union
(Societies for Ethical Culture)

THE Ethical Movement in the United States is held by many critics to be only what its name implies: an ethical, humanistic organization. It does, however, build its thought and program not only upon moral philosophy but upon the ethical traditions of the great religions of mankind as well. Broadly speaking, it has no formal creed or religious doctrine; the purpose of "ethical culture" is "to make men more aware of the intrinsic worth of human personality, of the uniqueness of every human being, of the interpenetration of one life with another, and of the possibilities of creative relationships among men." Stress is laid upon the development of conscience and a sense of responsibility as great creative forces among men. They seek actually a deepening of the spiritual life, and out of that spiritual life a practical expression in moral and social improvement.

There are seven active ethical culture societies affiliated in the Ethical Culture Union, located in New York (the first founded by Felix Adler in 1876), Chicago, Philadelphia, Los Angeles, South Orange, New Jersey, St. Louis, Washington, Brooklyn, and Westchester, New York—note that this is almost exclusively an urban movement and membership. Abroad there are active societies in England; there were others in Europe prior to World War II, which were banned by the Nazis and which have not yet been reorganized. An International Ethical Union was created in 1896, but because of the war and of postwar conditions it is not functioning at the present time.

Meetings of the societies feature inspirational music, readings, and addresses. There are no ministers in the usual sense. There are instead salaried leaders who serve as counselors, officiate at weddings and funerals, name children, and perform in general the functions of ministers. There are Sunday schools, young people's groups, and study groups; perhaps the most effective work is found in educational, philanthropic, and social efforts and projects. The New York society must be given credit for the start of settlement work in this country; at the present time the societies in New York, Chicago, and Philadelphia sponsor very effective settlement-house programs. Free kindergartens, visiting nurses, the Child Study Movement, the abolition of child labor, model tenements, and the inauguration of free public legal aid societies constitute ethical culture drives.

Within the movement outstanding schools have been developed at Central Park and Riverdale in New York City and at the Brooklyn Ethical Culture School; these are models in their fields, setting high standards in progressive education. The schools are popular with many not identified with the movement, and who many never become enrolled in it; no serious effort is made to proselytize among the children or their parents. There are approximately 3,500 members.

American Rescue Workers

THE American Rescue Workers originated with a dispute between Thomas E. Moore, leader of the Salvation Army in the United States, and the British founder of that Army, General William E. Booth. Moore, sent here to take charge of all Salvation Army work in 1880, felt that all money raised in the United States should be spent here; Booth, taking a more international view, demanded that part of it be sent to England. Moore withdrew in 1882 to start a separate group called at first the Salvation Army of America, then in 1913 the American Rescue Workers.

Doctrine and organization parallel that of the Salvation Army; this is a mission rescue group with a strong evangelical emphasis and preaching, and a program of practical assistance to the needy and unfortunate, to augment the preaching effort. About the only difference between the American Rescue Workers and the Salvation Army is that the former has the status of a regular Christian church, practicing the two sacraments of baptism and communion. Members join on confession of faith, which is followed by baptism. A board of directors, most of them laymen, directs the work and constitutes a general council, which also includes the Commander, staff and field officers, and corps representatives. As of 1943, the last year for which statistics are available, the group reported a budget of $165,994.52, a membership of approximately eight hundred, and twenty-seven mission homes, and service stations in twenty-two cities.

Apostolic Overcoming Holy Church of God

THE Rev. W. T. Phillips, a Negro preacher in the Methodist Episcopal Church, withdrew from that denomination in 1916 to join the Apostolic Faith Mission. Failing to find there the faith and liberty he sought, he led a large group out of the mission membership to organize the Ethiopian Overcoming Holy Church of God. The word "Ethiopian" was later changed to "Apostolic."

Found mostly in Kentucky, Texas, Oklahoma, and Illinois, this church is dominated by Bishop Phillips, who is also pastor of the largest church (Mobile, Alabama) in the group. The ministers are supported by the tithe payments of the membership; the clergy are likewise required to tithe. Worship includes foot washing and divine healing; services generally are very free, emotional affairs bordering on the bizarre, with the followers speaking in tongues and engaged in ecstatic dances.

It is claimed in this church that "even from the days of Enos" Christianity was in existence in Abyssinia. Marriage with unsaved men or women, the use of snuff, foolish talking, jesting, and the use of slang are strictly forbidden. Statistics are difficult to obtain; the last were for the year 1942, reporting two hundred churches; membership estimates vary from eight hundred to eight thousand.

Armenian Orthodox Church in America

ARMENIA claims to be the first Christian nation; the apostles Thaddeus and Bartholomew—sometimes held to be the same person—were there during the time of Paul, and Christianity was adopted as the state faith in A.D. 301. Gregory the Enlightener, preaching in Armenia during that century, became the first bishop of an apostolic succession of Catholicos, or supreme patriarchs.

The story of the Christian Church in Armenia has been written in blood; it suffered both in the inevitable conflict between the Byzantine Empire and Persia, and in numerous persecutions by the Turks. Thousands fled to America just before and after the First World War to escape the bloodshed, and formed themselves into what came to be known as the Armenian Orthodox Church in America. It cannot be called an Eastern Orthodox body, in as much as it rejects the doctrine of the two natures of Christ and the decisions of the early councils of the church. Headquarters for this church are in a monastery at the foot of Mount Ararat, but an American hierarchy of archbishops, priests, and deacons directs the work in the United States. Diocesan organization is under the direction of the Holy See of Etchmiadzin, Armenia, U.S.S.R.

Doctrine is based on the historic writings and declarations of the early church fathers; the saints and the Virgin Mary are venerated, but the Immaculate Conception is denied. A translation of the Scriptures by Sahak and Merob and other fathers of the Armenian Church is accepted as the only authoritative version of the Bible. There are seven sacraments: baptism, by immersion, eight days after birth; confirmation, immediately following baptism; Holy Communion, even for infants; penance; marriage; ordination; and prayers for the sick.

Government of the church affords something of a contradiction in terms; it is democratic in that all candidates for holy orders are elected by the people, and hierarchal in that all ministers must be ordained by bishops in the apostolic succession. Every province or diocese throughout the world has a constitution adapted to its peculiar needs, but which must be approved by the Catholicos. The principal services are the Holy Sacrifice, or Liturgy, on Sunday, and various feast-day services held during the week. The Bible is read in public at these services, in Armenian; language schools, Sunday schools, and a number of libraries help to keep the classic native tongue alive. There are, as of 1947, 18,787 members in the United States, out of between 150,-000 and 200,000 Armenians resident here.

Assemblies of God, General Council

THE LARGEST of the Pentecostal bodies, with 275,000 members and 5,950 churches, the Assemblies of God, General Council, is actually a combination of Pentecostal churches and assemblies accomplished at Hot Springs, Arkansas, in 1914. The founders were former ministers and pastors of evangelical persuasion who wished to unite into one body in the interests of a more effective preaching and an enlarged missionary crusade.

Ardently fundamentalist, its theology is Arminian; there is strong belief in the infallibility and inspiration of the Bible, the fall and redemption of man, baptism in the Holy Ghost and the gift of tongues, a life of holiness and separation from the world, divine healing, the second advent of Jesus, eternal punishment for the wicked and eternal bliss for the believers. Members stand officially opposed to war, but large numbers of their youth accepted noncombatant and even combatant service in World War II. They are especially insistent upon the teaching of the gift of tongues following Spirit baptism; no minister doubting that gift could hold credentials in this group.

The government of the Assembly is an unusual mixture of Presbyterian and Congregational systems. Local churches are left quite independent in polity and in the conduct of local affairs. District officers have a pastoral ministry to all the churches and are responsible for the promotion of home missions. Work is divided into forty districts in the United States, most of which follow state lines, each with a district Presbytery, which examines, licenses, and ordains pastors. In addition to these there are several foreign-language branches: German, Polish, Ukrainian, Latin American, and so on. All the ministers together constitute a general council, which in turn elects all general officers, sets the doctrinal standards, and provides for church expansion and development. Missionary work is under the care of a central missionary committee; there are more than six hundred foreign missionaries currently under appointment, and the missionary budget of the denomination runs close to two million dollars per year—unusually high among Protestant denominations.

Assyrian Jacobite Apostolic Church

FLEEING the persecutions of the Moslem Turks, large numbers of Syrians came to the United States in 1893 and during the years immediately following. They were Christians belonging to the Assyrian Roman Catholic Church, the Assyrian Protestant Church, the Assyrian Nestorian or Chaldean Church, and the Assyrian Jacobite Apostolic Church.

In 1907 one of these Assyrian groups raised the necessary funds to send Deacon Hanna Koorie, of Paterson, New Jersey, to Jerusalem for ordination as priest and bishop. He returned to supervise the establishment of the Assyrian Jacobite Apostolic Churches in Massachusetts, Rhode Island, New Jersey, and Michigan.

This church differs in liturgy from the Eastern Orthodox churches, but doctrine is based upon the Nicene Creed. It has seven sacraments: baptism, confimation, the Eucharist, penance, extreme unction, orders, and matrimony. Baptism is administered by pouring or immersion, and in the course of the baptismal ceremony, which comes several days after the birth of the child, the priest breathes upon the water and the child. The bread and wine at Holy Communion are considered to be the actual blood and body of Christ. The Virgin Mary is venerated, as are the saints of the church.

Fourteen hundred members were reported in 1946, and four local churches. The Assyrian Jacobite Patriarch of Antioch stands at the head of the church government; he resides at Homs, Syria, and his word is final on all church matters. Under him serve the metropolitan or mifrian, numerous iskiffs and mitrans, bishops, rhahibs, priests, and deacons. Every officer is elected to his office by vote of the people, which gives the body a democratic flavor under a hierarchal administration.

Bahá'is

THE SECT called Bahá'i aims at the universal brotherhood of man, the unity of all religions, and peace for the whole world. Its leader Bahá'u'lláh said, "The religion of God is for the sake of love and union; make it not the cause of enmity and conflict." To him the one universal spirit which is God spoke alike in Zoroaster, Mohammed, Buddha, Moses, and Jesus; their messages combined and revealed themselves in Bahá'u'lláh.

Originating in Persia in 1844, Bahá'i still bears something of an exotic flavor, although recent translations of its writings in English equivalents of the original thought make that element less conspicuous than it was. The founder was Mirzá 'Ali Muhammad, called the Báb (Arabic for "gate" or "door"). The Báb suffered fierce persecution at the hands of the Mohammedans and was executed in 1850. In the decade following his death over ten thousand of his followers were slain. His successor was Mirzá Husayn 'Ali, later called Bahá'u'lláh (Splendor of God). Imprisoned for forty years, Bahá'u'lláh announced himself as the Promised One; he also announced that a new day of God had come and that the age of brotherhood had arrived. The separate streams of Christian, Jewish, and Mohammedan faiths were to merge. He died in the Turkish penal colony of Akká in 1892, and his mantle fell upon his eldest son, Abbás Effendi, later known as 'Abdu'l-Bahá.

Like his father, the son spent forty

years in captivity; released in 1908 he toured Egypt, Europe, and the United States. At Wilmette, a suburb of Chicago, he broke ground for the first Bahá'i temple in the Occident; this is today the seat of all Bahá'i offices in the United States. He was knighted by the British for his services in Palestine during World War I, and died there in 1921.

The Wilmette temple is one of our most unique religious structures—a combination of mosque, cathedral, and synagogue. In its structure the numeral 9, the number of perfection in Bahá'i, is repeatedly emphasized; there are nine concrete piers, nine pillars or pylons symbolizing the nine living religions of the world, and nine arches; it is set in a park with nine sides, nine avenues, and nine gateways, and around it the sect plans to erect nine fountains. The building it is said will be completed in 1953, when public worship will start.

Local groups are officially recognized only when they have nine members or more; supervision of these groups is vested in a National Spiritual Assembly of nine members. Shoghi Rabbini, who succeeded Abdu'l-Bahá, is the present leader, spiritual head, and sole interpreter of Bahá'i writings; he has nine aides.

American Bahá'is have summer schools at Eliot, Maine; Geyserville, California; Davison, Michigan; and Colorado Spring, Colorado. There are centers in forty-six countries, and 5,232 voting members were reported for the year 1947. They use a calendar given by the Báb, consisting of nineteen months of nineteen days each, with New Year's Day falling on March 21. For the future they plan an International Spiritual Assembly to sit at Haifa; they also plan enlargement of their work at Wilmette, including schools, hospitals, and homes for the aged.

The Bahá'is have no ecclesiastical organization; there are only teachers instructing and discussing with local groups. It is considered in error to sell religious instruction. Their doctrine may be summed up in the following statement:

Unfettered search after truth and the abandonment of all superstition and prejudice; the oneness of mankind—all are "leaves of one tree, flowers in one garden"; religion must be a cause of love and harmony, else it is no religion; all religions are one in their fundamental principles; religion must conform with science, bringing faith and reason into full accord; and recognition of the unity of God and obedience to His commands as revealed through His Divine Manifestations.

There should be no idle rich and no idle poor; every one should have an occupation, for "work in the spirit of service is worship." Compulsory education is advocated, especially for girls who will be the mothers and the first educators of the next generation. In all walks of life, both sexes should have equal opportunities for development and equal rights and privileges.

An auxiliary international language should be adopted and taught in all the schools in order to bring men into closer fellowship and better understanding. In the interest of universal peace, there should be established a universal league of nations, in which all nations and peoples should be included, and an International Parliament to arbitrate all international disputes.

BAPTISTS

The Baptists constitute one of the major Protestant forces in the United States. Twenty-three Baptist denominations reported an approximate membership of 15,452,743 in 1947; there are perhaps 35,000 to 40,000 local Baptist churches, each one independent of the others, with members also completely independent of each other, yet bound together by an amazingly strong "rope of sand" in a great common allegiance to certain basic principles and doctrines based generally upon the competency of each individual in matters of faith.

It is often heard among them that they have no founder but Christ and that Baptists have been preaching and practicing from the days of John the Baptist. That is true in a limited sense; there were certainly men and women holding what have come to be considered distinctly Baptist principles, all across these years. But as a *church*, or as organized *churches*, they began in Holland and England.

When the Reformation set the Bible and men free early in the sixteenth century, scattered groups appeared advocating the convictions of faith which are today the warp and woof of Baptist theology and ideology. We find the name Baptist in various forms in Germany and Switzerland: Pedobaptists, among whom, however, there were no "Baptists in the modern sense," in as much as they baptized infants and children; Anti-Pedobaptists, who opposed infant baptism; and Anabaptists, who rebaptized adults once baptized as children. The Anabaptists were the left wing of the Reformation and held to a literal application of the Word of God in social matters; they were communistic and pacifistic, opposing capital punishment, oaths in court, the holding of public office, and the payment of taxes and interest. They rejected infant baptism as unscriptural, insisted upon the separation of church and state, and defended this belief heroically and to the point of fanaticism and martyrdom. Under persecution they spread all over Europe.

Some flew to Norway, others to Italy, Poland, Holland, and England. In Holland a remnant came under the influence of Menno Simons, who put the word "Mennonite" in the vocabulary of religion. A group of these Holland emigrees under the leadership of John Smyth, a Separatist minister, organized a Baptist church in 1608. They filtered across the channel and started another church in London.

These first two churches were General Baptist churches, believing in a general atonement for all men. In the course of time there arose a Particular Baptist Church, holding to the predestinarian teachings of John Calvin and preaching a limited atonement. The first Particular (British) Church dates back to 1638. Three years after their founding a third body, known as Immersion Baptists, broke away and wrote, in 1644, a Confession of Faith, which is still held by many modern Baptists. It was this confession that stamped these people popularly, for the first time, as Baptists.

These early British Baptists wielded a tremendous influence in their times and upon the future; it is claimed for them that "more than any king or Parliament, they set the heart and mind of England free." John Smyth's teaching that "the Magistrate . . . is not to meddle with religion, or in matters of conscience" has become one of mankind's great spiritual bulwarks. They sent William Carey to India in 1793, and Carey became the pioneer of modern missions. More than a century earlier, in 1631, they had sent Roger Williams to America, and Williams was to be the first great champion of freedom for faith and conscience on this side of the Atlantic.

Williams was not a Baptist but a Separatist minister when he arrived. History is well known; preaching "new and dangerous opinions against the authority of magistrates," he fled their courtly wrath and organized a Baptist church at Providence, Rhode Island. John Clarke established another Baptist church at Newport, Rhode Island, at about the same time. The Baptists are still arguing as to which church came first; many scholars put the Providence church in 1639, the Newport church in 1641.

These were Particular, or Calvinistic, Baptist churches. Their strength was challenged by the rise of interest in Arminian theology during the preaching of George Whitefield, but their Calvinism prevailed; it is the theological standard of most Baptists in the country today. Their progress was slow; a bitter persecution of their church ennobled them and left one of the darkest blots on colonial history.

Following the tour of Whitefield through the colonies a dispute arose among the Baptists, dividing them into Old Lights, or Regulars, who distrusted revivals and emotionalism, and New Lights, or Separates, who demanded a reborn membership in their churches. Separate Baptists were outstanding in the fight for religious freedom in the new land. The friction died down with the signing of the Constitution, however, and a new unity was found in a foreign-missions crusade. The first Protestant missionary board in America was the American Board, made up of Baptists, Reformed, Congregational, and Presbyterian churchmen. In 1814 the Baptists organized their own separate General Missionary Convention of the Baptist Denomination in the United States of America.

This convention, representing a national Baptist fellowship, marked the first real denominational consciousness of American Baptists. It was followed eventually by other organizations which welded them firmly together: a General Baptist Convention, a General Tract Society—later called the American Baptist Publication Society, various missionary societies for work at home and abroad, an Education Society, and the famous Baptist Young People's Union.

These organizations were on a national scale; their unity was disrupted first by a feeling that home-missions agencies within the body had failed to evangelize southern territory, and later by the question of slavery and the Civil War. The great division over slavery came in 1845, when the southerners "seceded" to form their own Southern Baptist Convention in order to carry on more effectively the work of the Southern Baptist churches. From this point forward there was to be a Northern, now the American, and a Southern Baptist Convention. The split is still in effect.

Various other Baptist groups, following to the logical end their love of independence, established themselves from East to West. While they differ in certain minor details, they are generally agreed upon the following principles of faith: the inspiration and trustworthiness of the Bible as the sole rule of life; the lordship of Jesus Christ; the inherent freedom of the individual to approach God for himself; the granting of salvation through faith, by way of grace and contact with the Holy Spirit; two ordinances—the Lord's Supper and baptism of believers by immersion; the independence of the local church; the Church as a group of regenerated believers baptized upon confession of faith; infant baptism as unscriptural and not to be practiced; complete separation of church and state; the immortality of the soul, the brotherhood of man, the royal law of God, the need of redemption from sin, and the ultimate triumph of God's kingdom.

These over-all doctrines have never been written by the Baptists into any official Baptist creed for all their churches, but they have been incorporated in two very important confessions of faith for the denomination. The Baptist churches of London wrote a Philadelphia Confession in the year 1689; this confession was enlarged by the Philadelphia Association in 1742; the New Hampshire State Baptist Convention drew up another famous confession in 1832. The older Philadelphia Confession is strongly Calvinistic in statement, the New Hampshire Confession only moderately so.

Baptists have insisted upon freedom of thought and expression in pulpit and pew; this has made them one of the most democratic religious bodies in America, and one in which liberal and conservative doctrine is preached freely. They have insisted too upon the absolute autonomy of the local congregation; each church arranges its own worship, examines and baptizes its own members. There is no age limit set on membership, but the candidate is usually of such an age that he can understand and accept the teachings of Christ. Candidates for the ministry are licensed by local churches and ordained upon recommendation of a group of sister churches.

Baptist churches are commonly found grouped into associations, local and state, for purposes of fellowship. National conventions are established among many of them to carry on educational and missionary work. Most state conventions meet annually, with delegates representing all Baptist churches in the given area. They receive reports and make recommendations, but they have no authority to enforce their decisions.

While Baptists in general have a reputation for exclusiveness, there have been in recent years several moves in the direction of interdenominational union. The American and Southern conventions have been discussing reunion for some time; in 1948 definite steps were taken toward the formation of a Baptist Alliance of North America. It was to be a nonlegislative alliance, providing an opportunity for all recognized Baptist bodies to give a united expression to their faith. In Washington, D.C., there is a Baptist Joint Committee on Public Affairs for both American and Southern conventions; it serves mainly to spread the Baptist conviction on public morals and to safeguard their principle of separation of church and state.

Finally there is the growing Baptist World Alliance, organized in 1905 and now including over fourteen million Baptists all over the globe. The Alliance meets every five years and is a purely advisory body, discussing the great themes and problems common to all Baptists. Headquarters of the Alliance are now located in Washington, D.C.

American Baptist Convention

UP TO the time of the Revolutionary War, Baptist work in the northern states was in the hands of the local churches, some few of which formed themselves

into associations, such as the Philadelphia Association or the Warren Association of Rhode Island. Beyond these associations, which were limited to Virginia, New Jersey, Pennsylvania, and Rhode Island, there was no central administrative body to bind the churches together. The association did well, building churches, colleges, schools, and libraries; by the time of the split with the Southern Baptists, about 1844, plans for a national co-ordinating body were under way.

In the early years of the nineteenth century there were three Baptist organizations in the North mutually maintained: the American Baptist Home Missionary Society; the American Baptist Missionary Union, later known as the American Baptist Foreign Missionary Society; and the American Baptist Publication Society. The deflection of the Southern Baptists served to intensify the efforts of these three bodies; they were separate corporations, but they often called annual meetings at the same time and place, and tended to work more and more co-operatively.

The women of the northern churches formed their own home and foreign missionary societies in the 1860's and 1870's. Separate appeals for funds to support all these competing societies created confusion and dissatisfaction, and led eventually to the incorporation of the Northern Baptist Convention in 1907. This convention, actually a corporation with restricted powers in conducting religious work, receiving and expending money and affiliating itself with other bodies, changed its name in 1950 to the American Baptist Convention.

The two women's missionary societies eventually joined the three larger societies already established in what are known as Co-operating Organizations within the convention, although they continue to work under their own charters and management. To these were added a Board of Education and a Ministers and Missionaries Benefit Board, the latter to give relief to needy clergymen and missionaries and pensions to retiring ministers and missionaries.

State conventions and city mission societies were drawn into closer unity by grouping them into affiliated organizations, through which they raise and distribute funds under a co-operative plan with a unified budget. A Council on Finance and Promotion supervises the collection of money for this unified budget. Numerous other councils and committees carry on the work of the convention under the supervision of the General Council, which functions between the annual gatherings of the convention. At the 1950 meeting for the first time a general secretary was elected.

The local church is still the basic and highly independent unit of American Baptist government and administration. There are 7,124 local Baptist churches in this convention, with 1,583,360 members. There are thirty-seven state conventions and fifteen Baptist city societies. The convention owns and controls eighteen homes for children, twenty-one homes for the aged, six hospitals, twelve theological seminaries, three training schools, ten academies, eight junior colleges, ten schools for Negroes, and nineteen colleges and universities. The American Baptist Foreign Missionary Society and the Woman's American Baptist Foreign Missionary Society support work in 114 stations in Burma, Assam, India, China, Japan, the Congo, and the Philippines; they also maintain a co-operative relationship in six European countries, to which eighteen missionaries are appointed. The American Baptist Home Missionary Society has workers in thirty-four states, Alaska, Latin America, Cuba, El Salvador, Haiti, Mexico, Nicaragua, and Puerto Rico; it supports Bacone College for the Indians of Oklahoma, seminaries in Mexico and Puerto Rico, colleges in Nicaragua and Cuba, an academy in Puerto Rico, and a pastors' training school in Haiti. The Woman's American Home Missionary Society maintains work in hospital visitation, Christian centers, bilingual churches, and Christian friendliness among Indians, Negroes, and Orientals resident in this country and in Alaska, Central America, Cuba, Mexico, and Puerto Rico.

In matters of faith every Baptist church of the convention speaks for itself, but there are certain Baptist doctrines held in common. The Bible is the foundation of their belief, and the individual conscience the interpreter of the Bible. There is the usual Baptist insistence upon the inspiration and validity of the Scriptures, the lordship of Christ, immortality and the future life, the brotherhood of man, and the need of man's redemption from sin. The ordinances of baptism and the Lord's Supper are considered more as aids than as necessities to the living of the Christian life.

By and large the Northern Baptists represented in the American Baptist Convention are more liberal in thought and theology than those in the Southern Baptist Convention; this gulf of theological difference, coupled with southern suspicion of northern social and economic liberalism, keeps the two largest Baptist conventions in the nation apart. Gestures at reunion are still frequent and still unsuccessful.

Independently Baptist as they are, there is still a clear trend among these northerners toward co-operation if not organic union with other churches, both Baptist and non-Baptist. The American Baptist Convention is a constituent body of the National Council of the Churches of Christ in the U.S.A., with several members on the council's executive committee. Its leaders were prominent at the world gatherings at Edinburgh, Utrecht, and Oxford, and they are well represented in the World Council of Churches. Moves have been made toward union with the General Baptists, the Disciples of Christ, the Southern Baptist Convention, and the National Baptist Convention. The Free Baptists have been received into full fellowship. Thus in the near future we are quite liable to find fewer and larger Baptist bodies in the northern states.

Southern Baptist Convention

It was inevitable that Northern and Southern Baptists should split over the slavery question, even before the outbreak of the Civil War. The friction between the two sections began a quarter of a century before Bull Run. The acting board of foreign missions of the Baptists in the country had its headquarters in Boston; being located there, it was naturally strongly influenced by the abolition movement. There was bitter debate among the board members, and in the early 1840's it became evident that this board would not accept slaveholders as missionaries. This question of missionaries, and of missionary money, was the immediate cause of the split. The "brethren of the North" first suggested separation; a month later, in May of 1845, the Southern Baptist Convention was organized, establishing at once its own boards for foreign and home missions.

Three hundred churches in Maryland, Virginia, North Carolina, South Carolina, Georgia, Louisiana, Kentucky, and Alabama entered the new organization. Up to the outbreak of the Civil War this convention met biennially; since 1869 it has met annually.

A hard struggle for existence lay immediately ahead. The new convention suffered badly in point of churches, membership, and finances during the war; homes, schools, churches, the livelihood of citizens, and the very pattern of southern society were destroyed, with devastating effects among all the churches. An anti-missionary movement decimated their ranks, and membership —not finances and leadership—was affected when the Negro Baptists withdrew to form their own convention. But the recovery of the Southern Baptist Convention was amazing. In 1845 there were 352,930 members in the convention, of whom 130,000 were Negroes. By 1890

there were 1,280,066 members, all of them white. In 1949 there were 6,761,265 members in 27,285 churches. Currently they outnumber Northern Baptists by almost five to one.

There was not at the start, and there is not now, any serious difference in doctrine between the American and Southern Baptist conventions. As a rule Southern Baptists are more conservative and more Calvinistic, and it is one of the ironies of Baptist history that the Southern Baptist Convention adheres more firmly to the New Hampshire Confession of Faith than the American. Church polity and government are the same in both conventions; membership and ministry are exchanged in perfect harmony and understanding.

Five denominational boards have charge of the work in home and foreign missions, Sunday schools, educational institutions, and ministerial relief. The Home Mission Board, with forty-six members, works throughout the South and in Cuba, Panama, Alaska, Costa Rica, and the Panama Canal Zone, with more than one thousand missionaries active in the field. It co-operates with Negro Baptists; works among migrants in the South and Indians in the West and Southwest, among several language groups and the deaf; operates several highly efficient mission schools in the Appalachians and the Ozarks; and provides loans for the erection of new church buildings.

Foreign missionary work is in twenty-two countries and three continents. Their record is a proud one, yet in comparison with their huge membership Southern Baptists rank third among the denominations in the number of missionaries sent overseas. With nearly 7,000,000 members, they have 700 foreign missionaries—American Baptists with 1,500,000 members have 550 missionaries, and the Presbyterians (U.S.A.) with 2,000,000 members have 1,300 missionaries. There are 304 schools supported in Southern Baptist mission fields with an enrollment of 26,733; medical work is found in five countries; total disbursements for 1949 reached nearly eight million dollars.

The Sunday-School Board of the Southern Baptist Convention is one of the ablest in America; it provides the literature and supervises the work of 4,643,650 students in 25,496 Sunday schools. The first chair of Sunday-school pedagogy was established at the Louisville Theological Seminary in 1915.

There are four theological seminaries supported and controlled by the Southern Baptist Convention: Southern Baptist Theological Seminary at Louisville, Kentucky; Southwestern Baptist Theological Seminary at Fort Worth, Texas; New Orleans Baptist Theological Seminary at New Orleans, Louisiana; and the American Baptist Theological Seminary at Nashville, Tennessee. There are twenty-nine colleges, twenty-four junior colleges, and seven academies, all under the control or sponsorship of various southern state conventions; twenty-six hospitals, twenty orphanages. There are 43,707 young people's societies with a membership of 693,186, and 46,722 missionary societies with a membership of 240,072 women and young people. A Baptist Brotherhood, with organizations in 4,153 churches and a membership of 142,402 men, promotes evangelism, stewardship, work for boys, and radio preaching.

The publishing work of the Southern Baptists is one of the best in Protestantism; the yearbook of the denomination lists nineteen weekly, eleven monthly or semi-monthly, and two quarterly publications; the Sunday School Board puts out sixty-three periodicals with a combined circulation of 37,894,147. A chain of thirty-eight bookstores provides distributing centers for books and supplies.

Relief work runs into high figures; the Relief and Annuity Board in 1949 paid out benefits amounting to $1,103,797.25 to 2,373 beneficiaries; the board now has assets of nearly $18,000,000.

Southern Baptists are the fastest growing religious group in the United States; they led all other churches in 1949 with a reported increase of 269,284 members, and they had an average gain of better than 200,000 a year for several years. Their convention is spreading not only in the South but all across the country. The 1950 Southern Baptist Convention was held in a northern city, Chicago, for the first time, and San Francisco was selected as the 1951 convention city. Two reasons are given for this. One is that there are no southern cities with hotel accommodations adequate to care for the ever-increasing numbers of delegates attending the conventions, and the other is that there are so many Southern Baptist churches in northern territory that northern cities from sheer force of membership are entitled to such conventions in their own states. State and territorial lines are being crossed, and it appears more and more that conservative Baptists are drifting into the Southern Baptist Convention and liberal Baptists into the American Baptist Convention from coast to coast.

Negro Baptists

THE FIRST Negro Baptist Church in America was organized at Silver Bluff, across the Savannah River from Augusta, Georgia, in 1773; other churches followed in Petersburg, Virginia, in 1776; Richmond, Virginia, in 1780; Williamsburg, Virginia, in 1785; Savannah, Georgia, in 1785; and Lexington, Kentucky, in 1790. It is interesting that Andrew Bryan, a slave, was the first pastor of the First African Baptist Church of Savannah, Georgia, and that its organization came about through the efforts of Rev. Abraham Marshall (white) and the Rev. Jesse Peter (Negro).

As early as 1700 white slaveholders in the South were providing religious teaching and places of worship for their slaves; at least most of them did little to prevent it. Usually, however, the Negro slave sat in the gallery of the white church, identified with the faith of his owner. White ministers, sometimes assisted by Negro helpers, moved from one plantation to another, holding services more or less regularly; occasionally a Negro minister was liberated to give full time to religious work among his people. These ministers had great influence; they were consulted by the whites as the respected leaders of their people and were a real power up to the time of the "slave rebellion" of 1831 led by Nat Turner. For a period following this disturbance it was illegal in some sections of the South for Negroes to become Christians or to build meetinghouses.

The great majority of Negroes in pre-Civil War days were either Baptists or Methodists. When Bull Run was fought in 1861, there were 200,000 Negro members of the Methodist Episcopal Church, South, and 150,000 Negro Baptists. In 1793 there were 73,471 Baptists in the United States, and one fourth of them were Negroes; in 1806 one third of the Baptists of North Carolina were Negroes. The lack of formality in the Baptist churches, together with the absence of ritual and with the freedom and democracy of the local congregation, appealed to the Negro more than the episcopal structure of the Methodists. This was accented at the end of the Civil War; a revival spirit swept the Negroes, creating thousands of new churches. Aided by the Freedman's Aid Society and various Baptist organizations, nearly a million Negro Baptists worshiped in their own churches within a period of fifteen years.

The first Negro Baptist association, the Providence Baptist Association of Ohio, was formed in 1836; the first attempt at national organization came in 1880 with the creation of the National Baptist Convention at Montgomery, Alabama. In 1886 the American National Baptist Convention was organized at St. Louis, and in 1893 the American National Educational Baptist Convention was organized in the District of Columbia. All of these conventions were merged into the National Baptist Convention of the United States of America at Atlanta in 1895 and

incorporated in 1915 under the laws of the District of Columbia. Three boards —foreign missions, home missions, and education—were established by the convention of 1895.

Today out of approximately fourteen million Negroes in the United States ten million are in the South, and 44 per cent of the total Negro population are church members as compared with 42.4 per cent of the whites. They are grouped into a bewildering number of churches and denominations. In Chicago in 1938 out of 266 "store-front" Negro churches a very large percentage averaged about 30 members each; in Harlem in 1930 out of 163 Negro churches 122 met in stores or residences. There are 34 recognized and entirely different Negro denominations, some of them with less than 20 members, but seven eighths of our total Negro population are either Methodist or Baptist.

Approximately 7,000,000 Negro Baptists are found in two conventions: the National Baptist Convention of the United States of America, Incorporated, with 4,385,206 members and the National Baptist Convention of America with 2,594,521 members. The latter is frequently referred to as the "Unincorporated" body; the former is the older and parent body. Both were formerly in the National Baptist Convention incorporated in 1915; they divided in a dispute in 1916 over the control of the publications of the conventions, in which the election and tenure of national officers was concerned.

Negro Baptist doctrine runs quite parallel to that of the doctrine of white Baptist churches; it is slightly more Calvinistic. The polity of the two larger white conventions prevails; local churches unite in associations, usually along state lines, for the purposes of fellowship and consultation. There are also state conventions concerned with missionary work and often extending beyond state boundaries.

Foreign missionary work of both conventions is especially strong in Africa,

32

nd home missionary efforts are largely hose expended in the direction of helping needy churches, schools, relief, and o on. The National Baptist Convenion, Incorporated, has several missionry stations in the Bahamas, reports five olleges, one theological seminary, and ne training school for women and girls. The old enmities between the two conventions seem to wane with the years, ut no reunion is looked for for some ime to come.

American Baptist Association

SOMETIMES called Landmarkers because of their historic adherence to the old apostolic order of church polity, the American Baptist Association members deny that those Baptists organized in conventions are faithful to Bible precedent. Maintaining that their own is the only true New Testament form, they hold themselves separate from all other religious groups.

Starting in 1905 as the Baptist General Association, they organized under their present name in 1924 at Texarkana, Arkansas–Texas. Denying all denominationalism, they seem to be quite denominational in their attitude in refusing to affiliate with any other group. Teaching that the great commission of Christ (Matthew 28:18-20) was given to a local congregation, they believe that the local congregation or church is the only unit authorized to administer the ordinances, and that it is an independent and autonomous body responsible only to Christ. Thus every church is equal "with every other like church"; they are often called Church-Equality Baptists.

Their doctrine is strictly fundamentalist; condemning "so-called modern science," they stand for the verbal inspiration of the Bible, the Triune God, the virgin birth and deity of Christ, the suffering and death of Christ as substitutionary, the bodily resurrection of Christ and all his saints. The second coming of Jesus, "physical and personal," is to be the crowning event of the "gos-pel age"; this second advent will be premillennial. There is eternal punishment for the wicked; salvation is solely by grace through faith and not by law or works. There must be absolute separation of church and state, and absolute religious freedom.

Government of the body is congregational. There are annual meetings composed of messengers from co-operating churches. Missionary work is carried on through county, state, interstate, and foreign missionary boards. Educational work is pursued in Sunday schools, in the Jacksonville Baptist College at Jacksonville, Texas, in one seminary—the Missionary Baptist Institute at Little Rock, Arkansas—and several minor Bible schools in Arkansas, Oklahoma, and Louisiana.

Most of the membership is found in the South, Southwest, and Southeast, but there are churches in California, Idaho, Colorado, Kansas, Massachusetts, and Pennsylvania. They have enjoyed a phenomenal growth during the past fifteen years; they now report 313,817 members and 2,460 churches. The membership is shifting rapidly from rural to urban.

Christian Unity Baptist Association

THE Christian Unity Baptist Association originated in a dispute over the question of open and close communion in the Mount Union Baptist Association of Regular Baptists in North Carolina. The dissenters believed that all Christians, in all denominations, should be admitted to participation in the Lord's Supper. They are one of the smaller groups, numbering 497 members and 11 churches.

They believe in one God and the Trinity and in the Bible as the inspired Word of God; that all mankind is fallen and helpless to save itself; in the redemption of the "bodies of the saints," infants, and idiots; that sinners reach God by way of repentance and faith; that the only two authorized ordinances are baptism of believers and the Lord's Supper; in foot washing, in the resurrection of the bodies of both just and unjust, in the everlasting reward of the righteous and punishment of the wicked.

Government is strictly congregational; there is one association, for advisory purposes only. Work centers largely in home missions, evangelism, revivals, prayer meetings, and Sunday schools.

Colored Primitive Baptists

THE NEGRO population of the South all through the years of slavery and the Civil War worshiped with the white population in their various churches. This was true of Colored Primitive Baptists, who attended white Primitive Baptist churches until the time of the emancipation, when their white brethren helped them to establish their own Colored Primitive Baptist churches, granting them letters of fellowship and character, ordaining their deacons and ministers, and helping in every possible way.

Their doctrine and polity are quite the same as in the white Primitive Baptist organization. Each church is independent, receiving and controlling its own membership; there is no appeal from a decision of the officers of the local church.

As of 1936 there were 43,897 members and 1,009 churches. Unlike the white Primitive Baptists they have since 1900 been establishing aid societies, conventions, and Sunday schools over the opposition of the older and more orthodox members.

Duck River and Kindred Associations of Baptists (Baptist Church of Christ)

CONFINED to five southern states, the Duck River Baptists originated in a protest movement in the old Elk River Association, which was strongly Calvinistic. This came in 1825; in 1843 the ranks of the dissenters were broken by a dispute over the legitimacy of mis-

sions and the support of a publicatio society and of a denominational schoo Those who withdrew were known : Missionary Baptists, sometimes as Sep arate Baptists. The division persists; ther are today two Duck River association

Doctrinally they are liberally Calvir istic; they hold that "Christ tasted deat for every man," that God will save thos who come to him on gospel terms, tha sinners are justified by faith, that th saints will "persevere in grace." The believe in believer's baptism by immer sion, and celebrate the Lord's Suppe and foot washing as as scriptural ordi nances. As they admit their close gospe ties with Regular, United, and Separat Baptists, there are growing sentiments i favor of union.

They are congregational in goverm ment, with four associations for fellow ship only; a general association include these four, together with three othe kindred associations. Membership i voted on by the local church; ordinatio of ministers is by two or more ministers There are 9,562 members and 9 churches.

Freewill Baptists

THE Freewill Baptists in this country have a Welsh background; they migratec from Wales in 1701, settling on a grant of land in Pennsylvania known as the Welsh Tract. Distinguished by their adherence to Arminian (freewill) doctrine rather than to the usual Calvinistic (predestinarian) tenets, they suffered badly during the rapid growth of the Calvinistic persuasion; at one time there were only four Freewill churches left But they rallied and grew; today they have a membership of 255,127 and 3,467 churches. They are confined for the greater part to the South; Freewill Baptists in the North have affiliated with the American Baptist Convention.

Doctrinally they are Arminian, holding that Christ gave himself as ransom for the many, not the few; that God calls all to repentance; and that all may

GENERAL SIX-PRINCIPLE BAPTISTS

be saved. Baptism is by immersion. They are one of the few Baptist churches practicing open Communion; they also practice foot washing and anoint the sick with oil. Their government is strictly congregational; there are quarterly conferences, which are grouped into state conferences and associations, and there is an annual conference representing the whole denomination. A publishing house is maintained, together with a theological seminary called Eureka College, at Ayden, North Carolina.

General Baptists

THE General Baptists claim their name and origin from the original Arminian Baptists of England and Holland. Their first minister in this country was an English immigrant, Robert Nordin; their first church was located in Vanderburg County, Indiana, in 1823, by Benoni Stinson. Their real strength developed in the Cumberland region of the South; their ranks were badly decimated by the early colonial interest in Calvinism, but a handful of churches held out and eventually spread into Kentucky, Illinois, Tennessee, and other states. Today they claim 39,600 members in 580 churches.

A confession of faith closely resembling that of the Freewill Baptists was drawn up by Stinson. It is an eleven-point confession, with the following cardinal tenets: Christ died for all men; failure to achieve salvation lies completely with the individual; man is depraved and fallen and completely unable to save himself; regeneration is necessary for salvation, except in the case of infants and idiots, who are not responsible for sin; salvation comes by repentance and faith in Christ; the Christian who perseveres to the end is saved, and the wicked are punished eternally; the dead, just and unjust, shall be raised at the judgment; the Lord's Supper and believer's baptism by immersion are the only authorized Christian ordinances and should be open to all believers. Some General Baptists practice foot washing.

There is a liberal and persistent interest among General Baptists in church union. A co-operative union with the American Baptist Convention was formed in 1915, and gestures of union have been made to Freewill and Separate Baptist groups without success.

Church polity is in accord with that of other Baptists; it is congregational, with local, state, and general associations for fellowship and advice. The separate churches must ratify the organic union of any association. Ministers are ordained in a council of sister churches; membership is by vote of the local church. The General Association, organized in 1870, exists to effect better relations and closer co-operation between "various bodies of liberal Baptists"; it binds together the local associations and supervises the work of the denomination in education, home and foreign missions, publications and literature. Foreign missions are confined to the island of Guam. There is one college, Oakland City College, in Oakland, Indiana. The official denominational magazine is the *General Baptist Messenger,* published at Poplar Bluff, Missouri.

General Six-Principle Baptists

FOUNDED in the United States in 1653 at Providence, Rhode Island, the Six-Principle Baptist Church claims as its charter the six foundation principles laid down in Hebrews 6:1-2—namely, repentance, faith, baptism, the laying on of hands, the resurrection of the dead, and eternal judgment. The question of the laying on of hands on admission to the church has been the occasion of a dispute among them, as among the first English Baptists; it is accepted not as a mere form but "as a sign of the reception of the gifts of the Holy Ghost."

Broadly speaking, they are Arminian in doctrine and congregational in polity. There are conferences, mainly for fellowship; there is no home missions work, but a few scattered contributions for foreign missionary work are reported.

A book and tract society distributes material published by the International Old Baptist Union, an international body with a bishop at its head, of which the American Six-Principle Baptists are a constituent body.

There are 269 members and 3 churches.

Independent Baptist Church of America

THIS IS a church of Swedish origin, founded in 1893 at Dassel, Minnesota, by a group of Swedish Free Baptist immigrants. A series of disagreements within the body brought about several changes in name and a split into two churches, which were united under the present name in 1927.

The Independent Baptist Church of America teaches faith in the Resurrection, that repentance and baptism by immersion are prerequisite to membership and participation in the Lord's Supper. They practice the laying on of hands at the time of admission into church membership. They are, generally, pacifists, but in all other matters they pledge obedience to the civil government.

No record of the work or organization of this church is available; in 1936 there were 129 members enrolled in 8 churches.

National Baptist Evangelical Life and Soul-Saving Assembly of the U.S.A.

THIS assembly was founded in 1920 at Kansas City, Missouri, not as another denomination but as an evangelical group working within the National Baptist Convention (Unincorporated). It had the endorsement of the parent body for seventeen years but became an independent group in 1937.

No new doctrine is set forth by this group; it has no doctrine except "the Bible doctrine as announced by the Founder of the Church, Jesus Christ." Concentration is mainly upon evangelical and relief efforts. The assembly maintains an Automatic Correspondence School, offering courses in evangelelology, deaconology, missionology, pastorology, and laymanology; degrees are granted in 60, 90 and 120 days.

In 1949 56,934 members and 235 churches were reported.

Primitive Baptists

THE Primitive Baptists have the reputation of being the most strictly orthodox and exclusive of all Baptists. Unique in that they have never been organized as a denomination and have no associations or administrative bodies of any kind, they represent a protest movement against missions and Sunday schools. Spearheading the antimissions crusade which gained headway in the middle and late nineteenth century, their first churches were in North Carolina and Georgia. The Kehukee Association in North Carolina in 1827 condemned all "modern, money-based, so-called benevolent societies" as contrary to the teaching of Christ. Within a decade several other Baptist associations, North and South, made similar statements and withdrew from association with other Baptist churches.

As the movement developed, each association began to print statements of its articles of faith and rules of order. Each statement was examined by every other association, and those associations not in general agreement with the rest were dropped from all fellowship. Fraternal visits were fairly frequent, and the lines of demarcation were not too clearly drawn, with the result that they were variously called Old School, Regular, Antimission, and Hard Shell Baptists, as well as Primitive. The latter name is the most widely accepted at the present time. The Primitive Baptists are the largest group of their kind, numbering 69,157 members and 1,726 churches as of 1936.

A strong Calvinism runs through their doctrine. In general they believe that by Adam's fall all his posterity became sinners; that human nature is completely corrupt, and that man cannot by his own efforts regain favor with God. God elected his own people in Christ before the world began and none of these saints will be finally lost. The two biblically authorized ordinances are the Lord's Supper and baptism of believers by immersion. All church societies are the invention of men and are to be denied fellowship; Christ will come a second time to raise the dead, judge all men, punish forever the wicked, and reward forever the righteous; the Old and New Testaments are verbally and infallibly inspired.

Ministers must be called of God, come under the laying on of hands, and be in fellowship with the local church of which they are members before they can administer the two ordinances; they are to deny to any other clergyman without these qualifications the right to administer such ordinances. No theological training is demanded of ministers among Primitive Baptists; while there is no opposition to such education, the position is that the Lord will call an educated man if he wants one but that lack of education should not bar a man from the ministry.

Some Primitive Baptists practice foot washing, but not all; the great majority are opposed to the use of instrumental music in the churches and opposed to Sunday schools and all secret societies as unauthorized by Scripture. All their churches are congregational in government; admission to membership is by careful examination and vote of the congregation. There is a persistent effort in evangelism within the denomination.

Regular Baptists

THE TERM "Regular" as applied to Baptists has been the cause of some confusion. Originally it was applied to the Baptists of the Northern, Southern, and National conventions; that usage ended about 1890, and the expression is applied now only to the denomination bearing that name, centering in North Carolina, Virginia, West Virginia, and Kentucky. These Regular Baptists claim to be the modern representatives of the original English Baptists, before the divisions into Particular (Calvinistic) and General (Arminian) Baptists were established. They are in close sympathy with the United Baptists and the Duck River and Kindred Association of Baptists.

Regular Baptists believe that men are responsible to all the commands of God, compliance always being by enabling grace; that with such grace all men may meet the conditions of salvation; that man through sin is completely depraved, with neither the power nor the will to save himself; that salvation is by grace alone, as a result of God's mercy and love; that on the basis of the sacrifice of Christ for all sin the gospel of God's grace must be preached to all men; that the lost are lost because of their unbelief. In general they hold a middle-of-the-road position on the Atonement, but a few of their churches are sympathetic with the views of the Primitive Baptists.

Each association has its own confession of faith; there is no over-all confession for all. Most of them are Arminian; a few lean toward Calvinism. They practice close Communion and foot washing. The governmental policy is strictly congregational, with associations meeting for fellowship only. Regular Baptists in 1936 numbered 17,186; there were 266 churches. A noticeable decline in both churches and membership is evident.

General Association of Regular Baptist Churches (North)

NOT A convention nor strictly a church, the General Association of Regular Baptist Churches (North) is a fellowship; any Baptist church may join on that basis.

The association subscribes to the New Hampshire Confession of Faith, with a premillennial interpretation of the final article of the confession. Members hold to the Bible as the Word of God, the Trinity, the personality of Satan as the author of all evil; they teach that man is the direct creation of God and that man is born in sin. There is conservative doctrine dealing with the virgin birth and the deity of Jesus; faith in Christ is held to be the way to salvation, through grace; the saved are in "everlasting felicity," and the lost suffer forever. There is a bodily resurrection; Christ rose and ascended and will return premillennially and reign in the millennium. Civil government is by divine appointment. There are only two approved ordinances: baptism by immersion and the Lord's Supper. Church government is strictly congregational.

There is no organized missionary work in this group, but missionary contributions are made through other Baptist agencies. There are about 80,000 members in 521 churches.

Separate Baptists

THE FIRST Separate Baptists arrived in the United States in 1695 as one refugee section of the separatist movement in England. They were especially active during the days of the blazing preaching of Whitefield, in the early eighteenth century, and in the conflict between Old Light and New Light sects. The Separate Baptist churches of this period were marked by their milder Calvinism and by an occasional use of infant baptism.

In 1787 Separate and Regular Baptist churches merged in Virginia in the United Baptist Churches of Christ in Virginia; there were other mergers and gestures toward union in New England and other states. But a few Separate Baptist churches maintained their independence; in 1947 there were 90 Separate churches, with 6,490 members.

All creeds and confessions of faith are rejected by Separate Baptists, but there is an annual statement of articles of belief by the several associations. These include statements of faith in the infalli-

bility of the Scriptures; the Trinity; three ordinances—baptism of believers by immersion only, the Lord's Supper, and foot washing; regeneration, justification, and sanctification through faith in Christ; the appearance of Christ on Judgment Day to deal with the just and the unjust. The election, reprobation, and fatality of Calvinism are rejected.

Separate Baptists are congregational in government, with associations for advisory purposes only. The associations carry on a limited home missions work; there are no foreign missions and no colleges, but there are good Sunday schools throughout the denomination. A denominational magazine called the *Messenger* is published at Kokomo, Indiana.

Seventh-Day Baptists

DIFFERING from other Baptists in their adherence to the seventh day as the Sabbath, Seventh-Day Baptists had thirty churches in New England, though they did not bear that name, before Stephen Mumford left the Newport, Rhode Island, church of John Clarke in 1671 to organize the first official Seventh-Day Baptist church on this side of the Atlantic. Others were organized in Philadelphia and in New Jersey, and from these centers they have spread into twenty-nine states; as of June, 1947, there were 63 churches and 6,283 members. They claim to have supplied the seventh-day teaching to ten other Protestant denominations, including the Seventh-Day Adventists.

Seventh-Day Baptists believe in salvation through faith in Christ, in believer's baptism by immersion, in soul and civil liberty, in a Bible free and open to all, and in the right of every man to interpret the Bible for himself. They have only two ordinances, baptism and the Lord's Supper. They hold open Communion and leave their members free to take Communion in other churches. They have an unusually broad policy in religious education and in co-operation in interchurch movements.

Local churches enjoy complete independence; they are organized into the usual associations. The general conference is the highest administrative body; for fellowship and co-operation all the churches in the country are organized into eight larger associations. Membership is by vote of the local church; elders, deacons, and ministerial candidates are approved by a council of sister churches. Of late years the general conference has approved the action of local churches in ordaining ministers.

Missionary, educational, and promotional work is carried on by the usual societies and boards; foreign missions are found in China, Java, India, Germany, the Netherlands, Africa, South America, and Jamaica. Alfred University is maintained at Alfred, New York, Milton College at Milton, Wisconsin, and Salem College at Salem, West Virginia.

Seventh-Day Baptists (German, 1728)

THE Seventh-Day Baptists (German, 1728) are not to be confused with the original Seventh-Day Baptist Church organized earlier in Rhode Island; this group was established by John Conrad Beissel, a Palatinate German, in 1728. Beissel worked for a while with Peter Becker, the Germantown mystic who founded the German Baptist Brethren, or Dunkards. He left Becker in 1732 to set up a monastic, communistic religious community at Ephrata, Pennsylvania. Goods were held in common, and men and women lived in separate houses under a regulation requiring celibacy.

The community declined late in the nineteenth century; by 1942 the church reported only 125 members in 2 churches. Generally they hold the usual Dunker doctrines, the inspiration of the Bible; one God, the Father, and Jesus Christ, his Son, the mediator; the Ten Commandments as the sole rule of righteousness for all men; baptism by trine forward immersion—the candidate is immersed three times, for Father, Son, and Holy Ghost. They practice foot wash-ing and anointing of the sick and the blessing of infants, observe Saturday as the Sabbath, and induct ministers by personal request rather than by congregational election.

A general conference meets annually; there is a small home missions program, but no educational or philanthropic work.

Two-Seed-in-the-Spirit Predestinarian Baptists

TRACING their thought back to the Waldenses, the Two-Seed-in-the-Spirit Predestinarian Baptists in this country began with the protests of Elder Daniel Parker in the late eighteenth century against missions and Sunday schools. Parker opposed the Arminian doctrine of the Methodists and based his dislike of the missionary effort and church schools on what he called his Two-Seed Doctrine. This, briefly, is the conviction that two seeds entered the life stream of humanity in the Garden of Eden. One seed was good, planted by God; the other was evil, from the devil. The two seeds have been in conflict in humanity ever since. Every baby is predestined, born with one seed or the other. Nothing can be done for him, one way or another. In as much as nothing can be done, missions are useless; they are, moreover, an institution which "usurps the privileges of God."

The seed is in the spirit, not the flesh. This is the cardinal point in the theology of the group. Other points include belief in the resurrection of the body of Christ, which is the Church, and salvation by grace alone. The church observes the Lord's Supper and practices foot washing. There is no paid ministry, "in as much as Christ came to save sinners, and He finished his work." Government is congregational; there are associations for fellowship only. There are no home missions nor benevolences. The membership is decreasing; there were 201 members and 16 churches in 1936,

United American Freewill Baptist Church (Colored)

WHILE THEY trace their history back to the same original sources of the white Freewill Baptist Church, the United American Freewill Baptists (Colored) have been independent since their official organization in 1901. Their members are found largely in North Carolina, Georgia, Florida, Mississippi, Louisiana, and Texas.

Although in general agreement with the congregational polity of other Baptist bodies this church grants a rather limited autonomy to the local church. There is a system of quarterly, annual, and general conferences, with graded authority. Doctrinal disputes may be carried up to the general conferences; district conferences may exclude members from fellowship.

Doctrinally they are in agreement with white churches of the same faith. There is one institution of higher learning— Kinston College, at Kinston, North Carolina. There were 75,000 members in 350 churches in 1944.

United Baptists

THE United Baptists represent a merging of several groups of Separate and Regular Baptists, mainly in the southern states of Virginia, the Carolinas, and Kentucky. While these groups were bodies holding both Arminian and Calvinistic theologies, they maintained a perfect freedom in preaching and polity. As the years passed, many of them found their way into either the Northern or Southern Baptist convention but they are still recognized as a separate denomination, organized in Virginia in 1794 and in Kentucky in 1804. There is close fellowship and much discussion of union with Regular Baptists and with the Duck River Baptists.

Doctrinally United Baptists hold that salvation is by grace and not works, and it is conditional upon gospel requirements; all men are commanded to repent, and they are led to repentance through the goodness of God or to rebellion by the devil; it is a matter of individual choice. They practice close Communion and in some instances foot washing. Government is strictly in the hands of the local congregation, with the usual associations for fellowship and counsel. There were 27,000 members and 277 churches in 1936.

BRETHREN (DUNKERS)

The terms Brethren and Dunkers have been the cause of much confusion; they call for careful definition. Dunker is a direct derivation of the German word *tunken*, "to dip or immerse." It is a word to be identified with the peculiar method of immersion employed by this group of churches: trine immersion, in which the believer, on his knees in the water, is immersed not once but three times, in the name of Father, Son, and Holy Ghost. Variously through their long history the Dunkers have been called Tunkers, Taufers, or Dompelaars. They were first called Brethren when their first church organization was established at Schwarzenau, Germany, in 1708.

It might be said generally that these Dunker or Brethren bodies are former German Baptists who took their theology and much of their practice from the Pietists of the seventeenth and eighteenth centuries in Germany. The Pietists, who were mostly Lutherans, became unhappy with the formalism of worship and ritual in their state church, and with the general "barrenness" of German Protestantism. They took the New Testament literally and endeavored to put its teachings into practice in the least detail of their living. They spurned the idea of apostolic succession, and at the heart of their practice they had a love feast or agape, which was the serving of the Lord's Supper preceded by a ceremony of foot washing. They saluted each other with a "kiss of peace," dressed in the plainest clothing, covered the heads of women at services, anointed their sick with oil for healing and consecration, refrained from worldly amusements, refused to take oaths, go to war, or engage in lawsuits. These doctrines and practices are held today by most Brethren, with certain modifications.

From these German Pietists came the Church of the Brethren (Conservative Dunkers), the Brethren Church (Progressive Dunkers), the Old German Baptist Brethren (Old Order Dunkers), and the Church of God (New Dunkers). Another Brethren group, unrelated historically to these and known as the River Brethren, also took its ideology from the German Pietists; this group includes the Brethren in Christ, the Old Order or Yorker Brethren, and United Zion's Children. A third Brethren body, known as the Plymouth Brethren, has a British rather than a German background.

The Brethren bodies beginning in Germany were known for years simply as German Baptist Brethren; that title has largely disappeared, except in the case of the Old German Baptist Brethren (Old Order Dunkers).

Church of the Brethren (Conservative Dunkers)

THE Church of the Brethren (Conservative Dunkers) began in 1708 with a church of eight persons in Schwarzenau, Germany. Persecuted and driven from Germany into Holland and Switzerland, one group of the church, in Crefeld, Germany, under the leadership of Peter Becker came to America in 1719 to take up free lands offered them by William Penn. They settled in Germantown, near Philadelphia, where they were joined in 1729 by fifty-nine families brought across the Atlantic by Alexander Mack. From Pennsylvania they spread across the country.

Their German speech, their opposition to war, and their insistence upon the inner Christian life as more important than church organization made them a suspected group from the start. Morally they opposed the Revolution; in the Civil War they opposed slavery—no member of this church ever held a slave—but took no part in the fighting. The suspicion and misunderstanding waned as time went on; today historians are generous in their praise of the contributions of the Brethren to American democracy. In our own day the work of their pacifists in World War II and their outstanding efforts in relief to Europe following that war have made them one of the most honored bodies in American Protestantism. In their earliest days at Germantown they printed the first German Bible in America and circulated the first American religious magazine.

In 1728 a group under Peter Becker and Conrad Beissel left the Church of the Brethren to found the famous Ephrata community and the Seventh-Day Baptists (German); in 1848 another break resulted in the establishment of the Church of God (New Dunkers); in 1881 a third group withdrew to organize the Old German Baptist Brethren (Old Order Dunkers); and in 1882 came the worst split of all in the organizing of The Brethren Church (Progressive Dunkers). Still another body, the Dunkard Brethren, was formed in 1926. The original body is known today as the Church of the Brethren (Conservative Dunkers); it had 185,088 members and 1,025 churches in 1949.

The Church of the Brethren (Conservative Dunkers) is conservative in doctrine. Its teaching is summarized in the following five divisions: (1) the doctrine of peace—they refuse to sanction all use of force in religion and will not go to war; (2) the doctrine of temperance—members are not to engage in the traffic of alcoholic liquors, and total abstinence is asked of all; (3) the doctrine of the simple life—worldly amusements and luxuries are to be shunned; (4) the doctrine of brotherhood—all class distinctions are unchristian and to be opposed; (5) religion means obedience to Christ rather than to creeds and cults. Christian living is stressed rather than forms. Baptism is by trine immersion; the love feast is observed, following the pattern of John 13:1-7. There is a waning adherence to the Brethren traditions of plainness in dress and the veiling of women in worship, as "commanded" in I Corinthians 2. They take no oaths and do not generally participate in lawsuits.

Church government is congregational, quite similar to that of the Baptists. Each member has an equal vote; there are elders, resident or nonresident, in charge of local congregations—elders not serving in the administrative work of the church—ministers, and deacons. Ministers are chosen by the ballot of the local congregation; they may in time become elders. The churches are divided into fifty districts, which in turn are integrated into five regions. Each district has an annual conference, and a general conference stands as the over-all, unifying body.

A General Brotherhood Board, composed of twenty-five members elected by the general conference, supervises the total church program. The board is subdivided into five commissions of five members each for administrative and promotional purposes. The Foreign Mission Commission administers the church's missions in India, China, Africa, and South America. The Brethren Service Commission represents the church in the field of social education, social action, and relief and rehabilitation, and carries on a world-wide program of peace and human welfare in America, Mexico, Puerto Rico, China, Africa, and Europe. The Christian Education Commission supervises church schools, weekday religious education, higher education in six colleges, fifty summer camps, and so forth. The Ministry and Home Mission Commission provides leadership and education in ministry and in locating and supporting new churches. The Finance Commission supervises the fiscal operations of the church and gives guidance to the other commissions in financial and business matters.

There is a large publishing house at Elgin, Illinois, where the church headquarters are located.

Brethren Church (Progressive Dunkers)

THE FIRST Brethren in Pennsylvania were largely farmers with little education. While there were a few men of real learning among them, they were for the most part earnest Christians who had been denied the benefit of schools. There came a growing dissatisfaction among them with this situation and with the failure of the church to provide schools of higher learning for clergy and laity. Dissatisfaction arose also over the strict enforcement of the traditions of plain dress, worship, and especially over the transfer of authority from the local congregations to the several conferences. The dissent swelled into a rebellion; the progressive leaders were at last expelled, and a considerable number followed them out to establish the Brethren Church (Progressive Dunkers) in 1882.

This body is quite specific in its doctrine, which is set forth in a *Message of the Brethren Ministry*, written about 1917. The message includes statements of belief in the infallibility of the Scriptures; the pre-existence, deity, and incarnation by virgin birth of Jesus Christ; the vicarious atonement of Jesus Christ, and his resurrection; the fall of man and the necessity of salvation; justification by personal faith in Christ; the resurrection of the dead; the judgment of the world and the life everlasting; the second coming of Christ; nonconformity with the world; believer's baptism by trine immersion; the ordinances of baptism, confirmation, the Lord's Supper, foot washing, and anointing the sick with oil.

In 1939 a split occurred in the Brethren Church which divided the church into what came to be known as the Ashland Group and the Grace Group. There is no formal division here; both groups still carry the name of the Brethren Church, but each group has its own annual conference, the Ashland body at Ashland, Ohio, and the Grace body at Winona Lake, Indiana. Each conference has its own executives; and since the government of the Brethren Church is congregational, it is possible for a congregation to support either one group or the other and still remain in good standing in the Church of the Brethren. Each group has its own seminary and missions boards. There has been no change in general doctrinal statement, but it is generally true that the Grace group represents the Calvinistic viewpoint and the Ashland body the Arminian viewpoint. A dispute over the necessity of baptism to salvation is still unsettled.

Polity in the Brethren Church is more congregational than in the Church of the Brethren (Conservative Dunkers). Each church is completely autonomous; there are ministers, elders, deacons, evangelists, and deaconesses. Deaconesses may become ministers. Churches are grouped geographically into nine district conferences. Membership is uncertain; the Grace group has about 17,500 members, and the Ashland group about 16,000. Ashland College is still supported by both bodies.

Old German Baptist Brethren (Old Order Dunkers)

WHILE THE Brethren Church (Progressive Dunkers) left the Church of the Brethren (Conservative Dunkers) because the latter body seemed too conservative, the Old German Baptist Brethren (Old Order Dunkers) left it because they considered it not con-

servative enough. The dissenters stood literally for the old order and the old traditions. The salient point of their opposition lay in their suspicion of Sunday schools, missions, higher education, and church societies. They withdrew in 1881.

They stand for a literal interpretation of the Scriptures in regard to the Lord's Supper and practice close Communion, which excludes all but their own members. They teach non-co-operation in war and in political and secret societies; their dress is the severely plain garb of the original Dunkers, and they frown on all amusements. They follow the other Brethren bodies in refusing to take oaths or engage in lawsuits, have no salaried ministry, enforce complete abstinence from alcoholic liquors, anoint the sick with oil, veil the heads of their women at worship, and refuse to perform the wedding ceremony for any divorced person. They have no Sunday schools, missions, or educational work. In 1947 they reported 3,254 members and 53 churches.

Church of God (New Dunkers)

DISAGREEMENT concerning the practices of trine immersion, the love feast, the veiling of women, and nonconformity in taking oaths brought about a schism among the first Dunkers in this country. A group led by George Patton and Peter Eyman withdrew to organize the Church of God (New Dunkers) in 1848. They held that "Bible things should be called by Bible names," and that the only name for a church authorized by Scripture was the Church of God.

This church accepts no human creed or confession of faith; it holds the Bible as the only infallible guide to Christian living. Members lay strong emphasis upon the Second Coming and upon future rewards and punishments. They do not believe in wars of aggression, but they will take part in wars for defense. They practice anointing the sick with oil; early in their history they also kept the Dunkard tradition of the holy kiss

43

at Communion, but the practice has now been discontinued. Baptism is in the name of the Father, Son, and Holy Ghost, but there is only one immersion. Governed strictly by the local congre-gation, this church has an annual conference and some home and foreign missionary work. There are no educational or philanthropic efforts. There were 526 members in 8 churches in 1944.

Plymouth Brethren

RESTLESS under the close connection of church and state in nineteenth-century England and Ireland, and opposing the stereotyped forms of worship in the Established Church, groups of Brethren began to meet for quiet fellowship and prayer. They had no connection whatever with the sects of Brethren in Germany but took their name from the Scriptures; at one time or another they were also called Christians, Believers, or Saints. The largest and most important meeting was held at Plymouth, England, hence the name Plymouth Brethren, which has never been officially accepted by any of the group.

These Plymouth Brethren set up their meetings on strictly New Testament lines. They had no ordained ministers, in as much as they held to the "priesthood of all believers." They put strong emphasis upon the second coming of Jesus—to be expected momentarily—and upon his deity, and they denied fellowship with all who were "not fundamentally sound as to doctrine and godly in walk." Differences arose over divergent views on the effects of unsound teaching in the Plymouth Assembly, and in 1848 there came a division into Exclusive and Open Brethren. The Open Brethren held that they should receive all persons personally sound in faith, even though they came from an assembly where error was taught, if they personally rejected the error. The Exclusive Brethren held that such reception disqualified the assemblies from participation in the Circle of Fellowship, which was, and is, a joint body of approved assemblies holding a corporate unity and responsibility made up of leaders who make decisions for all constituent assemblies.

The tendencies toward division followed the Plymouth Brethren to America when they came here in the late nineteenth century. Today there are eight bodies of Plymouth Brethren in this country, distinguished only by the Roman numerals I to VIII. Plymouth Brethren I and II, the two largest bodies, have practically dropped their differences and are in practice one body.

In doctrine the various bodies are in substantial agreement; the separation of these groups is caused mainly by conflicts in church discipline. Generally they acknowledge no creeds; they take the Bible as their own authoritative guide, believing it verbally inspired of God and inerrant. They are Trinitarians; they hold that Christ was begotten of the Holy Spirit and born of the Virgin Mary, and is true God and true man; that man is created in God's image; that by sin he has incurred physical and spiritual death, which is separation from God; that all men are sinners; that salvation and justification come through faith in his shed blood, apart from works; that Christ was resurrected and ascended into heaven to abide there as high priest and advocate for the redeemed. Christ's return will be premillennial; it is imminent and personal, and he will return in glory with all his saints to rule and judge the world. All who receive him by faith are born again and thereby become the children of God. There is a bodily resurrection for the just and unjust, eternal reward for the righteous and everlasting punishment for the wicked.

Plymouth Brethren hold that the true Church includes all regenerated believers; there are no specific requirements for membership, but all candidates are expected to give "satisfactory evidence of the new birth." They are received as "members of Christ" and do not join any organization. There are no ordained or salaried ministers in the usual sense; "personal gift and spiritual power" from the Holy Spirit are sufficient evidence of a call to ministry (I Corinthians 12:4-11). Hence they do recognize in certain men certain gifts of preaching and teaching, and those who devote their time to such work are supported by voluntary contributions. Gifted and godly men are acknowledged as elders and overseers, who hold no official position but who care for the spiritual needs of the saints.

Government among Brethren I and II is by individual assembly or congregation; these bodies hold that each assembly is responsible to the Lord alone as head of the Church. Brethren III to VIII, on the other hand, are joined in Circles of fellowship, as already described.

The idea of the "priesthood of all believers" is practiced in their meeting, service, and ministry. There is no ritual. The larger assemblies own church buildings, or gospel halls; smaller assemblies meet in rented halls or rooms, or in private residences. Baptism and the Lord's Supper are observed as ordinances; the Supper is celebrated each Sunday morning and the gospel preached at night. There are other meetings for prayer and Bible study, young people's meetings, missionary activities supported by voluntary subscription, tent meetings, evangelistic services, and the like.

Plymouth Brethren I follows closely the teachings of the English leader John Darby, of the original Plymouth congregation. It puts special emphasis upon the teaching that "eternal life in Christ is the common blessing of all believers of every age," in distinction to other Plymouth Brethren who restrict that blessing. There are about five thousand members.

Plymouth Brethren II is "open," hav-ing some fellowship with Christians beyond its own membership. Uniquely its members hold that ecclesiastical position in itself does not disqualify anyone. There is actually a variety of teaching here, some holding that an open ministry is obligatory, others that it is optional, and some others not tolerating it at all. This is the largest Plymouth body, claiming some fifteen thousand members. Plymouth Brethren I and II have a list of about 500 assemblies, 275 full-time ministers, and 200 foreign missionaries from assemblies in the United States and Canada.

Plymouth Brethren III had a thousand members and twenty-two assemblies, as of 1936; this might be called the high-church group, in as much as they believe that "absolute power of a judicial kind" has been assigned by Christ to the Christian assembly. They refuse fellowship with all of differing doctrine.

Plymouth Brethren IV refuses to be designated by any name, for this would make it a sect, and the Bible (I Corinthians 1:10-15) forbids all sects. Its differences with other Plymouth bodies are largely differences concerning government and discipline. There were 1,909 members and 56 assemblies, as of 1936.

Plymouth Brethren V clings closely to the doctrinal position of the original British (Plymouth) body. They do a widespread work in jails, hospitals, and so on, and distribute a large number of tracts and pamphlets. There were 1,776 members and 67 assemblies, as of 1936.

Plymonth Brethren VI is the smallest of all, with only two assemblies and thirty-four members in 1936. Their existence as a separate body goes back to the failure of an attempt to join all Plymouth Brethren bodies in England.

Plymouth Brethren VII and VIII are comparatively new organizations. Both were part of Plymouth Brethren I up to 1936. They have about two thousand members and a hundred assemblies.

Thus together all eight groups have an approximate membership in this country of 25,000. They are also found in Canada, Great Britain, and in various other countries. There is no unifying international bond or body.

RIVER BRETHREN

$\mathcal{A}$ considerable number of post-Reformation Pietists fleeing Europe settled in Lancaster County, Pennsylvania, in the year 1752. They were loosely grouped in a chain of brotherhoods—such as the ⁴Brotherhood in the North, the Brotherhood in Dauphin, and the Brotherhood in Bucks and Montgomery. The strongest group was known simply as the Brotherhood down by the River (the Susquehanna River), and later as River Brethren.

Various disputes, many of which would seem quite unimportant today, brought about the establishment of two smaller bodies—the Old Order or Yorker Brethren in 1843 and the Brinsers or United Zion's Children in 1853. The others remained in the original River Brethren body changing their name to the Brethren in Christ; they are today the largest of the three churches, which altogether number about 7,500 members.

Brethren in Christ

WITH THE outbreak of the Civil War the draft reached into the ranks of the River Brethren, and it became necessary for them to obtain legal recognition as an established religious organization in order to protect their objectors. Nonresistance had always been one of their cardinal principles. A council at Lancaster, Pennsylvania, in 1862 officially adopted the name Brethren in Christ, and the church was incorporated in 1904.

There is no allegiance to any written creed or confession in this church, but there is a strong statement of belief. It stands for justification by faith, holiness, divine healing, trine immersion, washing of the feet of the saints, the holy kiss, nonresistance, scriptural veiling of women, and the general resurrection of the dead. Members oppose all secret societies and frown upon worldly amusements. Many of the churches will not permit musical instruments within the sanctuary.

Government is in the hands of the local churches; the officers of the church include bishops, ministers, and deacons. There are district conferences and an annual general conference. Some of the churches have no stated ministerial remuneration, but in others regular salaries are paid.

A general executive board of seven members guides the over-all activities of the denomination; under this board a home missions board administers work in the United States and Canada, and a foreign missions board on work in Africa and India. There are four church schools: Messiah Bible College at Grantham, Pennsylvania; Beulah College at Upland, California; Bethany Bible School at Thomas, Oklahoma; and the Ontario Bible School in Ontario, Canada. Three philanthropic institutions are maintained, and a publishing house is located at Nappanee, Indiana. There are 5,319 members, and 98 churches.

Old Order or Yorker Brethren

THE Old Order or Yorker Brethren is the smallest of all River Brethren groups in the United States; they reported only 291 members and 7 churches in 1936. The primary reasons for their existence as a separate body lay in their feeling that the older River Brethren became lax in their enforcement of nonresistance and nonconformity to the world; they left the original body in 1843. Old Order in their name refers to their desire to keep the old traditions alive; Yorker resulted from the fact that most of them at the time of withdrawal lived in York County, Pennsylvania.

Their doctrine is identical with that of

other River Brethren bodies, except that they refuse to build or meet in church edifices; lacking these they meet usually in large barns owned by their members. There is no missionary or philanthropic program.

United Zion's Children

BISHOP MATTHIAS BRINSER was expelled from the River Brethren in 1855, together with about fifty others, for building and holding services in a meetinghouse; River Brethren were generally opposed to such edifices, preferring to meet in private homes in winter and small barns in summer. Within a few years after Brinser's expulsion, however, the older body began the erection of meetinghouses.

Essentially the same in doctrine as other River Brethren, they practice trine immersion, always preceded by "thorough repentance and remission of sins," and the usual foot washing at Communion, which is generally called a love feast.

Located today almost exclusively in Dauphin, Lebanon, and Lancaster Counties, Pennsylvania, they reported 1,240 members in 24 churches in 1936. There is a home for the aged, open to their own members and to members of other churches as well. No missionary work of their own is reported, but they support missionaries in other Brethren bodies. There is currently a strong interest in reunion with the Brethren in Christ; ministers are interchanged, as are delegates to their various conferences.

Buddhist Churches of America

BUDDHISM is found in real strength in this country in Utah, Arizona, Washington, Oregon, and California, and it represents the transplanting of the Buddhism of the East. Most of the Buddhists in the United States are Japanese or Japanese-Americans; there are, however, "English" departments in San Francisco, Los Angeles, and Tacoma, with American clergymen in charge.

The fact is built upon the teachings of the founder, Buddha—Siddartha Gautama, the Enlightened One (563-483 B.C.)—who attained his enlightenment in India and whose teachings have spread all over the Far East. Often challenged as a system of religious faith, it remains a most complex and involved pattern of thought and action. It is divided into two schools—Hinayana Buddhim, or the Lesser Vehicle, and Mahayana Buddhism, or the Greater Vehicle. These offer, on the one hand, a path of escape from suffering and, on the other, a thorough preparation for entry upon that path. Hinayana seems devised for those among its disciples who are satisfied with a comparatively modest attainment of Buddhist virtue, while

Mahayana is for those who would practice a more exacting discipleship. Buddha himself put the essence of his system in these words: "One thing only I teach. Sorrow [or pain], the cause of sorrow, the cessation of sorrow, and the path which leads to the cessation of sorrow." These are the Four Truths of Buddhism, the latter of which includes the actual means of arriving at these truths, by way of the "noble eightfold path"—"right views, right intention, right speech, right action, right livelihood, right effort, right mindfulness, right concentration." This description of the eight paths covers the whole training of the disciple who seeks nirvana, which means literally "blown out" or "extinguished." He strives to extinguish in his living all desire, hatred, and ignorance, and thus attain a nobler life.

There are no theories of creation, no miracles, and no divine being in Buddhism. Supreme reality is neither affirmed nor denied; it is only said to be beyond the comprehension of the human mind. It is actually a system of self-education in the conquering, or forgetting, of pain, sorrow, and suffering. Recognizing that this is a long process, the Buddha taught that man has an indefinite number of lives, or reincarnations, in which to accomplish it.

The titular head of American Buddhism bears the title of bishop superintendent; he is in charge of all religious activities, and he is authorized to transfer or dismiss the clergy under his jurisdiction. The first Buddhist church or temple in the United States was consecrated in San Francisco in 1905; the Buddhist Mission of North America was incorporated in 1942 as the Buddhist Churches of America. While no accurate figures on membership are available since the chaotic movements of our west-coast Japanese began with the opening of World War II, there are thought to be about seventy thousand Buddhists in the various groups. There are sixty-five ministers and two deans. Each church, of which there are forty-six, is autonomous, holding complete control of its own property. Weekly services are held, and Japanese language schools are maintained by many of the churches. Due to Buddhism's introspective nature and its lack of social outlook or endeavor, there are no hospitals or other philanthropic institutions, but a very active National Young Buddhist Co-ordinating Council has established district leagues in San Francisco, Seattle, Salt Lake City, Denver, and New York City.

Catholic Apostolic Church

THE FOUNDERS of the Catholic Apostolic Church never intended to establish a separate denomination. They were British millenarians who believed in the bestowal of the gifts of the Holy Spirit, their meetings characterized by speaking in tongues and prophetic revelations.

They also believed that a twelvefold apostleship was the only form of church government or supreme ecclesiastical authority authorized by Scripture, and that church officials should follow the order laid down in Ephesians 4:11. Accordingly they "set aside" twelve apostles who, being divinely called and not elected by the church, were "superior . . . to all other ministry." The movement began in England in 1830; their first church in America was established in 1851.

Their doctrine, based upon the Nicene, Apostolic, and Athanasian creeds, affirms belief in the authority and inspiration of the Bible, baptism, the Lord's Supper, the indissolubility of marriage short of death, the ordination of ministers (priests), the laying on of hands, the gift of tongues, the tithe—by which all their ministers are supported—and a strong insistence upon the premillennial appearance of Christ, who will raise the dead, translate the living, and establish peace on earth.

Church government, following the pattern of Ephesians, is in the hands of apostles, prophets, bishops (commonly called angels), evangelists, priests, and deacons. Only deacons are elected by the church; all others are chosen of God, but under the authority of the apostles. There are approximately 2,500 members in 7 churches in the United States. In as much as the last divinely chosen apostle died in 1901, there have been no ordinations of any sort since that year. There are no home or foreign missions, educational or institutional efforts, but there are a few Sunday schools. Worship and ritual are highly liturgical, laying great emphasis upon symbolism; their forms are borrowed from the great historic churches.

Christadelphians

DR. JOHN THOMAS came to the United States from England in 1844. He joined the Disciples of Christ but later became convinced that their doctrines

48

made them the apostate church predicted by Scripture, and that many other more important Bible doctrines were being neglected. He left the Disciples to organize a number of societies which under his leadership began preaching the need of a return to primitive Christianity. Loosely organized these societies bore no name until the outbreak of the Civil War, when their doctrine of nonresistance forced them to adopt the name Christadelphians or Brethren of Christ.

Christadelphians are both Unitarian and Adventist in theology. Holding that they alone interpret the Scriptures correctly, they reject the Trinity and belief in a devil; Christ is not God the Son but the Son of God, not pre-existent but born of Mary by the Holy Spirit. Man is mortal by nature, with Christ as his only means of salvation. Eternal life comes only to the righteous. Strong millenarians they believe that Christ will come shortly to reward the saints with immortality and destroy the wicked; he will take David's throne in Jerusalem, the twelve tribes will be gathered, and the world will be ruled from the Land of Canaan for a thousand years, after which a second resurrection will occur and judgment will be pronounced on all who have lived during the thousand years.

The church is congregational in polity; local organizations are known not as churches but as ecclesiae. Membership is by profession of faith and immersion. There are no paid or ordained ministers in the usual sense; each ecclesia elects serving brethren, among which are included managing brethren, presiding brethren, and lecturing brethren. Women take no part in public speech or prayer, though all vote equally. They do not vote in civil elections or participate in war, and they refuse to accept public office. There are no associations or conventions, but there are fraternal gatherings for spiritual inspiration. Meetings are generally held in rented halls, schoolhouses, or private homes; there are few church edifices.

Home missions work is local, usually in the form of lectures and instruction in Christadelphian doctrine. There are no foreign missions, but ecclesiae are found in several foreign countries. There is no educational work, with the exception of a summer Bible school in Arkansas. Found in 26 states from coast to coast in 1936, this church reported 2,755 members and 109 ecclesiae.

Christian and Missionary Alliance

THE Christian and Missionary Alliance, which prefers to be known not as a denomination but as an evangelistic and missionary movement, originated in 1881 under the leadership of the Rev. A. B. Simpson, a Presbyterian minister in New York City, who left that church to carry on independent evangelistic work among the unchurched. It was at first divided into two societies, the Christian Alliance for home missions work and the International Missionary Alliance for work abroad. The two bodies were merged in 1897 in the present Christian and Missionary Alliance.

Strongly evangelical and fundamentalist the alliance stands for the literal inspiration of the Bible, the atonement wrought by Christ, the reality of supernatural religious experience, separation from the world, the premillennial return of Jesus Christ, Spirit baptism, and practical holiness. While there is no creed as such, there is a formula of belief built upon a fourfold gospel of Christ as Saviour, Sanctifier, Healer, and coming Lord.

Work is carried on in 14 organized districts in the United States and Canada, with 939 churches fully or partially organized. Each of these churches or groups is a self-maintaining and self-governing unit engaged in missionary and evangelical activities. There is an over-all conference, which meets annually in various parts of the United States and Canada, called the General Council.

Foreign missionary work is carried on in South America, Africa, the Near East, India, China, Indo-China, Siam, the Philippines, and Indonesia. In 24 different mission fields are found 590 missionaries from the United States and 1,847 indigenous workers, and there are 796 organized churches with 74,062 members.

In addition to the organized church work in North America missionary work is carried on among Indians, Negroes, as well as in Mexico and the West Indies, and in certain other areas where there has not yet been full development. Bible training schools are maintained at Nyack, New York; St. Paul, Minnesota; Seattle, Washington; Regina, Saskatchewan, and Uree, North Carolina (Negro). In 1949 there were 45,348 members in North America in 879 churches. Thus the alliance has a larger constituency abroad than at home.

Christian Catholic Apostolic Church in Zion

JOHN ALEXANDER DOWIE, a Congregational minister in Scotland and Australia specializing in divine healing, came to the United States in 1888. Claiming to be Elijah III—Elijah II was John the Baptist—he organized the Christian Catholic Apostolic Church in Zion in 1896 at Chicago, where he conducted a series of startling mass healings, in a tabernacle. In 1901 he established Zion City, forty-two miles north of Chicago —a communistic sect and colony with communal businesses and industries, governed by a theocracy of which Dowie was "first apostle." The colony became notable for its code of "blue laws" and for an annual Passion play modeled on that of Oberammergau. Dowie was succeeded by Wilbur Glen Voliva, a former Disciples of Christ minister, as overseer of Zion. Under Voliva elders were appointed to carry on supervisory duties.

Religious thought in this church is extremely fundamentalist and literal; to this is added the practice of divine healing, a belief that the earth is flat and not round, a distrust of all modern science, and an expectation of the immediate second coming of Jesus Christ. The movement has failed to spread, though there are still a few missionaries at work. Zion City is no longer an exclusive community; both principles and laws have been greatly modified, and independent businesses and even churches have been welcomed. The community today bears little resemblance to the colony of Dowie and Voliva.

Christian Nation Church

ORIGINATING in a band of independent evangelists called equality evangelists, the Christian Nation Church was incorporated at Marion, Ohio, in 1895. By 1947 the membership was reported at 112 members in 5 churches in West Virginia and Ohio.

The church teaches a fourfold gospel: justification, entire sanctification, divine healing, and the second coming of Christ. Two ordinances, baptism and the Lord's Supper, are celebrated. Needless ornaments on clothing, worldly organizations and amusements, tobacco and liquor, Sabbath breaking, marriage with the unsaved and the remarriage of the divorced, jesting, foolish talking, and the singing of worldly songs are forbidden. Each family is encouraged to "raise just so large a family of children as God shall be pleased to give them"; tithing is practiced, and love for friend and enemy is emphasized. Days of fasting and prayer are observed, the sick and needy are assisted, and camp meetings are strongly supported.

Government is by the local churches, which are grouped into districts and which meet in annual conference. The licenses of all pastors expire at the end of each conference year.

Christian Union

CHRISTIAN UNION represents an attempt to unite all Christians on a scriptural basis, to provide within the union a larger liberty in thought and worship and freedom from ecclesiastical domination. Several independent groups, scattered from Vermont to Kentucky, were advocating these ideals prior to 1857; the strongly political and partisan preaching of the Civil War period brought to them many dissatisfied members from the larger Protestant churches, and Christian Union became an organized denomination in 1864. Among them were former Methodists, Brethren, Presbyterians, and Baptists. They are found today in seven states under two names: Christian Union and the Church of Christ in Christian Union. There were 15,400 members and 220 churches in 1938.

There is no one creed in this church; each member is left free to interpret the Scriptures for himself, but admission to membership requires a public confession of Christ as Saviour and acceptance of the Bible as the Word of God. Beyond this Christian Union stresses the oneness of the Church of Christ, Christ as the only head of the Church, the Bible as the sole guide to faith and practice, good fruits as the one condition of fellowship, Christian union without controversy, complete autonomy for the local church, and avoidance of all partisan or political preaching. Men and women are ordained ministers; ordinances include baptism—by any method, at the choice of the individual—the Lord's Supper, and occasionally foot washing.

While church government is congregational, a series of councils meet for fellowship and to conduct such business as concerns the entire church. Charge councils, made up of several churches served by the same pastor, meet quarterly; district councils, which are actually county units, meet semiannually; state councils meet annually and are composed of pastors and lay delegates; and a general council meets once every four years with both ministerial and lay delegates.

Local missionary work is largely evangelistic and is carried on by state missionary boards; a general mission board administers home missionary work and a small foreign missions effort through the Ceylon and India General Mission. The Chicago Tract Society engages in a work of Americanism and evangelism among the foreign-born. There are no colleges or other educational institutions; a home for aged clergymen is maintained at Excelsior Springs, Missouri.

Christ's Sanctified Holy Church (Colored)

THIS CHURCH began with the preaching of holiness and sanctification in the Colored Methodist Church in Louisiana by a small body of white evangelists; it was organized in 1904 as the Colored Church South. Its central theme is sanctification by faith, "as a distinct experience from justification by faith in Christ, which is not brought about by a growth in grace but is wrought instantaneously." There is emphasis on "one Lord, one faith, one baptism"; unequal persons, holy and unholy, should not marry; both men and women are ordained to the ministry; the strict observance of all church rules is required; no member using or selling tobacco or alcoholic liquors is acceptable; and members pledge that they will "ex-

51

pose all evil" to church officials. The governing body is a five-member Board No. 1, which ordains all deacons, deaconesses, and ministers, and supervises boards of extension, investigation, managers, ministers, and others. An an-nual conference meets in September, a district conference in June, a Sunday-school convention in March. The church, listing 884 members, is too small to maintain any sizable missionary, philanthropic, or educational work.

Church of Christ (Holiness), U.S.A.

C. P. JONES, a Baptist preacher in Selma, Alabama, and Jackson, Mississippi, left that denomination in 1894 to seek a faith which would make him "one of wisdom's true sons and, like Abraham, 'a friend of God.'" He called a convention at Jackson, enlisting the aid of men who like himself were interested in holiness, and founded there a holiness movement, which was at first completely interdenominational. By 1898, however, it had become a full-fledged denomination; in 1948 it reported some 7,685 members.

Doctrine in this church emphasizes original sin, Christ's atonement and his second coming; sacraments include the gift of the Holy Ghost, baptism by im-mersion, the Lord's Supper, foot washing, and divine healing. Episcopal in government, the church is led by bishops, one of whom is named senior bishop. The final authority in doctrine and church law is vested in the biennial annual convention.

The church is divided into seven dioceses, each under the charge of a bishop. A district convention meets semiannually, made up of elders, ministers, and local church representatives. A small missionary work is supported at home and abroad; there is a college, Christ Missionary and Industrial College, at Jackson, Mississippi, Boydton Institute at Boydton, Virginia, and a publishing house at Los Angeles, California.

Church of Christ, Scientist

AT Lynn, Massachusetts, in 1866, Mary Baker Eddy recovered almost instantly from a severe injury after reading in Matthew 9:1-8 the account of Christ's healing of the man sick of the palsy. Profoundly religious and a lifelong student of mental and spiritual causation, she came to attribute causation to God and to regard him as divine Mind. From these roots came Christian Science and the Church of Christ, Scientist.

Generally described as "a religious teaching and practice based on the words and works of Christ Jesus," Christian Science was regarded by Mrs. Eddy as "divine metaphysics," as the "scientific system of divine healing," and as "the law of God, the law of good, interpreting and demonstrating the divine Principle and rule of universal harmony." She believed the "Principle of all harmonious Mind-action to be God"; she wrote these definitions and descriptions of her faith in *Science and Health with Key to the Scriptures*, a famous volume which has become the textbook of Christian Science.

Like many other religious leaders and pioneers, Mrs. Eddy hoped to work through existing churches; she did not plan another denomination. But organization became necessary as interest in the movement spread, and under her direction the first Christian Science church was established at Boston in 1879. In 1892 this church was reorganized; it is still known as the First Church of Christ, Scientist, in Boston, Massachusetts, or more frequently as the Mother Church. All other Christian Science churches the world over are branches of this Mother Church.

Applied not only to the healing of sickness but to the problems of life gen-

CHURCH OF CHRIST, SCIENTIST

erally, the tenets and doctrines of Christian Science are often confusing to the non-Scientist and call for careful explanation. They start with the conviction that God is the only might or Mind; he is "All-in-all," the "divine Principle of all that really is," "the all-knowing, all-seeing, all-acting, all-wise, all-loving, and eternal; Principle; Mind; Soul; Spirit; Life; Truth; Love; all substance; intelligence." The inspired Word of the Bible is accepted as "sufficient guide to eternal Life." The tenets state: "We acknowledge and adore one supreme and infinite God. We acknowledge His Son, one Christ; the Holy Ghost or divine Comforter; and man in God's image and likeness." Jesus is known to Christian Scientists as Master or Way-shower. His chief work lies in the Atonement, "the evidence of divine, efficacious love, unfolding man's unity with God through Christ Jesus the Way-shower." Man, made in the image of God, "is saved through Christ, through Truth, Life, and Love as demonstrated by the Galilean Prophet in healing the sick and overcoming sin and death." The crucifixion and resurrection of Jesus are held as serving "to uplift faith to understand eternal Life, even the allness of Soul, Spirit, and the nothingness of matter."

This "nothingness of matter" involves the basic teaching of Christian Science concerning what is real and unreal. "All reality," says Mrs. Eddy, "is in God and His creation, harmonious and eternal. That which He creates is good, and He makes all that is made. Therefore the only reality of sin, sickness, or death is the awful fact that unrealities seem real to human, erring belief, until God strips off their disguise. They are not true, because they are not of God. "God forgives sin in destroying sin, with the spiritual understanding that casts out evil as unreal." The punishment for sin, however, lasts as long as the belief in sin endures.

It is a mistake to believe that the followers of Christian Science ignore that which they consider unreal; they rather seek to forsake and overcome error and evil by demonstrating the true idea of reality, with the help of spiritual law and spiritual power. Error is simply "a supposition that pleasure and pain, that intelligence, substance, life, are existent in matter. . . . It is that which seemeth to be and is not."

Certain terms are important in the exposition of Christian Science. *Animal magnetism* is the mesmeric action of erroneous belief; Christian Science is its antithesis. *Healing* is not miraculous but divinely natural; disease is a mental concept dispelled by the introduction of spiritual truth. *Heaven* is not a locality but "harmony; the reign of Spirit; government by divine Principle; spirituality; bliss; the atmosphere of Soul." *Hell* is "mortal belief; error; lust; remorse; hatred; revenge; sin; sickness; death; suffering and self-destruction; self-imposed agony; effects of sin; that which 'worketh abomination or maketh a lie.'" *Mortal mind* is "the flesh opposed to Spirit, the human mind and evil in contradistinction to the divine Mind." *Prayer* is "an absolute faith that all things are possible to God—a spiritual understanding of Him, an unselfed love." *Baptism* is not a ceremony in this church, but a spiritual experience in each individual, a "purification from all error."

All local churches in Christian Science, of which there are more than three thousand, as branches of the Mother Church are organized under the laws of the states or countries in which they exist. They enjoy their own forms of democratic government, but they are still subject to the bylaws laid down in the *Church Manual* by Mrs. Eddy. The affairs of the Mother Church are administered by the Christian Science Board of Directors, which elects a president, the first and second readers, a clerk, and a treasurer. The Board of Directors is a self-perpetuating body electing all other officers of the church annually, with the exception of the readers, who are elected by the board for a term of three years.

53

All-important in the continuing teaching of Christian Science are the reader, teacher, and practitioner. There are two readers in each church, usually a man and a woman; in all Christian Science services on Sunday and Thanksgiving Day they read alternately from the Bible and from *Science and Health;* the lesson-sermon of the Sunday service is prepared by a committee of Scientists and issued quarterly by the Christian Science Publishing Society. This system is followed by all Christian Science churches throughout the world. A midweek service, which is conducted by the First Reader alone, features testimonies of healing from sin and sickness.

Practitioners devote their full time to healing and are authorized to practice by the Board of Directors. There is a Board of Education consisting of three members, a president, vice-president, and teacher of Christian Science. Under the supervision of this board a normal class is held once in three years. Teachers are duly authorized by certificates granted by the Board of Education to form classes of pupils in Christian Science. One class of not more than thirty pupils is instructed by each teacher annually. Reading rooms open to the general public are maintained by all churches.

There is a Board of Lectureship consisting of nearly thirty members. These members are appointed annually by the Board of Directors. At the invitation of branch churches free lectures are given by these members all over the world. A Committee on Publication works to correct impositions or misstatements concerning Christian Science in the public press. The Christian Science Publishing Society is one of the most effective units within the church; it publishes very much and very well written literature, including the *Christian Science Sentinel,* the *Christian Science Journal,* the *Christian Science Quarterly,* the *Herald of Christian Science* in seven languages and in Braille, and the *Christian Science Monitor.* The *Monitor* is acknowledged in all journalism to be one of the finest newspapers in the world. There are two Christian Science Benevolent Association Sanatoriums and a home for elderly Christian Scientists, which are maintained by the Christian Science church.

The bylaws written by Mrs. Eddy prohibit the publishing of membership statistics; no comprehensive, accurate, or up-to-date figures are available. The government census of 1936 reported 268,915 members, but this figure has since been held inaccurate and not at all indicative of the total membership strength of the Mother Church and the branches. Actually today the figure would be much larger than this; in deference to the wishes of the officials of the church no estimate will be given here. It is enough to remark upon a strange situation, found here and probably in no other church in America: the number of people studying Christian Science and attending its services but not yet admitted to full membership exceeds the number who have been so admitted.

CHURCH OF GOD

*A*t least two hundred independent religious bodies in the United States bear the name Church of God in one form or another. Of these, five different Church of God groups have their headquarters in Cleveland, Tennessee. The Cleveland bodies have a common origin in the movement inaugurated by A. J. Tomlinson, an American Bible Society colporteur in North Carolina, who was general overseer of the movement from 1903 to 1923, when a disagreement arose over the form of government, elective versus appointive, of the group. A subsequent dispute over his successor, following Tomlinson's death in 1943, left the group divided into three main bodies: one, with H. L. Chesser as general overseer, has its headquarters at Cleveland; another, with Milton A. Tomlinson as overseer, also has headquarters in Cleveland; and a third, with Homer A. Tomlinson as general overseer or bishop, has its headquarters in Queens Village, New York.

There are minor differences in doctrine between these three groups, but generally they emphasize justification by faith, sanctification, baptism of the Holy Spirit, speaking in other tongues, being "born again," fruitfulness in Christian living, and a strong interest in the second coming of Christ. The Chesser group especially, while "relying upon the Bible as a whole rightly divided "rather than upon any written creed, is definitely Arminian in theology, Pentecostal, and holiness. The Queens Village body puts strong emphasis upon the fulfillment of Scripture "for the last days" and upon preparation now for the return of Christ.

The Cleveland bodies elect their officers; the Queens Village body appoints them. There are differences in licensing and ordaining ministers. Their ministry includes three orders: minister of the gospel, evangelist, and exhorter. Sacraments include baptism by immersion, the Lord's Supper, and foot washing.

Accurate membership statistics are difficult to obtain. The Church of God over which H. L. Chesser is general overseer claims 90,000 members in 2,200 churches; the Queens Village body claims 15,000 in 2,500 churches; the group under the supervision of Milton A. Tomlinson lists 2,200 churches and approximately 15,000 members. This would give them a total of 120,000 in the three branches.

The Chesser group holds state assemblies and an annual general assembly, maintains a General Bible School for the training of ministers, and several branch Bible institutes, an orphanage, children's home, and publishing house. Foreign missions are directed by a missions board, but home missions are in charge of a state superintendent and his council.

The claim is made that forty-four Protestant denominations have grown out of the labors of the common founder of the Church of God movement, A. J. Tomlinson.

Church of God (Anderson, Indiana)

THE Church of God, with headquarters at Anderson, Indiana, started about 1880 as a movement within existing churches. It prefers to have its name accepted in an inclusive rather than in a denominational sense and is actually a movement in the direction of Christian unity and the re-establishment of the New Testament standard of faith and life by realizing the identity of the visible and invisible church in the free fellowship of believers. The founders believed that the Church at large was too much restricted and overburdened with organization and ecclesiasticism; it should be "more directly under the rule of God."

Doctrine in this church includes belief in the divine inspiration of the Scriptures; the forgiveness of sin through the atonement of Christ and repentance of the believer; the experience of holiness; the personal return of Christ, which is not connected with any millennial reign; the kingdom of God as established here and now; the final judgment; the resurrection of the dead; the reward of the righteous and the punishment of the wicked.

Baptism is by immersion; members of this church also practice foot washing and observe the Lord's Supper, but not as conditions of fellowship. They believe the Church to be the body of Christ, made up of all Christians, and that all Christians are one in Christ. The confusion of sects and denominations, however, is an obstacle to this unity; being unscriptural it should be removed. God desires this restoration of the New Testament ideal in his church; it is a restoration based upon spiritual experience and not on creedal agreement.

There were 105,022 members reported in this church in 1949. They are governed by a congregational system; while they preach the idea of God governing his church, they agree that the aid of human personalities is quite necessary. Membership is not a formal basis, and hence no formal records are kept. Ministers meet in voluntary state and regional conventions, which are purely advisory. The General Ministerial Assembly meets annually in connection with the annual convention and camp meeting held at Anderson, Indiana.

(Original) Church of God

THIS CHURCH was organized in Tennessee in 1886 under the name Church of God after a difference of opinion in regard to doctrine and teaching brought about a split among the followers of the Rev. R. Spurling. The faction adhering to the original doctrines added the word Original to the name and incorporated in 1922.

The church believes in "the whole Bible, rightly divided"; in repentance, justification, and regeneration as defined by Martin Luther; in sanctification as defined by John Wesley; in divine healing; in the second coming of Christ; in eternal life for the righteous and eternal punishment for the wicked. Christian fruits alone stand as evidence of faithful Christian living; creeds that bind the conscience are considered unscriptural. Pentecostal experience and speaking with tongues are accepted; ordinances include baptism by immersion, the Lord's tithing, and free-will offerings.

Local churches, following the apostolic pattern, take local names, such as the Church at Corinth. Each local church is independent. The church recognizes the New Testament orders of ministers, apostles, exhorters, evangelists, bishops, and teachers, as given in Ephesians 4:11-14. A general convention meets annually; there is a general office and publishing house, and denominational headquarters, at Chattanooga, Tennessee. There are 5,000 members, 58 churches.

Church of God (Stanberry, Missouri)

AT THE the time of the Puritan migration to Massachusetts there were at least seven churches in London bearing the name Church of God; members of these congregations settled in Massachusetts, Pennsylvania, Rhode Island, and New Jersey between 1664 and 1800. Many drifted West and South after the Revolution; the Church of God at Shrewsbury, New Jersey, moved to Salem, West Virginia, in 1789; another group became strong in Missouri. Formal organization of these scattered churches was effected in Michigan in 1865, and headquarters were eventually established at Stanberry, Missouri.

These people constituted a Church of God that was a Sabbatarian, observing the seventh day as the true Sabbath. A large number of their membership joined the Adventist movement led by Ellen Harmon White, and changed the names of their churches accordingly; those who could not become Adventists reorganized under the old name, Church of God. A second withdrawal from their membership resulted in the organization of the Church of God (Seventh-Day) in 1933, with headquarters at Salem, West Virginia. These two latter bodies were reunited in August, 1949, under the present name, Church of God.

Details in doctrine and administration remain to be worked out in this merger. Generally, fundamentalist theology and doctrine prevail. The church believes in the infallibility of the Scriptures, in the natural sinfulness of man, the blood atonement of Christ on the cross for all men, the remission of sin by baptism, premillennialism, annihilation of the wicked and the reward of the righteous at the final judgment, the observance of the seventh day as the Sabbath, holiness in living, abstinence from tobacco, alcoholic liquors, narcotics, and so forth, and the use of only such foods as are classed as clean by the Scriptures.

A general conference will meet every two years; an executive board of twelve ministers accredited by the general conference will be the direct administrative body, and state conferences with executive boards of seven members each will be organized. In the general conference there will be seven departments of work, with a secretary in charge of each, under the supervision of the twelve member executive board. A ministerial council will restate the doctrine of the united church and pass upon the qualifications of its ministers.

Missionary work at home and abroad will be divided into districts, with a member of the national executive board in charge of each district. The reunited church has approximately 45,000 members and 1,250 churches.

Church of God and Saints of Christ

THE Church of God and Saints of Christ was founded in Kansas in 1896 by William S. Crowdy, a Negro cook on the Santa Fe Railroad who claimed visions from God, a divine commission to lead his people, and a prophetic endowment. He became the first bishop of the church and is still known as the prophet.

The members of the church, 34,610 in number, believe that the Negro people are descendants of the lost tribes of Israel. Sometimes called "Black Jews," they observe the Old Testament Sabbath and feast days, and use Hebrew names for the months of the year. Following the teachings of the Prophet, they call for literal interpretation and practice of the Ten Commandments. A pamphlet entitled *Seven Keys* is published, explaining to the faithful just which commandments are to be thus followed, and why. Members are admitted on confession of faith, repentance of sin, baptism by immersion, the taking of Communion, foot washing, instruction in prayer by an elder, and on promise to obey the Ten Commandments.

An executive board or council of twelve ordained elders or evangelists, usually called a presbytery, administers the general business of the church. A

Prophet, or successor to Crowdy, still stands at the head of the organization; he holds his position not by election but by divine call, and he is said to be in direct communication with God, to utter inspired prophecies, and to perform miracles. His office remains vacant on his death until another vision is given.

Other officers include ministers not fully ordained, elders fully ordained, evangelists, and bishops. Deacons supervise the temporal affairs of the church under the direction of annual district and general assemblies. Tithes are collected for the support of the ministry and the Prophet; "storehouses" are established by the district assemblies to receive the tithes and to distribute groceries and other necessities to the members. There is strong emphasis on temperance; marriage is permissible only between members of the church. The Belleville Industrial School and Widows and Orphans Home is located at Belleville, Virginia.

Church of God in Christ

ELDER C. H. MASON, a Tennessee Negro, severed his connections with the Baptists in 1897 and organized the Church of God in Christ, a name divinely revealed. He put strong emphasis upon "entire sanctification" and in a revival received the baptism of the Holy Spirit together with "signs of speaking with other tongues." His ardent preaching on these gifts aroused resentment and a subsequent division of followers.

Doctrine is Trinitarian, stressing repentance, regeneration, justification, sanctification, speaking in tongues, and the gift of healing as evidence of the baptism of the Holy Spirit. Holiness is considered a prerequisite to salvation. Ordinances include baptism by immersion, the Lord's Supper, and foot washing.

Church organization is held to have its authority in Scripture; it consists of a Chief Apostle—(or General Overseer)— apostles, prophets, evangelists, pastors, elders, overseers, teachers, deacons, deaconesses, and missionaries. Each local church has an overseer; a state overseer supervises groups of churches within each state and holds state and district conferences annually. A general convocation meets once a year; membership was 340,530 in 1949.

Church of the East and of the Assyrians

THIS IS an American branch of what was for many centuries the major part of the Christian Church, with its patriarch residing in Seleucia-Ctesiphon, Chaldea, Mesopotamia. It spread out from Urhai (Edessa) and Arbil, sending missionaries into Persia, India, China, and throughout all Asia during the first century and thereafter. It is an Aramaic-speaking church, recognized as a Nestorian body rather than as an Eastern Orthodox church; being monophysite—in opposition to the Council of Chalcedon it recognizes but one composite nature in Christ—it is not to be included among official Eastern Orthodox branches.

The chief officer of the church is Chief Bishop Mar Eshai Shimun XXIII, with headquarters in Chicago. About three thousand members were reported in 1949, in ten churches.

Church of the Nazarene

THE THEOLGICAL and doctrinal foundations of the Church of the Nazarene lie in the preaching of the doctrines of holiness and sanctification as taught by John Wesley in the eighteenth century revival in England. Its physical structure is the result not so much of schism as of the merging of three independent holiness groups already in existence in the United States. An eastern Holiness body, located principally in New York and New England and known as the Association of Pentecostal Churches in America, joined at Chicago in 1907 with a Western (California) body called the Church of the Nazarene; the two merging churches agreed on the name the Pentecostal Church of the Nazarene. The southern group, known as the Holiness Church of Christ, united with this Pentecostal Church of the Nazarene at Pilot Point, Texas, in 1908. In 1919 the word "Pentecostal" was dropped from the name, leaving it as we know it today, the Church of the Nazarene. This was primarily a move to disassociate in the public mind any connection with the other and more radical Pentecostal groups which taught or practiced speaking in tongues, a teaching and practice always opposed by the Church of the Nazarene.

The background of the Nazarenes is definitely Methodist; they adhere closely to the original Wesleyan ideology. Most of the early holiness groups in this country came out of the Methodist Episcopal Church; five of the original seven general superintendents of the Church of the Nazarene were ex-Methodist ministers, and the Nazarene *Manual* has been called "a rewritten and modified Methodist *Discipline*."

The doctrine of the church is built around sanctification as a second definite work of grace, subsequent to regeneration; all ministers and local church officials must have undergone this experience. Other doctrines include belief in the plenary inspiration of the Scriptures as containing all truth necessary to Christian faith and living; in the atonement of Christ for the whole human race; in the justification, regeneration, and adoption of all penitent believers in Christ; in the second coming of Christ, the resurrection of the dead, and the final judgment. Members of this church believe in divine healing, but never to the exclusion of medical agencies. The use of tobacco and alcoholic beverages is denounced. Two ordinances—baptism by sprinkling, pouring, or immersion, and the Lord's Supper—are accepted as "instituted by Christ." Members are admitted on confession of faith and on agreement "to observe the rules and regulations . . . of the Church." It is a middle-of-the-road church, neither extremely ritualistic on the one hand nor fanatically evangelistic on the other; one church historian calls it "the right ring of the holiness movement."

There are 3,469 local congregations grouped into 62 districts. Local pastors are elected by local churches; each district is supervised by a district superintendent elected annually by the members of the district assembly. Quadrennially the various districts elect delegates to a general assembly, at which general superintendents are elected for a term of four years to supervise the work of the entire denomination. All this closely resembles the Methodist system of administration; in general it may be said that the Nazarenes have the more democratic form and procedure.

The general assembly also elects a general board, consisting of an equal number of lay and ministerial members, which is in turn divided into six administrative departments: foreign missions, home missions and evangelism, publication, ministerial benevolence, education, and church schools. Foreign missionary work is conducted in twenty-three fields with two hundred missionaries and nine hundred native members at work. Home mission activities are carried on in all sixty-two districts and in five areas outside continental United States; strong emphasis is laid upon evangelism. Six liberal-arts colleges are maintained; there are a theological seminary in Kansas City, a Bible institute (Negro) at Institute, West Virginia, Bible colleges in Canada and the British Isles, and the Nazarene Samaritan Hospital and School of Nursing at Nampa, Idaho.

The books and periodicals of the church are produced at the Nazarene Publishing House in Kansas City, Missouri: thirty-five periodicals are published, and the annual volume of business exceeds $1,300,000.

Membership in the United States is reported at 220,042, with an additional 24,048 abroad. There are 3,751 churches at home and overseas, 4,415 ordained ministers, 3,395 Sunday schools, and 2,595 young people's societies with a membership of 71,979.

Churches of Christ

BORN IN the days of the antimissionary movement on the American frontier, the Churches of Christ represent a breach in the ranks of the Disciples of Christ. The dispute which brought about the breach and separation included objections to any church with a "money basis," organized missionary societies, closed versus open Communion, the use of the title "Reverend," the pastoral system and emphasis on the ordained ministry, the use of creeds, and the employment of instrumental (organ) music in the churches. The organ and missionary questions were the direct cause of the rupture.

The debate began in 1859; the two opposing parties, Conservatives and Progressives, remained within the Disciples of Christ Church until 1906, when the Conservatives reported for the first time as a separate denomination. The Magna Carta of the separating body may be found in its declaration: "Where the Scriptures speak, we speak; where the Scriptures are silent, we are silent." They demanded a biblical basis for all church worship and procedure, and reserved for themselves the right to say what was scriptural and what was not.

Doctrinally the Churches of Christ reject all human creeds and confessions, and emphasize the "Divine Sonship of Jesus" and the "divine personality of the

Holy Spirit." The Lord's Supper is observed every Sunday as a memorial rather than as a sacrament.

This church, "with such officers as belonged to it in apostolic times," is considered by its membership to be a divine institution; they do not think of the Churches of Christ as of recent origin, but as established on the first Pentecost after the resurrection and ascension of Christ. Paul speaks of the "churches of Christ" in Romans 16:16. They claim too to occupy the original ground on which Alexander Campbell, of the Disciples of Christ, stood when he "restored the ancient order of things." They do not think of themselves as being denominational but "rather desire to be as the church of the first century."

Local churches are completely independent, electing their own officers and ministers, who are called elders. They are strictly congregational, with no organization larger than the local church— no conferences, presbyteries, synods, or assemblies of any kind. The ministerial office is not emphasized, so there are no ministerial associations. While there is no publication house, there are six unofficial publications. The church practices open Communion and shuns all fraternization with other churches. There are no home or foreign missionary societies, but they not shun foreign missions as such; they have ministers serving as missionaries abroad, supported by individuals or local church congregations. There are about fourteen thousand churches with a membership of about one million, seven colleges, several academies and professional schools, two homes for the aged, and seven orphanages.

Churches of Christ in Christian Union of Ohio

A DIFFERENCE of opinion in the Council of the Christian Union Churches concerning holiness as a second definite work of grace subsequent to regeneration brought about the organization of the Churches of Christ in Christian Union of Ohio, at Washington Courthouse, Ohio, in 1909. When the majority of the council decided against those holding the second-blessing view, the minority withdrew.

Aside from this second-blessing doctrine the body has the usual fundamentalist theology; there is strong emphasis on divine healing and the second coming of Christ. Church administration is congregational; pastors, with the aid of first, second, and third elders, guide the spiritual affairs of the church, while trustees administer all business matters. Each local church is a member of a general council and is subject to the council's rulings; all ministers are ordained by the council's examining committee. Members are admitted on evidence of "good fruits" and "a personal experience of the new birth."

Foreign missionary work is conducted in India, Africa, South America, and Mexico; there is widespread work in the fields of home missions, youth, welfare, and publishing. Headquarters are located at the Mount of Praise Camp Ground, Circleville, Ohio. There are 4,797 members and 142 churches.

Churches of God, Holiness

THE Churches of God, Holiness, began in 1914 with a group of eight people in Atlanta, Georgia, under the preaching of K. H. Burrus. Large churches were founded in Atlanta and Norfolk, Virginia, in 1916, and by 1922 there were twenty-two churches in eleven states, Cuba, the Canal Zone, and the British West Indies. In 1922 these churches were incorporated into what is currently known as the National Convention of the Churches of God, Holiness.

All doctrine within this group is tested strictly by New Testament standards; the Scriptures are accepted as inspired, and the New Testament "gives safe and clearly applied instructions on all methods of labor, sacred and secular," and on the conduct of the whole of life. The churches believe in the Trinity, in justificaton, entire sanctification, and regeneration, and hold that the gift of the Holy Spirit is an act subsequent to conversion. Perfection is both *present* and *ultimate*. One must believe in divine healing to be acceptable as a member, but medicines and doctors are approved for those who desire them, not being expressly denounced by Scripture. Two ordinances, baptism and the Lord's Supper, are observed. The washing of feet is approved but not regularly practiced.

Pastors of all churches are assigned by the one bishop of the denomination; they are assisted in the local congregation by deacons. In direct supervision over the pastors is the state overseer, also appointed by the bishop. State conventions are held annually. The highest administrative body is the national convention, a delegated body that elects the national president, or bishop, who from the start has been the founder, K. H. Burrus. This church reported 5,872 members and 35 churches in 1936.

Churches of God in North America (General Eldership)

THE Methodist, Presbyterian, Baptist, and German Reformed churches among the Germans of Pennsylvania were active in the religious revival which swept this country in the early years of the nineteenth century. John Winebrenner, a German Reformed pastor in Harrisburg, aroused criticism and finally determined opposition by his ardent evangelical preaching during this period, and he severed his connections with his Reformed brethren in 1928. As early as 1825 he had organized an independent congregation, which he called the Church of God. Six other preachers joined with him in 1830 to organize the General Eldership of the Church of God, using the word "General" to distinguish it from local church eldership. The words "in North America" were added in 1845, and "Church" became "Churches" in 1896.

Arminian in theology, these churches have no written creed; the Bible is considered the sole rule of faith and practice. "Bible things, as church offices and customs, should be known by Bible names, and a Bible name should not be applied to anything not mentioned in the Bible." Sectarianism is held to be anti-Scriptural; "each local church is a church of God and should be so called," and this church in a denominational sense is the only true church. Three ordinances are "perpetually obligatory" —baptism by immersion only, the Lord's Supper, and foot washing; the last two are companion ordinances, observed together and in the evening. There is strong insistence upon the Trinity, human depravity, the sacrificial atonement of Christ, the office and work of the Holy Spirit, man's moral agency, justification by faith, repentance and regeneration, practical piety, Sabbath observance, the resurrection of the dead, the eternal nature of the soul, and final judgment.

The church is organized into seventeen elderships, or conferences, in as many states. Over these is a general eldership, composed of an equal number of lay and ministerial delegates from the lower elderships, which meets triennially and has charge of the general interests of the church. In local affairs the churches are presbyterian in government, but ministers are appointed to their churches by the annual elderships.

Home and foreign missionary work is under the supervision of the Board of Missions, elected triennially. Home missions are confined principally to the West and Southwest; foreign mission stations are found in India and other fields.

There is one college, at Findlay, Ohio, and a publishing house at Harrisburg, Pennsylvania. There were 372 churches and 33,831 members in this group in 1949.

Churches of the Living God

Two NEGRO churches, similar in type but differing in details, are found under the general title Churches of the Living God: the Church of the Living God, Christian Workers for Fellowship; and the Church of the Living God, the Pillar and Ground of the Truth.

The first and parent body was founded at Wrightsville, Arkansas, in 1889 by Elder William Christian, who was known as Chief of the church, a title which still persists. Leadership and control seem to have been held firmly by members of the Christian family to the present time. Their rulings are final; while there is a general assembly, nothing may be done without their approval. In many ways the body is exactly what its name implies—a fellowship, as much fraternal as religious. Doctrine includes belief in baptism by immersion, the use of water and unleavened bread at the Lord's Supper, and "many other fraternal points of doctrine known only to members of the organization." Attention is given to the care of the sick and the burial of the dead along the lines of strictly fraternal societies. Local congregations are grouped not into churches but into temples. The ministry includes ambassadors (assistants to the acting head of the church), evangelists, pastors, and missionaries. A House of Refuge for the aged is maintained at Memphis, Tennessee.

Membership in this parent church has declined swiftly, from 4,525 in 1936 to a reported 120 in 1944, because of a series of deflections and divisions. In 1925 a number of withdrawing churches were united under the name the Church of the Living God, the Pillar and Ground of the Truth. It was joined in 1926 by another seceding body, the Church of the Living God, General Assembly, and by a group of churches in Texas known simply as the Church of the Living God.

The main differences between the two existing bodies lie not in doctrine but in government. The Church of the Living God, the Pillar and Ground of the Truth, is episcopal, having three bishops who hold annual assemblies in three dioceses. A general assembly meets every two years to elect such bishops as are necessary and to supervise generally the work of the church. There are a Booker T. Washington Home for the Aged at Oklahoma City and a secondary school and orphanage, The Edmondson Institute and Orphanage, at Athens, Texas. The official organ of the church, the *Western News Review*, is published at Oklahoma City. There are 3,185 members grouped in 85 churches.

Churches of the New Jerusalem

COMMONLY called Swedenborgian, the Churches of the New Jerusalem are based on the teachings of Emanuel Swedenborg and are actually two denominations rather than one. The older body is the General Convention of the New Jerusalem in the United States of America; the General Church of the New Jerusalem broke from this body in 1890.

Swedenborg, who was born in Stockholm in 1688 and died in London in 1772, was a Swedish scientist distinguished in the fields of mathematics, cosmology, and anatomy before he turned seriously to theology. Interested in the relation of these sciences to the spiritual life of man, he experienced a series of dreams and visions which resulted in an illumination of the things

CHURCHES OF THE NEW JERUSALEM

and ways of the spiritual world. He claimed to have had communication with the other world and to have witnessed certain stages of the last judgment there. He taught that with this judgment a first dispensation of the Christian Church had come to an end, and a new dispensation which he called the New Jerusalem or the Descent of the Holy City, was beginning. While he said that he was "dead on this side of the world," he still continued his usual activities in the world, including participation in the Swedish Parliament, of which he was a member.

Certain that he was divinely commissioned to teach the doctrines of the New Church, Swedenborg taught divinity in man—that God *is* man, meaning that the origin of all that is truly human is in God. The Divine Humanity is, however, Christ's glorified and risen humanity, in which God is manifested and which is God's. These doctrines were accepted and preached by his followers, who considered him to be a divinely illuminated seer and revelator. With the help of his concept of "correspondence" with the spiritual world he expounded a deeper and additional sense of the Scriptures than was offered by most interpreters of his time. Swedenborg himself never preached, and he preferred to leave his followers in the churches of which they were already members; he never intended to found a new sect or church.

The New Church as an organization started in London in 1783 when Robert Hindmarsh, a printer, gathered a few friends together to read and discuss the writings of Swedenborg; they formed a general conference of their societies in 1815. The first Swedenborgian Society in America was organized at Baltimore in 1792; in 1817 the General Convention of the New Jerusalem in the United States of America was established.

The doctrines of the General Convention as given in the *Liturgy* are as follows:

1. That there is one God, in whom there is a Divine Trinity; and that He is the Lord Jesus Christ.
2. That a saving faith is to believe on Him.
3. That evils are to be shunned, because they are of the devil and from the devil.
4. That good actions are to be done, because they are of God and from God.
5. That these are to be done by a man as from himself; but that it ought to be believed that they are done from the Lord with him and by him.

The societies are grouped into a general convention meeting annually; there are also state associations. Each society is self-regulating, with general pastors (actually bishops) supervising the work of the whole body. A distinction is made among ministers (ordained but without assigned pastorates), pastors (in charge of local societies), and general pastors (bishops). Services are liturgical, using chants extensively but with wide latitude, and based on the *Book of Worship* issued by the general convention.

The general convention now has 4,621 members active in 52 societies; it carries on a home mission program in the United States and a foreign missions program in fourteen countries abroad. A theological school is located at Cambridge, Massachusetts, and the Swedenborg Foundation in New York City distributes Swedenborg's writings. The church publishes two weeklies, a young people's monthly, and a quarterly.

The General Church of the New Jerusalem holds the same doctrine, emphasizing the "original" teachings of Swedenborg. There is no fixed constitution in this church; polity is based on "practical unanimity" in council and assembly. There are ministers, pastors, and bishops, the latter being chosen by a general assembly; there are 1,496 members in 10 societies. There are a theological school, one college, an academy for boys, and a seminary for girls. Headquarters are at Bryn Athyn, Pennsylvania, where a cathedral church has been built.

CONGREGATIONAL CHRISTIAN CHURCHES

*M*erged in 1931, the Congregational Church and the Christian Church, separated by many years in their establishments, were nevertheless almost identical in their ideals and principles. Both have been deeply influential in this country, and both have made significant contributions to our way of life. Their development, important and inspiring, must be traced separately.

Congregational Church

CONGREGATIONALISM "has been implicit in Christianity from the beginning; it began, as Gaius Glenn Atkins suggests, "without a name and with no sense of its destiny." Even before the Reformation broke over Europe, there were little dissenting groups of churchmen in England "seeking a better way" than that of the Established, or Anglican, Church of England. As the Reformation developed in England, they became Separatists, differing from both Anglicans and Puritans in their contention that the whole idea of an Established or State Church was inherently wrong, that to attempt to reform it from within was hopeless, and that the only course for a true Christian to take was to separate himself from it completely.

Meeting and worshiping under constant threat of persecution and even death, they were strengthened by the publication of Robert Browne's *Reformation Without Tarrying for Anie*, the first basic statement of Congregational principles. Browne's church at Norwich, established in 1581, was the first regularly constituted Congregational church; its congregation, unable longer to endure persecution under the Elizabethan Act of Uniformity, fled to Holland within a year. They were joined in 1609 by the congregation from Scrooby, under the leadership of John Robinson.

For twelve years they enjoyed peace and perfect freedom under the Dutch, but haunted by the conviction that their children would not grow up as Englishmen, they sailed for America in 1620 aboard the historic "Mayflower." In a hostile new world, the wilderness before them and the sea at their backs, they helped lay the foundations of the American commonwealth; the democratic ideals of their Plymouth colony, worked out slowly and painfully, were the cornerstone of the structure which gave us our free state, free schools, and free social and political life.

Other Separatist churches were established at Barnstable, Salem, and elsewhere along the Massachusetts coast. Between 1630 and 1640 twenty thousand Puritans came to Massachusetts Bay; and while the "Bay People" had at first no intention whatsoever of joining forces with the Independent or Separatist "Plymouth people," it was inevitable under the drive for self-preservation that they should join forces. Join they did, establishing with their merger an all-powerful, theocratic government over both settlements.

Church and commonwealth were this theocracy's two instruments, with the church dominant. It was a stern and at times an intolerant regime. Suffrage was limited to church members; Anne Hutchinson and Roger Williams were banished; Baptists were haled into court, and four Quakers were hanged on Boston Common. It was a dark period, with the church fighting to maintain supremacy. And it was a comparatively short period, ending with the Act of Toleration in 1689.

From the first, dissenters arose among the dissenters. Quarreling with the Boston hierarchy in 1636, Thomas Hooker led a company of one hundred to what is now Hartford, Connecticut. The freeman's constitution drawn up by Hooker and his associates was to become the model of the American Constitution. Dissenting from the rigidity of current church worship, Congregationalists such

Is Jonathan Edwards of Northampton played leading roles in the Great Awakening which broke in 1734; that revival was marked not only by the eloquence of George Whitefield, but by the vigorous preaching of Edwards, whose theological writings are still regarded as American classics.

Emerging stronger than ever from the Revolution, in the preparation of which it played a great heroic part, Congregationalism was concerned for the next century with five significant developments: higher education, missions, the Unitarian separation, the formation of a national council, and the production of a uniform statement of belief. In the field of education this church had already made tremendous contributions; it had founded Harvard in 1636; Yale (1701) was a Congregational project for the education of its clergy; Dartmouth (1769) developed from Eleazer Wheelock's School for Indians. These, with Williams, Amherst, Bowdoin, and Middlebury, were the first seven colleges in New England. By 1948 we find forty-six colleges and ten theological seminaries in the United States claiming Congregational-Christian origin or connection.

Interest in missions among American Congregationalists began the day the Pilgrims landed at Plymouth. The Mayhews, David Brainerd, and John Eliot were soon at work among the Indians; Eliot spent seven years mastering the Indian tongue, put the Bible in their language, and published an Indian catechism in 1653, the first book to be printed in their language. By 1674 there were four thousand "praying Indians" in New England, with twenty-four native preachers. When the wagon trains went West after the Revolution, the families of Congregational ministers and missionaries were prominent. Manasseh Cutler, a preacher from Hamilton, Massachusetts, was instrumental in framing the famous Northwest Territory Ordinance of 1787, and other ministers led in the founding of Marietta, Ohio, the first permanent settlement in the Northwest Territory.

The American Board of Commissioners for Foreign Missions was organized in 1810 and concerned at first with both home and foreign missionary work. On it served not only Congregationalists but representatives of Presbyterian, Dutch Reformed, and Associated Reformed churches. This was the first foreign missionary society in the country, and it was interdenominational. The first five men ordained were the five young men who had participated in the famous "haystack" meeting at Williams College. The "haystackers" went to India; after them came missionaries to more than thirty foreign countries and in American territories, not the least of which is Hawaii, where Congregational Missionaries within twenty-five years taught a whole nation of people to read and write, laid the foundations of a constitutional, democratic government, and made of their beautiful islands a sociological laboratory filled with many races living together in a racial harmony and understanding. The Congregational achievement in Hawaii is one of the greatest in the whole history of Protestant missions.

The rise of denominationalism worked against the interdenominational complexion of the American Board, and by mid-century the non-Congregationalists had all withdrawn to go their separate ways. It is still known as the American Board, but it is no longer interdenominational.

Moving westward, Congregationalists from New England came into contact with Presbyterians moving out from the middle and southern states; to avoid competition and duplication of effort a Plan of Union was worked out, under which ministers and members from both churches were exchanged and accepted on equal basis. Adopted in 1801, the plan eventually worked out to the advantage of the Presbyterians; it was discontinued in 1852, leaving the Presbyterians stronger in the West and the Congregationalists with a virtual church monopoly in New England. But the plan did much to inspire new Congregational missionary work. In 1826 the American Home Missionary Society was founded; it was active in the South before the Civil War, and especially effective there toward the end of that conflict with its "contraband" schools for Negroes, one of which became Hampton Institute.

Meanwhile differences of opinion between theological liberals and conservatives were developing within the church. Strict Calvinists and Trinitarians were opposed by Unitarians, and a famous sermon by William Ellery Channing at Baltimore in 1819 made a division inevitable. The American Unitarian Association was established in 1825. One third of all existing Congregational churches went Unitarian; only one Congregational church was left in Boston. Debate and legal action over property and funds were not finished until about 1840.

In spite of the Unitarian deflection Congregationalism continued to grow. It assumed such proportions that a national supervisory body became necessary, and a series of national conventions or councils evidenced the growing denominational consciousness of the widely scattered independent local churches. A national council held at Boston in 1865 was so effective that a regular system of councils was established. Following conferences between the associations into which the churches had grouped themselves the first of the national councils was called at Oberlin, Ohio, in 1871. Known today as the General Council of the Congregational Christian Churches, it meets biennially and acts as an overall advisory body for the entire fellowship.

The council of 1913 at Kansas City adopted a declaration on faith, polity, and wider fellowship which has been accepted by many churches as a Statement of Faith. While it did not in any way modify the independence of the local churches, it did give a new spiritual unity to the church. It reads as follows:

Faith. We believe in God the Father, infinite in wisdom, goodness, and love; and in Jesus Christ, His Son, our Lord and Savior, who for us and our salvation lived and died and rose again and liveth evermore; and in the Holy Spirit, who taketh of the things of Christ and revealeth them to us, renewing, comforting, and inspiring the souls of men. We are united in striving to know the will of God, as taught in the Holy Scriptures, and in our purpose to walk in the ways of the Lord, made known or to be made known to us. We hold it to be the mission of the Church of Christ to proclaim the Gospel to all mankind, exalting the worship of the true God, and laboring for the progress of knowledge, the promotion of justice, the reign of peace and the realization of human brotherhood. Depending, as did our fathers, upon the continued guidance of the Holy Spirit to lead us into all truth, we work and pray for the transformation of the world into the kingdom of God; and we look with faith for the triumph of righteousness and the life everlasting.

Polity. We believe in the freedom and responsibility of the individual soul and the right of private judgment. We hold to the autonomy of the local church and its independence of all ecclesiastical control. We cherish the fellowship of the churches united in district, State, and national bodies, for counsel and co-operation in matters of common concern.

The wider fellowship. While affirming the liberty of our churches, and the validity of our ministry, we hold to the unity and catholicity of the Church of Christ, and will unite with all its branches in hearty co-operation; and will earnestly seek, so far as is in us lies, that the prayer of our Lord for His disciples may be answered, that they all may be one.

The "wider fellowship" is taken seriously; unity and co-operation across denominational lines have been outstanding characteristics of Congregationalism all through its history. Christian Endeavor, the largest young people's organization in all Protestantism, was founded by a Congregationalist, Francis E. Clark, in 1881; by 1885 it had become an interdenominational organization known all over the world as the United Society f Christian Endeavor. In 1924 the Evangelical Protestant Church of North America was received into the National Council of Congregational Churches as the Evangelical Protestant Conference of Congregational Churches; in 1931 the union with the Christian Church, already described, was effected; a merger with the Evangelical and Reformed Church has been under consideration since 1944, and interest in that possible merger is still strong in spite of the reversal by a court decision in 1950. Congregationalists have given able and continuous leadership in such interchurch movements and organizations as the National Council of the Churches of Christ in the U.S.A. and the World Council of Churches. Within their own church, while steadily developing boards and commissions to carry on their work, they have shown a marked tendency to avoid multiplication and duplication. This is especially clear in the creation in 1936 of a Missions Council to co-ordinate better the work of their various missionary agencies, the Council for Social Action, and so forth.

In the publishing field the *Missionary Herald,* the oldest missionary periodical with continuous publication in the United States, and the monthly *Advance* are acknowledged leaders among church magazines. The Pilgrim Press, a division of the Board of Home Missions, is the official agency for publishing religious books and educational literature.

Christian Church

THE Christian Church, like the Congregational, was born in protest against ecclesiasticism and the denial of individual freedom in the church. There were actually three revolts which resulted in the establishment of Christian churches in New England and in the South.

The first came in 1792, when James O'Kelley, a Methodist minister in Virginia, withdrew from that church in protest against the development of the superintendency into an episcopacy, especially in so far as it gave the Methodist bishops absolute power in appointing ministers to their charges. O'Kelley and his followers organized under the name Republican Methodists; this was later changed to "Christian," with the new church insisting that the Bible be taken as the only rule and discipline, and that Christian character be made the only requirement of church membership.

Abner Jones, convinced that "sectarian names and human creeds should be abandoned," left the Vermont Baptists to organize at Lyndon, Vermont, in 1801 the First Christian Church in New England. This was done not so much in objection to Baptist organization or doctrine as in a desire to secure a wider freedom in religious thought and fellowship. Like O'Kelley, Jones insisted that piety and character were to be the sole test of Christian fellowship.

In the Great Awakening which swept Tennessee and Kentucky in 1801 there was a great deal of preaching which either ignored the old emphasis on the doctrines of the various denominations involved or was often in direct contradiction. Barton W. Stone, accused of anti-Presbyterian preaching, led a number of Presbyterians out of the Synod of Kentucky to organize a Springfield Presbytery. This presbytery was discontinued as its members gradually came to accept the ideology of James O'Kelley and Abner Jones, and adopted the name "Christians." Stone, an ardent revivalist, was deeply influenced by the preaching of Alexander Campbell and led many of his followers and churches into the fold of the Campbellites, or Disciples of Christ. But the large majority of his Christian churches remained with the original Christian body. There are still, however, in this territory many Disciples churches called Christian churches though they actually have no connection with the Christian denomination.

The groups under O'Kelley, Jones, and Stone engaged in a long series of

67

conferences which resulted in their union on six basic Christian principles:

1. Christ, the only head of the Church
2. The Bible, sufficient rule of faith and practice
3. Christian character, the measure of membership
4. A right, individual interpretation of the Scripture, as a way of life
5. "Christian," the name taken as worthy of the followers of Christ
6. Unity, Christians working together to save the world

No council or other body in the Christian Church has ever attempted to draw up any other creed or statement. Their creed is the Bible. Their interpretation of Bible teaching might be called evangelical, but no sincere follower of Christ is barred from their membership because of difference in theological belief. Open Communion is practiced; baptism is considered a duty, but it is not required; immersion is used generally, but any mode may be employed.

The union of the Congregational and Christian churches has been thoroughly democratic, leaving both free to continue their own forms of worship and each with its own polity and doctrine. Adhering strictly to the congregational idea, each local church is at liberty to call itself either Congregational or Christian, and the same choice is found in the self-governing district and state associations into which the churches are organized. The general council is made up of delegates from state and district conferences; they have no authority over the churches but act in an advisory, co-ordinating capacity in promoting the work of the churches represented in their national, international, and interdenominational relations. Between sessions of the general council an executive committee chosen by the council attends to business details and correlates the work of the churches and agencies.

With 5,715 churches and 1,184,661 members the Congregational Christian Churches are the eleventh largest Protestant group in the United States. Their contributions to our national development have been unique and vital. They are characterized by their faith in God, their broad Christian fellowship, and their freedom in the Spirit; and they insist that in the church nothing trivial or sectarian be exalted and that dogmatism and all legislative control of the spiritual life be repudiated. Marked by their educational efficiency, evangelistic zeal, missionary passion, and a continuing interest in Christian union, religious progress, and social reform, they constitute one of the most effective religious bodies in modern America.

Congregational Holiness Church

FOUNDED in 1921 by a group of ministers withdrawing from the Pentecostal Holiness Church in an effort to retain holiness doctrines and to establish a more democratic church polity, this church is Trinitarian, emphasizing the inspiration of the Scriptures, justification, sanctification, divine healing (without objection to medicine), the second coming of Christ, eternal punishment and reward, the merits of the Atonement, and the salvation of the entire church.

The Bible is held as the sole rule of conduct; slang, tobacco, membership in oath-bound secret societies, and other forms of worldliness are condemned. Ordinances include baptism, foot washing, and the Lord's Supper. The crowning blessing of religious experience is held to be the baptism of the Holy Ghost and speaking with other tongues "as the Spirit [gives] utterance."

Church government is, as the name suggests, congregational. Local churches are grouped in annual associations, from which delegates are elected to a general association. Local church officers, elected annually, consist of deacons, trustees, a secretary, and a treasurer. Pastors are called by a majority vote of the congregation; women are licensed to preach but are not ordained. There are 103 churches and 3,399 members in the United States; the Congregational Church in India, with 250 churches and 30,000 members, was united with the American body in 1949.

Disciples of Christ

THE REVIVAL movements of the early nineteenth century in the United States had both positive and negative results and influence: while inspiring new consecration and zeal in the established churches, they also resulted indirectly in the creation of new, smaller churches breaking from the larger bodies. One of these was the Disciples of Christ.

Thomas Campbell, a clergyman of the Secession branch of the Presbyterian Church in Ireland, settled in western Pennsylvania in 1807 and started preaching on a Presbyterian circuit. Almost immediately he was in trouble. Finding many people with no church affiliation, he invited them to attend his services and to partake of the Lord's Supper offered in his churches. He wanted closer relations with Christians in other churches than the Seceders permitted; he preached that acceptance of the creed, or of any creed, should not be a condition of church communion or fellowship, and appealed from the creed to the Bible; he was restive under the domination of the church by the clergy; and he taught that all men who believed were saved by Christ. All this challenged ecclesiastical authority and the Calvinistic doctrine of the Presbyterian Church, and Campbell was censured for his departure from the paths of orthodoxy. Appealing from his Presbytery to the higher Associate Synod of North America, he succeeded in having the censure removed, but so severe was his criticism of the whole idea of sectarianism and denominationalism that further service with the Presbyterians was impossible. With his son Alexander Campbell he withdrew in 1809 to establish the Christian Association of Washington, Pennsylvania. His "declaration address" on this occa-

sion has become an ecclesiastical document of historic importance.

Campbell made it plain that what was sought in this move was not so much reformation as restoration—restoration of the New Testament polity and ideal. There ought to be, Campbell declared, "no schisms, or uncharitable divisions" among the churches; such divisions were "anti-Christian, anti-Scriptural, anti-natural" and "productive of confusion and every evil work"; they were a "horrid evil, fraught with many evils." The Church, and membership in the Church, should be based solely upon the beliefs and practices of primitive New Testament Christianity. The articles of faith and holiness "expressly revealed and enjoined in the Word of God" were quite enough without the addition of human opinions or the creedal inventions of men.

As the Campbells insisted thus upon the unity of believers, the last thing in their minds was the founding of still another Protestant church; to avoid it overtures were made to the Presbyterian Synod of Pittsburgh in the hope that the two groups could work together. This gesture failed, and in 1810 "the First Church of the Christian Association of Washington, meeting at Cross Roads and Brush Run, Washington County, Pennsylvania," was organized. A working unity with the Redstone Baptist Association was established and lasted nearly ten years, but eventually points of disagreement arose and the two groups drifted apart. The separation was gradual, becoming complete about 1830, after which time the followers of the Campbells were known as Christians, or Disciples of Christ.

The name "Christian" was used by

Barton W. Stone, a Presbyterian minister in Kentucky (see Congregational Christian Churches). Stone's followers entered into a partial union with the Campbells in 1832. Stone felt that the whole church should be called simply Christians, and Campbell favored the name Disciples. No final decision was reached; both names were used intermittently; a church was generally called a Christian church or a Church of Christ.

The first national convention of the Disciples and the first missionary society, the American Christian Missionary Society, were organized in 1849; state conventions and societies also began meeting in that year. The church developed rapidly through and after the Civil War period; unlike Methodists, Baptists, and Presbyterians, the Disciples did not divide on the issue of slavery. Especially in the Midwest, in Ohio, Indiana, Illinois, Tennessee, and Missouri, the church gathered impressive strength in membership in spite of the persistent inherent objection toward any emphasis on denominationalism or ecclesiastical organization. This objection became acute in differences between Conservatives and Progressives over the development of missionary societies and the use of instrumental music in the churches. Out of this long debate came the Churches of Christ.

The Disciples believe that the Bible is divinely inspired, and they accept it as their only rule of faith and life; neither Trinitarian nor Unitarian, they urge a simple usage of New Testament phraseology as to the godhead. They believe that Christ is the Son of God, that the Holy Spirit is at work in the present world, that sin has alienated every soul from its maker. They feel that baptism and the Lord's Supper are divine ordinances, and that it is a sacred duty to observe the Lord's Day. They believe that holiness is a necessity for every believer, and that there is a final judgment with reward for the righteous and punishment for the wicked.

In detail their characteristic beliefs are set forth as follows:

1. Feeling that "to believe and to do none other things than those enjoined by our Lord and His Apostles must be infallibly safe," they aim "to restore in faith and spirit and practice the Christianity of Christ and His Apostles as found on the pages of the New Testament."

2. Affirming that "the sacred Scriptures as given by God answer all purposes of a rule of faith and practice, and a law for the government of the church, and that human creeds and confessions of faith spring out of controversy and, instead of being bonds of union, tend to division and strife," they reject all such creeds and confessions.

3. They place especial emphasis upon "the Divine Sonship of Jesus, as the fundamental fact of Holy Scripture, the essential creed of Christianity, and the one article of faith in order to receive baptism and church membership."

4. Believing that in the Scriptures "a clear distinction is made between the law and the gospel," they "do not regard the Old and New Testaments as of equally binding authority upon Christians," but that "the New Testament is as perfect a constitution for the worship, government, and discipline of the New Testament church as the Old was for the Old Testament church."

5. While claiming for themselves the New Testament names of "Christians," or "Disciples," "they do not deny that others are Christians or that other churches are Churches of Christ."

6. Accepting the divine personality of the Holy Spirit, through whose agency regeneration is begun, they hold that men "must hear, believe, repent, and obey the gospel to be saved."

7. Repudiating any doctrine of "baptismal regeneration," and insisting that there is no other prerequisite to regeneration than confession of faith with the whole heart in the personal living Christ, they regard baptism by immersion "as one of the items of the original divine system," and as "commanded in order to the remission of sins."

8. Following the apostolic model, the Disciples celebrate the Lord's Supper on each Lord's Day, "not as a sacrament, but as a memorial feast," from which no sincere follower of Christ of whatever creed or church connection is excluded.

9. The Lord's Day with the Disciples is not a Sabbath, but a New Testament institution, commemorating our Lord's resurrection, and consecrated by apostolic example.

10. The Church of Christ is a divine institution; sects are unscriptural and unapostolic. The sect name, Spirit, and life should give place to the union and cooperation that distinguished the church of the New Testament.

Strictly congregational in polity, each Disciples church elects its own officers—pastors, elders, and deacons—and acknowledges no outside ecclesiastical authority. Baptism by immersion follows the reception of candidates for church membership, who are received on profession of faith in Christ. Ministers are ordained usually by the local church and sometimes by a committee from neighboring churches. The minister is a member of the church in which he serves as pastor or evangelist. Ministerial associations are employed for mutual help and supervision, but they have no authority.

Churches are grouped into district and state conventions, which, like all others, have no final authority. There is no national ecclesiastical organization of the churches, but there is an International Convention of Disciples of Christ, meeting annually with advisory powers only

and composed of individual members of the churches.

The supervision of denominational activities is placed with the usual boards, which, however, are more unified than in most Protestant bodies. The American Christian Missionary Society was formed at Cincinnati in 1849 to "promote the preaching of the Gospel in this and other lands." The Christian Woman's Board of Missions was organized in 1874. Other boards, organized to supervise ministerial relief, social action, benevolences, higher education, and church extension, were grouped, together with the missionary societies in a new United Christian Missionary Society at the International Convention at Cincinnati in 1919.

In 1949 there were 7,771 Disciples churches and 1,738,605 members. In 1949 a total of $1,529,188.46 was spent for foreign missions in Africa, China, India, Japan, Latin America, Puerto Rico, and the Philippines.

The Board of Higher Education had under its supervision some thirty-four colleges, universities, Bible schools, and foundations with 30,056 students. There are six homes for children, six homes for the aged, and Valparaiso Christian Hospital at Valparaiso, Indiana. *World Call*, the church magazine, reports a circulation of 67,067.

Divine Science College and Church

CONVINCED that she had been healed from a very serious illness through her realization of God's presence, Malinda E. Cramer founded this movement in 1885. The core of its teaching, which is quite similar to that of the New Thought Movement, is the principle of the all-inclusive God-mind:

God [is] the Omnipresence, the Universal Presence, Substance, Life, and Intelligence; man, a child of God, lives in God, is of God, is like God; knowledge of this truth used in our living frees us from sin, sickness, and death; the practice of right thinking, or thought training, results in the

elimination of fear, doubt, anxiety, and other wrong mental habits, and the establishment of love, faith, joy, and power in the consciousness; evolution is God's method of accomplishing, and love, conscious unity, is the fulfilling of the law.

Healing through thought training is the cleansing of the inner man from all that is unlike God. Sickness, sin, and death exist because of man's ignorance of the truth; they vanish when man knows God and lives by that knowledge. Divine Science does not deny the existence of visible matter but interprets both form and force as manifestations of God.

The church claims to have been recently formed into "a federation for the purpose of strengthening the work of its many branches of church, college, publication, and field activities." It also claims that its publications circulate around the world. Headquarters are in Denver, Colorado, where the official church organ, *Divine Science Monthly*, is published. While no statistics are published, it is estimated that there are over nine thousand followers in the movement; the monthly lists thirty-six churches, colleges, and centers in the United States, and two in London, with forty-six practitioners, ministers, teachers, and workers in the United States.

EASTERN ORTHODOX CHURCHES

*W*hen Constantine in A.D. 330, moved his capital from Rome to Byzantium and began to rule his vast empire from the new Constantinople, the most important split in the history of Christianity was under way. Up to this time the church in the West, centered at Rome, and the church in the East, with headquarters in Byzantium, were one church. Both accepted the Nicene Creed; both were sacramental and apostolic. But there were also certain basic differences which made for confusion; racially, socially, linguistically, mentally, morally, and philosophically there were deep gulfs between the two. The East was Greek in blood and speech; the West was Latin. The transference of the capital from Rome to the East meant a shifting of the center of political, social, and intellectual influence. When the Goths swept down upon Rome, that city turned for help not to Constantinople but to the Franks; in gratitude for his aid the pope crowned Charles the Great as emperor on Christmas Day in 800, and the die was cast.

Conflict deepened between the pope at Rome and the patriarch at Constantinople. In 857 Ignatius in Constantinople refused to administer the sacrament to Caesar Bardas on the ground that he was immoral; tried and imprisoned, Ignatius was succeeded by Photius, an intellectual giant for whom the weaker pope was no match. Their increasing friction broke into flame at the Council of St. Sophia, where Photius bitterly condemned the Latin Church for adding the word "filioque" to the Nicene Creed. The Eastern Church held that the Holy Spirit proceeded directly from the Son; the Western Church held that it came from the Father *and* the Son—filioque. Political and ecclesiastical jealousies fanned the flame, the pope excommunicated the patriarch and the patriarch excommunicated the pope, and the result of the long friction was that there were two churches, Eastern and Western, instead of one. The pope remained head of the Western Church; in the East four of the five patriarchs remained Orthodox, and there were finally five Patriarchs, or heads, in Eastern Orthodoxy. This is important in an understanding of the Eastern Church. It is not a monarchy with one all-powerful ruler at the top; it is "an Oligarchy of patriarchs." It is based on the body of bishops, but the rule of the bishops, holding power variously as metropolitans, primates, and exarchs, is conducted finally through the sovereignty of the five patriarchal thrones. Each patriarch is to his diocese what the pope is to the Roman Catholic Church. He is not responsible to any of the other patriarchs, yet he is within the jurisdiction of an oecumenical synod.

Today Christendom remains divided into three great sections: Roman Catholic, Eastern Orthodox, and Protestant. Eastern Orthodox Churches consist of those churches which accept all of the decisions and decrees of the first seven general councils—two at Nicea, three at Constantinople, one at Ephesus, and one at Chalcedon—and of such other churches as have originated in the missionary activities of these parent churches or have separated from them but still maintain communion with them.

Claiming to be the "direct heir and the true conservator" of the original primitive church, Eastern Orthodoxy has tended historically to divide into independent national or social bodies—Russian, Serbian, Syrian, Bulgarian, Romanian, Albanian, Greek, Georgian, and so forth. These bodies have had a bitter struggle for existence, caught as they have been between Arab, Turkish, and Western armies in their endless wars. Generally it may be said that Greek Christianity became the faith of the people of the Middle East and of the Slavs in Europe, while Latin Christianity became the religion of the Germans. There are at present five large eastern patriarchates: Constantinople, Alexandria, Antioch, Jerusalem, and Moscow, with the lesser patriarchates of the Serbs, Romanians, and Georgians. Mount Sinai, Greek Cyprus, Greek Athens, Bulgaria, Japan, and Albania constitute autonomous archbishoprics, or n a t i o n a l churches. The First World War and the Russian Revolution of 1917 greatly depleted the power and prestige of the mother church of Constantinople, and with the disruption of the Russian empire Eastern Orthodox Churches in Poland, Finland, Estonia, Latvia, and Lithuania became free and independent. Widely separated they are still in essential agreement in doctrine and worship, and together make up what we know as the Holy Eastern Orthodox Churches; the above churches now submit to the patriarch of Moscow.

In the United States today Albanian, Bulgarian, Greek, Romanian, Russian, Serbian, Ukrainian, Carpatho-Russian, and Syrian churches are under the supervision of bishops of their respective nationalities. Romanian and Serbian bishops are under their respective patriarchs. Syrians are under the supervision of Antioch. The patriarchs of Alexandria

and Jerusalem have no jurisdiction in the United States; their churches here are under the supervision of the Greek church.

In addition there are several groups which have no connection with valid, recognized, ancient Orthodoxy: the American Holy Orthodox Catholic Eastern Church, the Apostolic Episcopal Church (also called the Holy Eastern Catholic and Apostolic Orthodox Church), and the Holy Orthodox Church in America. To be Orthodox a church must be under the jurisdiction of a legal Orthodox bishop, who is in turn under the legal jurisdiction of a historic patriarch or autocephalous synod. These irregular Eastern churches might be called autogenic, or self-starting. They are comparatively small bodies.

Doctrine in Eastern Orthodoxy is based on the Bible, on the holy traditions, and on the decrees of the seven early councils. The Nicene Creed is recited in all liturgies, vespers, and matins, but generally the Eastern Churches hold that "a creed is an adoring confession of the church engaged in worship"; its faith is expressed more in public testimony than in written statements. Actually the basis lies in the decisions and statements of the seven councils—in the oecumenical creeds of the early undivided church and in the later statements defining the position of the Orthodox Church of the East with regard to the doctrine and faith of the Roman Catholic and Protestant churches. The Niceo-Constantinopolitan Creed is still held in its original form without the filioque clause. The dogma of the pope as the sole "Vicar of Christ on earth" is rejected, together with the dogma of papal infallibility. The only infallibility recognized is found in "the whole assembly of true believers." Members of this church accept the virgin birth but do not dogmatize the immaculate conception, and they honor nine orders of saints and angels. They reject the teaching of the surplus merits of the saints and the doctrine of indulgences, but reverence relics of the saints, pictures of holy objects, and the cross. The use of carved images, except for the crucifix, is forbidden. Bas-relief is permitted in some of the Orthodox groups.

They have seven sacraments: baptism, anointing (confirmation or chrismation), Communion, penance, holy orders, marriage, and holy unction. Both infants and adults are baptized by threefold immersion, although other forms are sometimes used when necessary, as in the baptism of a convert who has been previously baptized. The sacrament of anointing with "chrism," or holy oil (confirmation), is administered immediately after baptism. Holy Unction is administered to the sick, but not always as a "last rite." Transmutation is taught; purgatory is denied. There are prayers for the dead by the living, and it is believed that the dead pray for the living. For justification both faith and works are considered necessary.

Government is episcopal, but organization differs in different countries. There is usually a council at the head of the church, of which the bishop, elected by ecclesiastical representatives, is president. This presiding bishop has been known historically, and is still known in most instances, as the "patriarch of the church." There are three orders in the ministry: deacons, who assist in parish work and in administering the sacraments, priests, and bishops. Deacons and priests may be either secular or monastic; candidates for the diaconate and the priesthood may marry before ordination, but they are forbidden to marry thereafter. They may be widowers, however. Bishops are members of the monastic communities or engage in missionary work. All are of one order, under vows of obedience, chastity, prayer, fasting, and poverty, following the rule laid down by Basil the Great.

Church services are elaborately ritualistic. Of their worship Frank Gavin says:

In the details of Eastern worship is a rough epitome of the history of Eastern Christendom: the *ikons*, about which a bitter controversy was once waged; the service in the vernacular as against Latin; the existence of both a married and a celibate priesthood; the strong and passionate loyalty to the national allegiance evidenced by the provision of special prayers for the rulers by name—all these mark the characteristics, peculiarities, and contrasts with the customs of the West.

In the United States they do, however, pray for the President, Congress, the armed forces, and for all in places of lawful civil authority.

Membership statistics are confusing and often unreliable, in as much as membership has different meanings to different Eastern churches. All baptized persons are confirmed immediately after baptism and are given their first sacrament, and are from that moment considered as communicant members of the church. But parish membership is more frequently determined by the number of males over twenty-one than by communicants (the male head of each family is the voting member in the parish organization). There are well over three million Orthodox church members in the United States.

On the whole Eastern Orthodox Churches seem to be gaining rather than losing in spite of the obstacles placed in their paths. Their clergymen have attained higher and higher standards of education, the number of schools and seminaries is steadily growing, and church leaders and theologians are in prominent places here and abroad.

Albanian Orthodox Church

CHRISTIANITY reached Albania in the first century, finding the oldest existing race of people in Europe with a language older than classical Greek. The church grew slowly, not gaining any impressive strength until the fourth century; this was due in part to the refusal of the Patriarch of Constantinople to allow the Albanians the use of their native tongue in their services. When the Turks made Constantinople a Turkish province in 1478, the majority of the population accepted Mohammedanism. But some Ghegs in the north and some Tosks in the south remained Christian. Today three quarters of Albania is still Mohammedan. Of the other one quarter the majority are Greek Orthodox in the South, and the minority in the north are Roman Catholics.

The Albanian Orthodox Church is autocephalous—ecclesiastically self-controlling. Its bishops and churches recognize the jurisdiction of no other bishops or patriarchs than their own. The Albanian language is used in all services, and all church books have been put in the same tongue; otherwise it is similar in dogma, doctrines, rites, and ceremonies to the other Eastern Orthodox Churches.

Albanians never came to the United States in large numbers; most of them came during the unrest which followed the First World War, but many returned to the old country when Albania gained her independence. There are now approximately 25,000 Albanians in this country, of which about half are members of the Albanian Orthodox Church. It is a church very active in the sponsoring of national, educational, and musical societies and clubs, one of which, the Albanian Federation, Vattra, was influential in the fight for Albanian freedom. Thirteen local churches are reported, under the jurisdiction of Bishop F. S. Noli of Boston, Massachusetts; he is in close touch but not under the direction of the Holy Synod of Albania. Officially it is a branch of the Eastern Orthodox Church ministering to Albanians in the United States. There is a strong sentiment in favor of placing its churches under the spiritual jurisdiction of the Holy Synod of Albania, with an administrator to be appointed by that synod.

American Holy Orthodox Catholic Apostolic Eastern Church

INSTITUTED in 1932 and incorporated in 1933, this church is self-governing, "maintaining the Eastern Orthodox faith and rite for all men indiscriminately." Spiritually it "owns no head but the head of the Christian faith, Jesus Christ our Lord," and considers itself "inseparately joined in faith with the great church of Constantinople and with every other orthodox eastern church of the same profession." The Greek rite is used in all worship services, but it receives into communion and affiliates with other churches of Eastern Orthodox persuasion and belief which desire to retain their national and individual characteristics.

This church is autocephalous; the archbishop does not acknowledge the authority or jurisdiction of any other church or bishop. He is responsible to a national council, which is the supreme legislative, administrative, and judicial authority. The national council is made up of bishops, clergy, and laity; it meets every third year. Two lower ecclesiastical bodies, the Holy Synod and the Supreme Ecclesiastical Council, manage the affairs of the church between councils. There were in 1947 two thousand members and seven churches reported.

The work of the church is not only religious but social and educational. It represents an effort, fairly successful, to draw together those of Eastern Orthodox faith into one group regardless of race, nationality, or language. A provisional synod has been set up to encourage coordination between the national groups in the various Eastern Orthodox churches. The church has five bishops, sixteen clergymen, nine parishes and missions.

Apostolic Episcopal Church

ACKNOWLEDGING the historic Eastern confession and order, the Apostolic Episcopal Church claims apostolic orders through the Chaldean succession. It was constituted in 1925 at the ordination of its first bishop, Arthur Wolfort Brooks, who at the time was a priest in Anglican orders. It is "an English-speaking primitive Catholic Church of Apostolic Eastern Orthodox faith and order, an American church free from all ecclesiastical and political [and foreign] alliances."

Differing little in belief from other Eastern Orthodox churches, it is distinguished by the use of English in its worship; foreign language services, however, are occasionally provided. A Primate Bishop is the ecclesiastical administrator; other bishops appoint priests to local parishes. The church is divided into two provinces, the Province of the East and the Province of the West. Each province is completely autonomous and has its own primate, but the primate of the West presides over the general (joint) synods. A section of the church has been established in continental Europe; this section is also autonomous, under its own primate. A merger with the Ancient Christian Fellowship, a group formerly associated with the Old Catholic Church of America, was effected in 1947; the name "Apostolic Episcopal Church, Province of the West" was adopted for the two merged bodies.

Both sacerdotal and evangelical, this church ordains men as readers, preachers, teachers, evangelists, and priests; women may become deaconesses or messengers. The clergy may marry. Remarriage after divorce is permissable on dispensation from an ecclesiastical court. The church ministers not only to Anglo-Saxon but to Irish, Germans, Armenians, and Syrians. There were 7,086 members and 46 churches in 1947.

Bulgarian Orthodox Church

BEFORE THE outbreak of the Macedonian revolution of 1903 there was very little Bulgarian immigration to the United States; up to 1909 there were never more than ten thousand a year entering this country, and in 1940 there were only nine thousand Bulgarians resident here. Coming out of the Bulgarian Orthodox Church, which is the state religion of the country, they brought with them memories of the long struggle for the independence of that church from the domination of Constantinople. The first free Bulgarian church under the name of Exarchate was established in 1872.

The church started in this country as the Bulgarian Orthodox Mission in 1909 and established a bishopric in 1938. The church is attached directly to the Holy Synod of Bulgaria, with a membership made up of immigrants from Bulgaria, Macedonia, Thrace, Dobrudja, and other parts of the Balkan peninsula. Services are in the Bulgarian language, and doctrine is in accord with that of other Eastern Orthodox churches. Membership is apparently dwindling; in 1936 there were 5 churches with 969 members; in 1948 there was 1 church with 150 members.

Greek Orthodox Church (Hellenic)

GREEKS arrived in the United States in increasing numbers between 1890 and 1914, coming from the Greek mainland, the Greek islands in the Aegean, Dodecanese, and Cyprus, and from Constantinople, Smyrna, and other sections of Asia Minor. They asked for and secured the services of Orthodox priests sent to them by the Holy Synod of Greece or the Ecumenical Patriarchate of Constantinople. Each priest maintained his relation with the synod or patriarchate from which he came; there was at first no central organization to unite them.

Following a period of confusion (1908-22), during which jurisdiction of the American churches was shifted from the Ecumenical Patriarchate of Constantinople to the Holy Synod of Greece and then back again, an act known as the Founding Tome of 1922 established the Greek (Orthodox) Archdiocese of North and South America, consisting of four bishoprics under the supervision of Archbishop Alexander and the patriarchate of Constantinople. Alexander's successor, Archbishop Athenagoras, was elected patriarch of the Greek Orthodox Church in 1948, thus heading a body which has more than 100,000,000 adherents around the world. Centered in Istanbul, formerly Constantinople, this body established a strong hold of Eastern Orthodoxy sympathetic with Western ideals as a counterbalance to the Soviet domination of the Russian Orthodox Church.

A new constitution and bylaws have been adopted for the Greek Orthodox churches in the United States. Doctrine, polity, and worship are of the usual Eastern Orthodox patterns. There were 300,000 members in 286 churches in 1947, 450 parochial schools, 306 Sunday schools, a theological seminary at Brookline, Massachusetts, and a teachers' college for girls, known as St. Basil's Academy, at Garrison, New York, under the jurisdiction of the Greek Archdiocese of North and South America, now headed by Archbishop Michael.

Holy Orthodox Church In America (Eastern Catholic and Apostolic)

AN INTERCHURCH movement rather than a denomination, this body was instituted in 1927-28 to present the Eastern liturgies in the English language and offset the disadvantages of the use of foreign languages in America, and to establish an autocephalous Orthodox church in America for English-speaking people with American customs and traditions.

The movement stems from the authorization of the late Patriarch Tikhon of the Russian Orthodox Church and the acts of his successors to propagate Orthodoxy among English-speaking people throughout the world. For its first fifteen years in this country it was a program of translating, lectures, classes, and writings.

Services are based on the original liturgy composed by St. James, first bishop of Jerusalem, as abbreviated and arranged in the fourth century by St. John Chrysostom into the local usage it has today in all Orthodox bodies, varying only in local custom and language. This liturgy is used throughout the year with the exception of the weekdays of the Great Feast (Lent). The liturgy of St. Basil the Great is used ten days of the year.

The faith and order of the Holy Orthodox Church in America rest on the Holy Scripture, holy tradition, the canons of the seven councils, and the teachings of the ante-Nicene Fathers. Concessions have been made to Western custom in the installation of seats in its churches, in the use of organs and mixed choirs, and in conformity to the Western calendar with the single exception of Easter, which is celebrated according to the Julian calendar. It wishes to be known as an independent unit of the Holy Eastern Orthodox Greek-Catholic Church, following strictly, however, the ancient traditional doctrines and dogmas of that church. In 1944 there were 1,300 members in 14 churches.

Romanian Orthodox Church

THERE ARE about 150,000 Romanians in the United States, spread over thirteen states and coming principally from the provinces of Transylvania, Banat, and Bukovina. Since April of 1929 the Orthodox Parish churches of the United States and Canada have been united in the Romanian Orthodox Episcopate (Diocese) of America, with headquarters in Detroit, Michigan.

In matters of faith and doctrine this church recognizes the spiritual and canonical authority of the Holy Synod (House of Bishops) of the Romanian Orthodox Church of Romania, of which body the titular bishop of the American diocese is a *de jure* member. In administrative matters the episcopate is an autonomous organization having the "Church Congress," a yearly convention, as its supreme administrative body and a Council of the Episcopate as the executive body of the congress. The episcopate adheres to the same doctrine as all other Eastern Orthodox churches and respects the canon laws governing them all. Only 1 local church reported on membership in 1946, listing 390 members.

Russian Orthodox Church

EASTERN ORTHODOXY came to what is now Russia with the baptism of Vladimir in A.D. 988. Government of the church at first was by metropolitans appointed or approved by the Patriarch of Constantinople. About five hundred years ago Job became the First Patriarch of All-Russia. The patriarchate was suppressed, and a Holy Synod was instituted during the reign of Peter the Great; the other Orthodox churches recognized this synod as being patriarchal in effect. From 1721 to 1917 the Holy Synod was made up of three metropolitans and several bishops from various parts of Russia, who sat alternately at its sessions. In this Holy Synod also sat a civil officer of the czar, known as the Chief Procurator of the Holy Synod. To all intents and purposes, while the czar himself was not head of the church, this pre-1917 church was dominated by the czarist régime.

In 1917 dramatic changes were instituted by the Great Sobor, or council. Administration was changed, the office of chief procurator was abolished, and plans were made to return to the old patriarchal form of government. The reforms were put into effect. As the Great Sobor held its sessions, however, the gunfire of the revolutionists was heard in the streets, and once the followers of Lenin had taken over the state, they soon took over the church. During these revolutionary days and in the early postrevolutionary days a small group of married priests, aided by a few bishops, formed what they called the Living Church. They were aided and upheld by the Soviet government, which saw in the group a means of splitting the historic church in Russia. The Living Church consecrated married priests as bishops, permitted remarriage after divorce or death, even after ordination as priests, and extended the same privileges to bishops. This departure from Orthodox law was in itself sufficient to cause excommunication. No lawful Orthodox church ever recognized this new group; they misled some of the people of Russia with their close adherence to the ancient Orthodox rituals and vestments, but eventually the people recognized the deception and returned to the mother church. Laxity in discipline and in canonicity soon divided the Living Church into warring factions; thousands deserted the membership until the Living Church ceased to exist, and in spite of pressure from the government the old patriarchal administration of the old church was fully restored.

The main efforts of the Russian Orthodox Church have been in North America; an Orthodox mission in Japan, still strong and influential, has become schismatic since World War II. Eight Russian Orthodox monks entered Alaska in 1792 before its purchase by the United States; they established headquarters at Kodiak and built there the first Eastern Orthodox church in America. Twelve thousand natives were baptized within two years. Orthodox monks and bishops printed an alphabet and grammar in the Aleutian language, translated the catechism and portions of the Bible, and built a cathedral at Sitka.

With its purchase by the United States many Russians left Alaska, funds for missionary work became difficult to secure, and the influence of the church deteriorated. The Episcopal see was moved to San Francisco in 1872, and in 1905 to New York City. The diocese was extended to include Canada and the eastern states of the United States.

Increase in immigration from Russia, Serbia, Syria, and Greece since 1885 has brought new difficulties to the Russian Church in America. Many Orthodox adherents of the old Austro-Hungarian empire, where a Uniat church had grown to impressive numbers, came to this country and found themselves in an embarrassing situation. Uniat churches abroad, under the influence of the Polish domination, became a compromise between Eastern Orthodoxy and Roman Catholicism, accepting the supremacy of the pope but retaining their Eastern Orthodox rites and customs. Finding themselves free from the yoke of a state-dominated church, many of these Uniat churches in the United States returned to and remained in the jurisdiction of the Russian Orthodox Church.

The bitterness and confusion of the divided church in Russia followed the Russian immigrants to this country. Today the church in the United States is separated into three competing groups: the canonical church under Archbishop Makarios, an autonomous church but submitting to the spiritual authority of the Patriarch of Moscow; the Platonites, led by Archbishop Platon and now about to elect a successor to the late Metropolitan Theophilus Pashkovsky, who acknowledged the Patriarch of Moscow but refused to obey him; and the Church Abroad, headed by Archbishop Vitaly, who in turn represents Archbishop Anastasy and a few surviving bishops who left Russia shortly after the revolution, settling first in Serbia and then in Munich, Germany. This group repudiates any allegiance whatever to the Patriarchate of Moscow and opposes the Platonite group. Both Platonite and Church Abroad bodies are condemned as schismatic by the Patriarch of Moscow and create an embarrassing problem for the Orthodox in America.

The church in America is governed by an archbishop and a council, lay and clerical, elected by a convention, with vacancies filled by the archbishop. There are also two vicars, one at San Francisco and the other having the title of "Philadelphia of the Carpatho-Russians." The American Church is recognized canonically by all Eastern Orthodox patriarchs; the present ruling primate is

the Most Rev. Macarios, Archbishop of the Aleutian Islands and North America.

Missionary work is carried on by the American church in Alaska; church services and liturgies are increasingly held in the English language, and church periodicals are published in both Russian and English. There is a theological seminary in New York City, a seminary at the Holy Trinity Monastery in Jordanville, New York, and a pastoral school for priesthood candidates at South Canaan, Pennsylvania. Doctrine is in complete agreement with that of all Eastern Orthodox churches. A membership of 300,000 is reported in 300 churches as of 1942.

Serbian Orthodox Church

THE CHURCH in Serbia from the seventh century to the thirteenth was under the jurisdiction of the Greek Patriarchate of Constantinople and then became the independent National Serbian Church in 1219. It made notable contributions to art and architecture, and played an important part in the Serbian struggle for independence all through the long period of Turkish invasion and domination (1389-1876), during which it suffered an unbelievable persecution.

Serbian immigrants to the United States, coming here more for political than for economic reasons, began to arrive in large numbers about 1890. They worship at first in Russian churches, accepting the ministrations of Russian priests and the supervision of Russian bishops. The Serbian Patriarchate of Yugoslavia approved the organization of the diocese of the United States and Canada in 1921, and sent its first bishop in 1926. Headquarters were established, and still remain, at St. Sava's Serbian Monastery at Libertyville, Illinois. There are today fifty parishes and eighty thousand members, an increase of over fifty thousand since 1936. Doctrine and polity are in harmony with other branches of the Eastern church.

Syrian Antiochian Orthodox Church

UNDER THE jurisdiction of the Patriarch of Antioch this church is made up of former residents of Syria, Lebanon, Palestine, Egypt, and Iraq now living in the United States. Prior to 1914 it was under the supervision of a Syrian coadjutor of the Russian Orthodox Church and five bishops of that church. Three of the bishops died between 1933 and 1934, and the other two were excommunicated. In September of 1934 the Patriarch of Antioch appointed the Very Rev. Archimandrite Antony Bashir as patriarchal vicar for all Syrian Orthodox people in North America, with authority to unite all parishes in America in one organization, to be known as the Syrian Antiochian Orthodox Archdiocese of New York and all North America. In February of 1936 at the request of both clergy and people he was elected and consecrated as the Metropolitan-Archbishop of the Archdiocese.

Work is maintained in the United States, Canada, Mexico, and Central America. The usual Eastern Orthodox patterns of belief and ritual are used. In 1942 there were 20,300 members enrolled in the church, and 76 parishes.

Ukrainian Orthodox Church of America

EASTERN ORTHODOXY was established as the religion of the state in the Ukraine by a unique procedure. In the tenth century Vladimir the Great, ruler of Kiev, sent investigators abroad to study the doctrines and rituals of the various churches of the East and West; they came back to report that the Eastern Orthodox faith was best suited to the needs of their people. Ulolodimir was immediately baptized, and by 988 the entire Ukraine had become Christian.

For more than six hundred years the Ukrainian Church was under the jurisdiction of the Oecumenical Patriarchate of Constantinople; in 1686 it was placed under the supervision of the Russian Patriarch of Moscow.

Ukrainians in the United States have shown the same spirit of independence. They formed their own church independent of Moscow in 1928 and held their first convention in 1931. Their first bishop died within two years of his consecration, and in 1937 the Right Rev. Bishop Bohdan was elected the second bishop of the Ukrainian Orthodox Church of America and confirmed in this office by the Oecumenical Patriarchal Synod of Constantinople. At a special convention convoked by Athenagoras I, Oecumenical Patriarch, and held in Allentown, Pennsylvania, the Most Rev. Mstyslaw Skrypnyk, Archbishop of Winnepeg and all Canada, was elected to be the ruling hierarchy of the church. The confirmation of that election pending, another special convention was held at Wilmington, Delaware, April 18-19, 1950. It recognized the church as autonomous in its government, confirmed the preceding election, and authorized Archbishop Mstyslaw to enter immediately upon the performance and discharge of his duties as the head of the church. The same convention removed Bishop Bohdan from his office. While the church recognizes the spiritual authority of Constantinople, it is completely independent in all matters of administration. Subscribing to Eastern Orthodox doctrine, it has instituted certain variations in worship and polity to meet the needs of its people living in the United States. As of 1945 there were 39,500 members and 44 parishes.

Erieside Church on the Boulevard

ORGANIZED IN 1933 to minister to "Bible-believing Christians of the deeper sort" who were moving from Cleveland to the rural areas, the Erieside Church on the Boulevard in Willowick, Ohio, is modeled on the Gospel Church of Cleveland. It is unique among rural churches for its complete independence in both faith and government, and for its strong missionary interest.

With a membership of 140 there is an average attendance at services of 275. Two missionaries are supported abroad, and seven are now in preparation for missionary work. It is described as "a Bible-teaching ministry for all ages, missionary and premillennial, strongly fundamental [Baptistic]." Its creed is deeply concerned with salvation through faith in Christ's atonement, the doctrine of the Trinity, and the verbal inspiration of the Bible. The ruling body of the church is an official board made up of elders, trustees, deacons, secretary, treasurer, Sunday-school superintendent, pastor, and church clerk. Baptism and the Lord's Supper are accepted as "simple rites," and members are accepted on confession of faith after examination by a membership committee and by a two-thirds vote of the congregation.

Evangelical Congregational Church

OBJECTING TO "the usurpation of powers in violation of the discipline" by bishops and district superintendents, seven annual conferences and from sixty to seventy thousand members of the Evangelical Association—later known as the Evangelical Church—withdrew from that body in 1894 to organize the United Evangelical Church. The two churches were reunited in 1922, but again a minority objected and remained aloof from the merger. The East Pennsylvania Conference, together with several churches in the Central, Pittsburgh, Ohio, and Illinois conferences, continued its separate existence under the old name. This was later changed to the Evangelical Congregational Church.

Today the boundaries of the East Pennsylvania Conference are the same as at the time of the merger; the midwest churches are joined in a western conference. They are, like their parent Evangelical church, "Methodists in polity, Arminian in doctrine." There is strong emphasis on the inspiration and integrity of the Bible and the "fellowship of all followers of Christ." There are annual and general conferences with equal lay and clerical representation, bishops and district superintendents, and an itinerant ministry. Pastors are appointed yearly by the annual conferences, with an eight-year limit set on their pastorates. Local congregations, as the name of the church implies, have more freedom, especially in temporal matters, than congregations in either Evangelical or Methodist churches. A Society of Home and Foreign Missions supervises work in those fields, with sixty-one missionaries at work at home and twenty-one abroad. Large summer assemblies are held in three parks owned by the church in Pennsylvania; church headquarters and a publishing house are located at Myerstown, Pennsylvania. In 1949 there was a total membership for both eastern and western conferences of 27,093 members and 163 churches.

Evangelical and Reformed Church

THE Evangelical and Reformed Church is the product of a union established at Cleveland, Ohio, on June 26, 1934, between two bodies of Swiss and German background with basic agreements in doctrine, polity, and culture—the Evangelical Synod of North America and the Reformed Church in the United States. The Evangelical Synod was the younger of the two bodies, originating with six ministers who met at Gravois Settlement near St. Louis in 1840 to form the Evangelical Union of the West. They were ministers of Lutheran and Reformed churches in the Evangelical United Church of Prussia. Two had been sent to America by the Rhenish Missionary Society and two by the Missionary Society of Basel; the other two were independent, one coming from Bremen and the other from Strassburg.

The Evangelical Union of the West was a co-operative ministerial association until 1849, when the first permanent organization was established. As the movement spread to the East and Northwest among German-speaking Lutheran and Reformed peoples, headquarters were established at St. Louis and a new name, the German Evangelical Synod of North America, adopted. A series of amalgamations with four other bodies of similar belief and polity—the German Evangelical Church Association of Ohio, the German United Evangelical Synod of the East, the Evangelical Synod of the Northwest, and the United Evangelical Synod of the East—resulted in the formation of the Evangelical Synod of North America, giving it a membership of 281,598 at the time of the merger with the Reformed Church in the United States.

The Reformed Church in the United States had its origin in Switzerland, Germany, and particularly in the flood tide of German immigration to Pennsylvania in the eighteenth century. More than half of the Germans in Pennsylvania in 1730 were of the Reformed persuasion; their congregations were widely separated along the frontier, and lacking ministers they often employed school teachers to lead their services. Three of their pastors, Johann Philip Boehm, George Michael Weiss, and Johann Bartholomaeus Rieger, were deeply influenced by Michael Schlatter, who had been sent to America by the Synod (Dutch Reformed) of South and North Holland; with him they organized in 1747 a *coetus* (synod) in Philadelphia. It was a synod directly responsible to and in part financially supported by the synod in Holland, from which it declared its independence in 1793, taking the name of the German Reformed Church, and in that year it reported 178 congregations and

15,000 communicants. The word "German" was dropped in 1869; from that time on the denomination was called the Reformed Church in the United States.

Reformed Church missionaries went early across the Alleghenies into Ohio and south into North Carolina. An overall synod of the church divided the country into eight districts or classes in 1819, and an independent Ohio classis was formed in 1824. Franklin College (now Franklin and Marshall) was founded at Lancaster, Pennsylvania, with the support of Benjamin Franklin; a theological seminary was opened at Carlisle and later moved to Lancaster; an academy which later became Marshall College was established in 1836. The Synod of Ohio established a theological school and Heidelberg University at Tiffin, Ohio, in 1850. The mother synod in the East and the Ohio Synod were united in the General Synod in 1836, which functioned until the merger with the Evangelical Synod of North America in 1934.

Difficulties arose in the early years of the last century over the languages used in the Reformed Church; the older Germans preferred the use of German, and the second-generation members demanded English. Inevitably in a church of such mixed membership there were conservatives and liberals in conflict. Some of the churches withdrew and formed a separate synod but returned in 1837 as wiser heads prevailed and compromises were made. New district synods of both German-speaking and English-speaking congregations were created, and two Hungarian classes were added in 1924 from the old Hungarian Reformed Church.

By 1934 the boards of the church were directing a widespread home missions work and foreign missionary work in Japan, China, and Mesopotamia. There were twelve institutions of higher learning, three theological seminaries, and three orphanages. There were 348,-189 members in the Reformed Church at the time of the 1934 merger, largely concentrated in Pennsylvania and Ohio.

Few difficulties were encountered in reconciling the doctrines of the two bodies when the union was finally accomplished. Both churches were German Calvinistic; the Reformed Church had been based historically on the Heidelberg Catechism and the Evangelical Synod on the Heidelberg Catechism, the Augsburg Confession, and Luther's Catechism. These three standards of faith were woven into one in the new constitution of the Evangelical and Reformed Church in these words:

The Holy Scriptures of the Old and New Testaments are recognized as the Word of God and the ultimate rule of Christian faith and practice.

The doctrinal standards of the Evangelical and Reformed Church are the Heidelberg Catechism, Luther's Catechism, and the Augsburg Confession. They are accepted as an authoritative interpretation of the essential truth taught in the Holy Scriptures.

Wherever these doctrinal standards differ, ministers, members, and congregations, in accordance with the liberty of conscience inherent in the Gospel, are allowed to adhere to the interpretation of one of these confessions. However, in each case the final norm is the Word of God.

Two sacraments, baptism, usually administered to infants, and the Lord's Supper, are accepted; confirmation, generally before the thirteenth or fourteenth years, ordination, consecration, marriage, and burial are considered as rites. Although hymns and forms of worship are provided for general use, a wide freedom of worship is encouraged.

Church polity is modified Presbyterian; each local church is governed by a consistory or church council elected from its own membership. Local churches form a synod, of which there are thirty-four, each made up of a pastor and lay delegate from each charge. The synod meets twice a year, has jurisdiction over all ministers and congregations, examines, licenses, and ordains all pastors, and elects its own officers. It appoints the committees necessary to the work of the congregations united in the synod.

The general synod is the highest body of the church; it consists of an equal number of lay and clerical delegates, meets every three years, and elects a general council of twenty-one members to supervise the work of the denomination and to act between sessions of the general synod. The general synod also elects the denominational boards and commissions; there are eight boards and five commissions, charged with the development of work in missions, education, publication, business management, pensions and relief, investments, evangelism, and social action. Together the general synod, the synod, and the consistory or church council are known as judicatories; the boards and commissions are called agencies. The judicatories create the agencies, and they work in perfect harmony together, bringing into the activity of the church the whole of its membership.

It is interesting that while the union of the two churches came in 1934, the constitution of the new church was not put into effect until 1940, and the boards were not unified until 1941. The procedure of union was completely democratic; both churches considered and approved a plan of union before the constitution, statement of doctrine, and *Book of Worship* were drafted or adopted. It was the first time that such a method of procedure had been employed in the history of Protestantism.

Home missions work covers a wide area; it is found in the Ozarks, among American Indians, Volga Germans, Hungarians, Czechs, and among Japanese in various cities and rural communities. Foreign missions are maintained in India, China, Japan, Honduras, Iraq, and Africa. There are eight colleges, three theological schools, and two academies. The *Messenger* is the leading denominational paper; there is one periodical in the German language. In 1949 there were 714,583 members and 2,754 churches.

Evangelical United Brethren Church

THE YOUNGEST of the major Protestant churches in Amercia, the Evangelical United Brethren Church was born in a merger at Johnstown, Pennsylvania, in 1946, uniting bodies previously known as the Church of the United Brethren in Christ and the Evangelical Church. Both churches originated in Pennsylvania and were quite alike in doctrine and polity.

Jacob Albright (1759-1808), founder of the Evangelical Church, was reared and confirmed a Lutheran and later confirmed as a Methodist exhorter. He began to preach in 1796 among the German people in Pennsylvania; and while he had no intention of forming a new church, his work was so successful that an ecclesiastical organization was effected in 1803, and he was ordained as an elder. He brought his Methodist ideas and ideals to this organization; the circuit system was adopted and an itinerant ministry instituted. At the first annual conference, held in 1807, Albright was elected bishop, and articles of faith and a book of discipline were adopted. The name Evangelical Association was approved by the first general conference in 1816.

Gradually, as the church spread, the German language was displaced by English. Missionary work under a society organized in 1839 was developed in Germany, Switzerland, Russia, Poland-Latvia, Africa, China, and Japan. A division rent the church in 1891, resulting in the organization of the independent United Evangelical Church. It was not healed until 1922 when the two churches were reunited under the name Evangelical Church.

The body held an Arminian doctrine, closely resembling that of the Methodists. The deity of Jesus and his perfect humanity and the divinity of the Holy Ghost were stressed. There was strong emphasis laid upon Christian perfection; entire sanctification was based upon this perfection.

The government was Methodistic. A quadrennial general conference elected the bishops of the church, who, however, were not ordained or consecrated as such; they presided at the general conference, which was a delegated body.

The Church of the United Brethren in Christ had a similar development; it began in the work of Philip William Otterbein, a German pastor who reached Pennsylvania in 1752 at the invitation of Michael Schlatter, a minister of the Reformed Church of Holland. Otterbein, already an ardent evangelist, joined with Martin Boehm, a Mennonite preacher, in an evangelistic work among the German settlers of Pennsylvania, Maryland, and Virginia. They held two-day "great meetings," which produced thousands of converts but which seemed so irregular to Otterbein's fellow ministers that he left their fellowship to organize an independent congregation in Baltimore in 1774.

Neither Otterbein nor Boehm had any intention or desire to create a new denomination, but such a move became imperative. Other evangelistic preachers working with them held a conference in 1800 which resulted in the establishment of the United Brethren in Christ; Boehm and Otterbein were elected bishops. It was not so much a schism as a fellowship of evangelists; they held their first general conference in 1815 and in the conference of 1817 ordered a confession of faith and book of discipline printed in both German and English.

As had been the case in the Evangelical Church, doctrine followed Methodist and Arminian patterns, with stress upon the Trinity, the authority of the Scriptures, justification, regeneration, the Sabbath, and the future state. Modes in baptism and the Lord's Supper, accepted as sacraments, were left to individual preference. There were the same Methodistic quarterly, annual, and general conferences, but the ministry had but one order, that of elders. The deflection of the Church of the United Brethren in Christ (Old Constitution) in 1889 constituted the only serious break in the ranks of this church up to the time of its union with the Evangelical Church.

The Evangelical United Brethren Church in October of 1949 reported 711,537 members in 4,460 churches, working and worshiping as one body and with no essential changes in the basic doctrines or polities of either of the two merged churches. Their doctrines admittedly stem from the articles of the Methodist Church and in turn from the Thirty-Nine Articles of the Church of England, with a Reformed flavor or emphasis. Prominent among them are convictions on the sinful state of man and the saving grace of God. The sacrament of baptism is obligatory for membership, and the Lord's Supper is conceived "in a Calvinistic sense to provide the spiritual, yet nevertheless real, presence of Christ for the believer." It is usually celebrated quarterly. Liturgically the church belongs to the free tradition; orders of worship are optional; the rituals of the two sacraments are derived from the *Book of Common Prayer.*

The church is divided into fifty-two annual conferences under which are quarterly conferences supervised by district or conference superintendents. There are seven bishops, who serve as general superintendents. The general conference meets every four years and is the final authority in all matters pertaining to the work of the church. Laymen have theoretically equal representation in the annual and general conferences, and there is parity among the clergy—no ecclesiastical power is granted to anyone beyond the authority of

ordination. All general church officers are elected quadrennially by the general conference.

The General Council of Administration acts as a co-ordinating body, recommends benevolence budgets and appropriations, assembles and prints the reports and memorials of the general conference, and so forth. Various boards —publication, missions, pensions, education—function under the general conference; there are also commissions on Christian social action and evangelism. The two denominational publishing plants, the Otterbein Press and the Evangelical Press, are still at work; there are other publishing houses in Germany and Switzerland. Pensions were paid in 1949 to more than one thousand annuitants, the payments reaching a total of $341,865. Home missions have been established among the Italians of Wisconsin and in Kentucky, Florida, and New Mexico; and foreign missionaries are stationed in Sierra Leone, West Africa, the Sudan, Central China, Japan, Puerto Rico, Santo Domingo, and Ecuador. There are sixteen Bethesda Deaconess hospitals in Germany, France, and Switzerland. The Department of Church Extension in 1949 aided forty-five church and parsonage building projects in grants totaling $118,000. The church supports eight colleges and three theological seminaries, two children's homes, and seven homes for the aged. The women of the church are organized into the Women's Society of World Service, composed of 3,054 societies and 101,997 members, for aid to missionary work; the laymen are banded in the Brotherhood, which in 1949 contributed $300,000 to the denomination's Kingdom Advance program.

EVANGELISTIC ASSOCIATIONS

$\mathcal{M}$any religious bodies in the United States are of such a nature as almost to defy classification. Some are called churches which are not churches at all in the accepted sense of the word. Some known as associations or bands or societies should be called churches, yet for all practical purposes they are denominations. Twelve of these have been grouped in this section as evangelical associations, in as much as they are, while separate and distinct from the churches, to be recognized by their common evangelistic nature and effort rather than by any ecclesiastical or doctrinal distinction. They are small groups, variously organized and supported, engaged primarily in evangelistic or missionary work.

Apostolic Christian Church (Nazarean)

THE Apostolic Christian Church (Nazarean) began in this country with the arrival of a Swiss, S. H. Froehlich, about the year 1850. Froehlich went to work immediately among Swiss and German immigrants, founding a number of small churches among those nationalities in the Midwest. Many of the early members were former Mennonites.

Distinguished in doctrine chiefly by their insistence upon entire sanctification, the local churches are independent in polity but united in a loose organization. Nearly half the membership, approximately 1,663, is found in Illinois; small bodies are found in nearly all the northern states, from New England to the West Coast. They report thirty-one churches.

Apostolic Christian Church of America

THE Apostolic Christian Church of America began with the labors of Benedict Weyeneth, a Swiss who came to America about 1847 and organized a number of Swiss-German churches. Its doctrine is based largely on the teaching of entire sanctification, aiming "solely at the saving of souls, a change of heart through regeneration, and a life of godliness guided and directed by the Holy Spirit." Members are noted for their pacifism; they will not bear arms but will engage in any service in support of the government "which is compatible with the teachings of Christ and the Apostles."

There are seven thousand members and fifty-five congregations, each of which is directed by an unpaid minister. There is currently a widespread interest in a closer unity and a more definite organization.

Apostolic Faith Mission

REFUSING to call itself a church or denomination but holding that it is "an evangelistic movement on a Scriptural plan," the Apostolic Faith Mission is a big-city, mission-type religious body with an ultraconservative evangelical message. The members devote all their time to the work with no remuneration of any kind.

Suspicious of churches, the mission is ardently evangelistic. Sanctification, the gift of tongues, baptism of the Holy Spirit, a strong faith in the literal accuracy and truth of the Bible, a distrust of scholarship, foot washing, and millennial preaching feature its beliefs and worship. Healing is most important; it is accomplished either by the laying on of hands or by sending to the sick a handkerchief or other object that has been specially blessed.

The movement is led by two women pastors, Mrs. Martha White and Miss Minnie Hanson. Miss Hanson, a former Lutheran, became a Methodist and went through a series of intensely emotional experiences in which she was "overwhelmed by the Holy Ghost" and received directly the power of God; as a result she was able to speak in strange tongues. Her type of experience and conversion has become typical of the Apostolic Faith Mission. Membership is less than two thousand, confined mostly to the state of Oregon, and fourteen congregations are reported.

Christian Congregation

THE PHILOSOPHY and work of the Christian Congregation, formed in Indiana in 1887, revolve about the "new commandment" of John 13:34-35. It is a fellowship of ministers, laymen, and congregations seeking a noncreedal, nondenominational basis for union. It opposes all sectarian strife, insisting that according to the new commandment "the household of faith is not founded upon doctrinal agreement, creeds, church claims, names, or rites," but solely upon the relation of the individual to God. The basis of Christian fellowship is love toward one another, the actual relations of Christians to each other transcending in importance all individual belief or personal opinions. Free Bible study is encouraged, and the Bible Colportage Service in Augusta, Texas, circulates the *Christian Indicator* quarterly publication series and other Bible helps and literature for field workers.

Churches and pastorates are established largely in the areas in which Barton Stone preached and in which the original Christian Connection congregations were located—Kentucky, Virginia, the Carolinas, Pennsylvania, Ohio, Indiana, and Texas, and in a few states west of these. In many respects the work of Christian Congregation is identical with that of the Stone movement and with his original Christian Church, although Christian Congregations were established and at work when the Christian Church was organized. The membership of 5,272 is 90 per cent rural. Polity is "that of a centralized congregational assembly"; congregational assemblies and a general assembly are held annually. Ministerial titles and forms of worship common to Presbyterian and Episcopalian churches are employed. Political and sectarian controversies are avoided, and members refuse to contract debts of any kind. Listed often as an evangelical association, it has now reached the proportions of a regular Protestant denomination.

Church of Daniel's Band

ONE OF the smaller sects of American Protestantism, the Church of Daniel's Band had 131 members in 3 churches in 1944. Incorporated at Marine City, Michigan, in 1893, it stresses evangelism, Christian fellowship, abstinence from all worldly excess, and religious liberty. It is quite similar to the Methodist Church in form and organization, and is generally believed to have grown out of the Methodist class meeting. It strives to revive primitive Wesleyanism, and the preaching of the church is strongly perfectionist. Sunday-school work is carried on in union schools with other churches. There is a small missionary work in Canada.

Church of God (Apostolic)

ORGANIZED in 1897 at Danville, Kentucky, by Elder Thomas J. Cox, this body was first known as the Christian Faith Band. It was incorporated under its present name in 1919. Its members believe that admission to the church must be only after repentance for sin, confession, and baptism; they teach holiness and sanctification, practice foot washing, and observe the Lord's Supper with unfermented grape juice and unleavened bread.

The general assembly is the governing body; under it serve officers known as the apostle or general overseer, the assistant overseer, district elders, pastors, evangelists, and local preachers. The church is divided into districts, each with an annual ministerial conference. There are about three thousand members.

Church of God as Organized by Christ

A MENNONITE preacher, P. J. Kaufman, withdrew from the Mennonite body in 1886 to protest against the ecclesiasticism of Protestantism and the lack of scriptural authority in Protestant organizations, and to found the Church of God as Organized by Christ. Kaufman and his followers held that membership in the church is not dependent on human choice but that all true Christians "have equal rights with all in the services and are members of His church." A spirit birth constitutes church membership; there is no formal joining of the church as other denominations know it. Ordination for church service is by Christ alone, but the ministry may, if it desires, be licensed and ordained for the purposes of public recognition.

Positively members of this church teach repentance and "restitution so far as restitution is possible," nonresistance, and complete obedience to Christ; they practice the sacraments of baptism, the Lord's Supper, and foot washing. Negatively they stand opposed to "denominationalism, churchianity, or sectism," union meetings and interdenominational co-operation, tobacco, secret societies, going to courts of law, church schools and Sunday schools, revivals, emotionalism, theaters, amusements, fine clothing, jewelry, human traditions and creeds, and "a hireling ministry." There were 14 congregations and 2,192 members in 1938.

Hephzibah Faith Missionary Association

THIS IS a loosely bound group of churches founded at Glenwood, Iowa, in 1892 for the purpose of preaching holiness and developing missionary and philanthropic work at home and abroad, and advocating "the establishing of independent, nonsectarian, full-salvation local churches and missions." It was reorganized in 1935 and again in 1948.

While there is a central executive committee with headquarters at Tabor, Iowa, to supervise general activities, each church, called an assembly, maintains its own work, establishes its own polity, and keeps its own records. There is no formal statement of creed or belief, but the group as a whole is strongly conservative and evangelical, emphasizing the emotional aspects of the influence and power of the Holy Ghost. Members, known as communicants, are required to give evidence of a new birth and of acceptance of the teachings of Scripture, and must be amenable to group discipline; many of them retain their affiliations with other churches. Ministers receive no salaries; they engage in other occupations and are in part supported by freewill offerings. Approximately a hundred ministers, evangelists, and deaconnesses are at work. Foreign missionary work, begun in 1894, is maintained in Japan, China, Africa, and India. There were seven hundred members and twenty assemblies in 1946.

Metropolitan Church Association

SPRINGING from a revival in the Metropolitan Methodist Church of Chicago in 1894 and sometimes known as the Burning Bush, the Metropolitan Church Association was originated primarily to carry on a local evangelistic work in the poorer and more densely populated sections of the city. It has since grown into a widespread work in the United States and abroad; in 1936 it was supported by nearly 961 members in 14 churches.

This is a "faith" organization in every sense of the word. No worker receives any salary or remuneration, and the membership as a whole takes seriously the command, "Sell all that thou hast, and distribute unto the poor," in that they hold no property which can be sold for the support of the work; all money raised goes into a common treasury.

Foreign missionaries are stationed in India, the Union of South Africa, and Brazil; evangelistic work is conducted in Norway and Sweden. At home workers go out into the cities in bands of from one to five on evangelistic missions wherever and whenever they feel the need of such work, often leaving a pastor in charge of groups organized during these campaigns. Four Bible training schools or institutes—in Glasgow; Capetown; Siwait, India; and Waukesha, Wisconsin—are maintained; no charges are made in any of these schools for board or tuition.

The founders of the association sought a return to the teachings of primitive Wesleyan holiness, and that emphasis is still strong. There is no creed "except such as may be found in the Scriptures themselves." As the association is an off-shoot of Methodism, government closely resembles the Methodist pattern, with stewards and trustees as the ruling units of the local church. The association was chartered under the laws of Wisconsin in 1918 and has its headquarters in Waukesha.

Missionary Bands of the World

MORE OF a missionary movement than a church, the Missionary Bands of the World constitutes a deflection from the Free Methodist Church under the leadership of the Rev. Vivian A. Dake in 1885. It became a separate body in 1898, adopting the name Pentecostal Bands of the World. The present name was adopted in 1925.

In common with the regularly established churches it has a regular membership, church buildings, pastors, evangelists, and missionaries. Foreign mission projects are located in India and Jamaica, staffed by unsalaried workers and supported by freewill offerings. Both doctrine and government correspond to those of the Methodist Church, with the local congregations enjoying slightly more freedom in the management of their churches. There were two hundred members and six churches in 1946.

Missionary Church Association

INTERDENOMINATIONAL, highly evangelistic, and conservative, this association was founded at Berne, Indiana, in 1898. Moderately perfectionist and premillenarian, its members believe that they have in Acts and in the New Testament Epistles the ideal patterns of Christian faith, evangelism, and church organization.

Prominent in their beliefs are the doctrines of the plenary inspiration of the Bible, the virgin birth and deity of Jesus, the Atonement, divine healing, premillenarianism, the immortality of the just, and the everlasting punishment of the wicked. Participation in war is opposed, but obedience to civil law is urged upon the membership. Baptism by immersion and open Communion are practiced.

Local churches are quite independent in managing their own affairs, but they recognize the authority of a general conference made up of ministers, missionaries, and appointed delegates. A general committee of eleven supervises the work of the whole church. The majority of missionaries abroad—in India, China, Africa, Jamaica, South America, the Dominican Republic, and Hawaii—serve under the Christian and Missionary Alliance, and the rest under various denominational boards. Church headquarters and a Bible institute are located at Fort Wayne, Indiana. Five thousand members and fifty-eight churches were reported in 1942.

Pillar of Fire

THE Pillar of Fire originated from the evangelistic efforts of its founder, Mrs. Alma White. The wife of a Methodist minister in Colorado, Mrs. White often preached from her husband's pulpit. Her fervent exhortations on regeneration and holiness, and especially her habit of organizing missions and camp meetings on her own authority, brought her into sharp conflict with the bishops and other leaders of Methodism, and she withdrew to become an evangelistic free lance. She established the Pentecostal Union in 1901 and changed that name to Pillar of Fire in 1917.

Mrs. White's first headquarters were located at Denver; they were later moved to Zarephath, near Bound Brook, New Jersey. In both Denver and Zarephath the body has a college, preparatory school, Bible seminary, radio station, and publishing plant. Other schools are located in Cincinnati, Los Angeles, Jacksonville, and London.

Modernism in theology is condemned by Pillar of Fire; its teaching is based upon primitive Wesleyanism, with doctrines on the inspiration and inerrancy of the Scriptures, repentance, justification, second blessing holiness, premillennialism, and future judgment. Sacraments include baptism and the Lord's Supper; marriage is a "divine institution."

Mrs. White was the first bishop of Pillar of Fire; on her death authority passed to her two sons. The membership is divided into four classes: proba-

tionary, associate, regular, and full, with only regular and full members being allowed to vote on administrative matters. There are deacons and deaconesses, and both men and women are ordained as ministers; there are also consecrated deaconesses, licensed preachers, and missionaries, and, as in Methodism, presiding elders (district superintendents) and bishops. Considerable literature is printed and distributed in the United States, and there are regular broadcasts from WAWZ, Zarephath, and KPOF, Denver. There are approximately five thousand members and sixty-one churches.

Faith Tabernacle

A ONE-CHURCH body organized by Pentecostalists in 1924 and located in Los Angeles, Faith Tabernacle reports about two hundred members. Its stated purpose is "to establish and maintain a place for the worship of God and to propagate the Gospel at home and in foreign

lands." The Bible is recognized as the "revealed will of God, superior to conscience and reason but not contrary to reason." Baptism of the repentant is by immersion, and believers practice foot washing and observe the Lord's Supper.

Federated Churches

FEDERATED CHURCHES in the United States are largely a rural or village phenomenon, strongest in New England and the West. They are churches, two or more in number and representing different denominations, which unite for mutual conduct of their work while continuing their connections with the denominations involved. The first federated church of which we have any record was formed in Massachusetts in 1887; another was founded in Vermont in 1899. By 1936 there were 508 federated churches in 42 states, with 88,411 members. There may be double that number now; further statistics are unavailable because of the lack of any national organization or office.

Economic pressure, conviction that the community is overchurched, flow of population, the inspiring example of the consolidated school, and the increased cost of church maintenance have been influential in forcing such federations. Ralph A. Felton in *Local Church Co-*

operation in Rural Communities (Home Missions Council, 1944) describes the usual circumstances under which the average federated Church is created:

Two churches in the same locality begin to have financial difficulties. Their memberships are too small to carry on thriving individual churches. They feel that if they could unite into one local congregation they could provide a more efficient religious program. Neither church wants to give up its affiliation with its denomination. For years they have been saying, "We should unite, but who's going to give up?" Finally they unite locally, hire one minister instead of two, but continue their separate "overhead" or denominational affiliations. The two or more separate churches thus become a federated church.

Usually there are joint religious services and a common Sunday school, and policy is determined by a joint official board. In some cases one minister is chosen to serve continuously; in others the minister is chosen alternately from the denominations represented. In approximately half of the federated churches in this country all of the Protestant churches in the community have entered the federation. Presbyterians seem to have the highest percentage of co-operation, with Congregationalists and Christians, Methodists, and Baptists following, in that order. There is still a real conflict of loyalties in the federated churches; its conclusion depends upon a slow educational process. Missionary giving and education are also unsolved problems. There is a noticeable trend toward eventual denominationalization; majority groups have a way of absorbing minorities, and usually when denominationalization comes, people go to the denomination that continues to provide a minister. It is also clear that if a federated church lasts five years, it is seldom abandoned.

Doctrine, polity, and membership requirements correspond in some cases to the standards of the denominations included; in other instances they are completely independent. No blanket statement is possible in these matters.

Fire Baptized Holiness Church of God of the Americas

A NEGRO Pentecostal sect, this church was for the first ten years of its existence a part of the white Fire Baptized Holiness Association of America; the Negro membership separated in 1908. In 1922 it became the Fire Baptized Holiness Church of God; the words "of the Americas" were added in 1926.

This church teaches the standard Pentecostal and holiness doctrines of repentance, regeneration, justification, sanctification, Pentecostal baptism, speaking with other tongues, divine healing, and the premillennial Second Coming. It stands opposed to the "so-called Christian Scientists, Spiritualists, Unitarians, Universalists and Mormons." Adventism, immorality, antinomianism, the annihilation of the wicked, the glorification of the body, and "many other modern teachings of the day" are denounced as false, wicked, and unscriptural. Government is by a bishop, two overseers, a general secretary, treasurer, and a board of trustees. Ruling elders, ordained ministers, and pastors are in charge of local churches; and a general convention is held yearly. In 1940 six thousand members were reported in three hundred churches. Headquarters are in Atlanta, Georgia.

Free Christian Zion Church of Christ

LED BY E. D. Brown, a local Methodist missionary, a small group of Methodist and Baptist Negro ministers formed this church in 1905 at Redemption, Arkansas. They objected to the taxing of any church membership to provide support for any ecclesiastical organization, feeling that the care and relief of the needy and the poor were the first responsibility of the church. Such relief activities characterize their local churches today.

Doctrine is completely Methodist, and so is government except for minor titles and details. Chiefs or superintendents perform the functions of bishops; a chief pastor is chosen as top administrative officer, making all assignments to pastorates and appointing all church officers. Pastors and deacons head local churches and are responsible for the aid of the poor in their congregations. Laymen share in the conduct of the churches and in the annual general assembly. The latest membership report, in 1944, listed 2,478 members and 37 churches.

91

FRIENDS

*W*ith a membership in the United States of only 115,000 and with 160,000 around the world the Religious Society of Friends, better known as Quakers, has had a deep and lasting influence upon Western society. Contributions in both religious and humanitarian spheres have won the Quakers universal respect and admiration, and their amazing history and loyalty to their quiet faith offer a challenge and inspiration seldom paralleled among the churches.

Their vicissitudes and victories began with George Fox (1624-91), a British "seeker" after spiritual truth and peace. Failing to find such in the churches of his time, Fox found them in a new intimate, personal relationship with Christ. He said: "When all my hopes in [churches and churchmen] were gone . . . then I heard a voice which said, 'There is one, even Christ Jesus, that can speak to thy condition.'" This is the Inner Voice or Inner Light of Quakerism, based upon the description of John 1:9—"the true Light, which lighteth every man that cometh into the world"— a voice available to all men, having nothing to do with outward forms or ceremonies, rituals or creeds. Every man to the Quaker is a walking church; every heart is God's altar and shrine.

Quakerism was revolutionary, and it was treated as revolution by the state Church of England. To tell this united state and church that they were both wrong, that their theology and dogma meant nothing, that men need not attend the "steeple-houses" to find God, and that it was equally wrong to pay taxes in support of state church clergymen—this was rebellion.

Fox and his early followers went even further. They not only refused to go to church but insisted upon freedom of speech, assembly, and worship; they would not take oaths in court; they refused to go to war; they doffed their hats to no man, king or commoner; they made no distinctions among people, in sexes or social classes; they condemned slavery and England's treatment of the prisoner and the insane. The very names they took—Children of Truth, Children of Light, Friends of Truth, and finally the Religious Society of Friends—roused ridicule and fierce opposition. Fox, haled into court, advised one judge to "tremble at the Word of the Lord" and heard the judge call him "Quaker." It was derision, but it was not enough to stop them. Persecution unsheathed its sword.

The Quakers were whipped, jailed, tortured, mutilated, murdered. Fox spent six years in jail; others spent decades, dying there. From 1650 to 1689 fifteen thousand of them died for their faith. Thanks to that persecution they prospered, founding the Society formally in 1666. When Fox died, there were fifty thousand Quakers.

Some were already in America. Ann Austin and Mary Fisher arrived in Massachusetts from Barbados in 1656, were promptly accused of being witches and deported; two days later eight more came from England. Laws were passed hastily to keep them out; the whipping-post was worked overtime and failed. Four were hanged in Boston. Quakers kept coming into New England, New York, New Jersey, Maryland, Virginia, and Pennsylvania. Only Rhode Island at first welcomed them. The long horror ended finally with the passage of the Toleration Act of 1689.

With Fox's death and the Act a new phase began; persecution waned and died—and so did a great deal of Quaker zeal. They settled down, looked within rather than without, and began enforcing discipline on their membership so strictly that they became in fact "a peculiar people." Members were disowned or dismissed for even minor infractions of the discipline; thousands were cut off for "marrying out of Meeting." Pleasure, music, and art were taboo; sobriety, punctuality, and honesty were demanded in all directions; dress was painfully plain, and speech was biblical. They held no public office. They were different and dour; they gained few new converts and lost many old members. It was a dark era from 1691 to 1835.

But there were lights in the darkness. Quaker philanthropy became highly respected, and their ideals on prison reform began to take effect. Quaker schools increased; as early as 1691 there were fifteen Quaker boarding schools in England. And William Penn came to Philadelphia. He sat under an elm at Shackamaxon and made a treaty with the Indians—"the only treaty never sworn to and never broken." Treated like human beings, the Indians reacted in kind. If all our cities had been Philadelphias and all our states Pennsylvanias, our national history would have been vastly different. But even there the holy experiment came to an end in 1756 when, rather than pay a tax to finance a war against the Shawnees and the Delawares, the Quakers stepped down and out of power.

Some few "fighting Quakers" went to battle in the American Revolution, but they were few; most of them remained pacifists. They worked quietly for peace, popular education, temperance, democracy, and against slavery. In 1688 the Friends of Germantown, Pennsylvania, said that Negro slavery violated the Golden Rule and encouraged adultery; they protested against the "traffic in the bodies of men" and called it unlawful. An attitude of toleration changed slowly to one of outright opposition; it took nearly a century for the Quakers to rid their society of slavery, but they did it, years in advance of any other religious body in America. Sellers or purchasers of slaves were forbidden membership in the Society by the close of the eighteenth century. Persistently all across these years the Quakers dropped their seed of antislavery agitation into the body politic; first John Woolman and then the poet Whittier wielded tremendous influence in the fight, and once the Civil War was over, they threw their strength into such organizations as the Freedman's Aid Society. Ever since, they have been active in education and legislative protection for the free Negro.

Serious divisions arose within their ranks in those years; the Hicksites separated in 1827, the Wilburites in 1845, and the Primitives in 1861. (These movements are considered under special paragraphs in this section.)

The twentieth century thus far has been a century of Quaker unity and outreach. A Five Years Meeting was organized in 1902, merging most of the orthodox groups. The two Philadelphia yearly meetings, separated since 1827, have been drawing closer together, and the two New York yearly meetings have been meeting in joint session during recent years. Eleven Quaker colleges have been built and strengthened; all but two of them are coeducational. On all levels Quakers schools have drawn students from other communions; their ideal of education for character is becoming increasingly popular.

In 1917, before the guns of World War I had stopped firing, Friends from all branches of the Society were at work in the American Friends Service Committee in relief and reconstruction efforts abroad; the A.F.S.C. remains today one of the most effective of such agencies in the world. Its volunteers erected demountable houses, staffed hospitals, plowed fields, reared domestic animals, and drove ambulances. Famine relief and child-feeding programs were instituted in Serbia, Poland, Austria, Russia, and Germany. Greek refugees, earthquake victims in Japan, needy miners' families in Pennsylvania, West Virginia, and Kentucky were helped. Millions would have perished but for A.F.S.C.

Quakers drove ambulances and served in the medical corps of both world wars, and some were in combat; one Quaker authority says that "more Quakers went to World War II than didn't." They also worked to relieve our displaced Japanese-Americans, and they co-operated with Brethren and Mennonites in locating our conscientious objectors in work of real national importance on farms, in reformatories, hospitals, and insane asylums. They were in Spain soon after the outbreak of the Spanish Civil War and later fed the child victims of war in Spain, southern France, Italy, Austria, Holland, North Africa, and Finland. In one year, 1945, they sent 282 tons of clothes, shoes, bedding, and soap to Europe and still more to China and India. The A.F.S.C. in 1948 had a budget of five million dollars. At home and abroad summer work camps of young volunteers have inspired an incalculable good will among nations and minority groups within nations.

Nor have they been satisfied to work merely in relief. Peace conferences have been a prominent part of their work, conferences ranging from local to international and covering all age groups. Lake Mohonk in New York was founded by a Friend. Scores of youth conferences and camps at home and in foreign fields testify to their devotion to the way of Christ; it is little wonder that they are known as a "peace church."

All worship and business in the Society of Friends is conducted in a series of four meetings: the preparative or congregational meeting, the monthly, quarterly, and yearly meetings. The monthly meeting is the basic unit, made up of one or more meetings in a neighborhood. It convenes for business and worship once a month, keeps records of membership, births, deaths, and marriages, appoints committees, considers the queries on spiritual welfare, and transacts all business of the group. Monthly meetings in a district join four times a year in the quarterly meeting to disburse funds, enroll elders and ministers recommended by the monthly meetings, and to summarize and pass on whatever business is thought worthy of the attention of the yearly meeting. The yearly meeting corresponds to a diocese in an episcopal system; there are twenty-eight of them in the United States and Canada. They are in touch with Friends all over the world and have standing committees on publications, education, the social order, missions, peace, charities, and national legislation; they allocate trust-fund incomes and generally supervise the joint work of the Society.

No vote is ever taken in any of these meetings; decisions await "the sense of the meeting." Lacking any unity of opinion, the meeting may have a "quiet time" for a few minutes until harmony is restored, or it may postpone consideration of the matter. Minorities are not outvoted but convinced. Every man, woman, and child is free to speak in any meeting; delegates are appointed to quarterly and yearly meetings to ensure adequate representation, but they enjoy no unusual position or prerogatives. Women have as much power as men; they hold a position of absolute equality in Quaker polity.

There are, contrary to popular misunderstanding, church officers—elders and ministers—among the Quakers. These are simply men or women of recognized ability in spiritual leadership, chosen by acclamation. But they stand on equal footing with the rest of the membership; *all* members are priests to the Quaker. A few full-time workers are paid a modest salary by the Society, and "recorded" ministers serving as pastors in the orthodox branch of the Society receive salaries.

Quaker worship is characterized by its silence and by its custom of "inquiring into the condition," lacking usually any established order of service, ritual, rites, or sacraments. There are no organs, choirs, collections, pulpits, or altars in the Conservative and Hicksite branches, though all of these exist in the orthodox or larger branch. Orthodox Friends also use the term church while meetinghouse is always used by the other branches. There are spontaneous prayer, scripture, reading or recitation, testimony, preaching, and singing as the spirit moves them, and there is often frank inquiry into the conduct of their businesses, their treatment of others, their use of narcotics or intoxicants, and their reading habits or recreation. No real Quaker gambles, plays the stock market, patronizes a movie theater to excess or owns one, bets, owns race horses, or engages in raffles, lotteries, or the liquor business. All controversy is avoided. Some follow conservative religious or theological patterns, and others are liberal; all are guided by the Inner Light and choose their own way.

The Inner Light is the heart of Quaker belief. Grace, power from God to help man resist evil, is to them universal, among *all* men. They seek not holiness but perfection—a higher, more spiritual standard of life for both society and the individual—and they believe that the truth is unfolding and continuing. Christ holds authority above that of the Bible; the Quaker should know his Bible well, but he puts "the Word of God which was Christ above the Word which is the Bible."

Rufus Jones says:

They believe supremely in the nearness of God to the human soul, in direct intercourse and immediate communion, in mystical experience in a firsthand discovery of God. . . . It means and involves a sensitiveness to the wider spiritual Life above us, around us, and within us, a dedication to duty, a passion for truth, and an appreciation of goodness, an eagerness to let love and the grace of God come freely through one's own life, a reverence for the will of God wherever it is revealed in past or present, and a high faith that Christ is a living presence and a life-giving energy always within reach of the receptive soul.

All members are considered priests or ministers. They are pacifist-minded, and many oppose all war; many still refuse to take oaths. Marriage is not a ceremony to be performed by a minister; the Quaker bride and groom simply stand before a meeting and make mutual vows of love and faithfulness and are thereby married, though the minister may officiate in the orthodox branch.

They have never been primarily interested in recruiting membership, depending almost entirely on birthright membership and membership by convincement. Every child born of Quaker parents is declared a member of the Society. This has resulted in a large number of nominal or paper members who contribute little; efforts are being made to correct this custom by establishing a junior or associate membership for children. This reliance upon birthright membership, plus the "purges" of membership which expelled hundreds for offenses against their discipline, has seriously depleted their membership; there are only about half as many Quakers in Philadelphia today as there were in 1830.

A total of 115,000 Quakers in the United States are found in approximately 1,000 congregations; 20,000 more are in the British Isles, 700 in continental Europe, 2,000 in the Far East, and about 23,000 in Australia, New Zealand, Madagascar, Palestine, Alaska, Cuba, Mexico, Guatemala, Canada, South Africa, and Kenya Colony. Never strong in foreign missions, American Friends do, however, maintain foreign work in Alaska, Cuba, Guatemala, Mexico, Japan, China, Palestine, and Africa.

Society of Friends (Five Years Meeting)

WITH ABOUT seventy thousand members this is the largest single Quaker body in the United States. Twelve of the fourteen yearly meetings in the country were united in this body in 1902; two of them Kansas and Oregon, later withdrew, and Ohio and Philadelphia-and-Vicinity never joined. Together these yearly meetings, aside from the Philadelphia Yearly Meeting, Race Street, and the Five Years meetings, constitute what is known as the Orthodox Friends. In the Five Years Meeting are included the Baltimore, California, Indiana, Iowa, Nebraska, New England, New York, North Carolina, Western, Wilmington, and Canada yearly meetings. Each of these yearly meetings remains independent but meets in the gathering held every five years for advisory purposes.

Religious Society of Friends (General Conference)

THIS IS a national organization of six yearly meetings, including the Hicksite branch, which was estabilshed with the great separation of 1827. Elias Hicks was a rural Long Island Quaker with a liberal and rational theology who came into conflict with those of more orthodox and evangelical persuasion. He and his followers resented the exercise of authority by certain of the orthodox leaders, especially those in Philadelphia; personalities had much to do with the split, as did rural restlessness under "city" authority. Basically, however, the split was due to the widespread nineteenth-century conflict between liberalism and rationalism on the one hand and an orthodoxy based on the Methodist ideas of evangelism and salvation on the other. The Methodist plan influenced Quakerism deeply. Two thirds of the Philadelphia Yearly Meeting withdrew with the Hicksites (a nickname never officially adopted by any Quaker body), and similar divisions followed in the New York, Ohio, Indiana, and Baltimore yearly meetings.

The history of the Hicksite groups since 1827 has been the history of the orthodox branches, except that there has been little emphasis upon evangelism. There are today many signs of reunion; a Philadelphia General Meeting of the Religious Society of Friends, including but not liquidating the two yearly meetings in that city, was organized in 1946, and beginning that year, as already stated, the two New York yearly meetings have met in joint session. There are currently some 19,016 members in the general conference.

Religious Society of Friends (Conservative)

KNOWN ALSO as Wilburites, this group represents a second serious division. It resulted from the preaching of Joseph John Gurney, a British evangelical Quaker who came to America teaching doctrine which conservative John Wilbur of Rhode Island considered a menace to Quakerism, advocating as it did the final authority of the Bible and acceptance of the doctrine of the Atonement, justification, and sanctification. Wilbur felt that this meant the substitution of a creed for the inner experience of the heart; with his followers he broke ranks to establish new yearly meetings in Kansas, western Iowa, Canada, New England, and Ohio between 1845 and 1881. Their doctrinal pattern was that "set forth by the Society in the beginning"; it was a movement back to the earliest and most conservative Quakerism. There are said to be about 4,000 Wilburites in the United States, but only 1,014 are reported as of 1949. In New England in 1945 the Wilburite controversy seemed resolved at last in the reunion of all Friends in that area in the New England Yearly Meeting.

Primitive Friends

THE Primitive Friends were even more insistent upon "the ancient testimonies of the Society." They separated from the Wilburites in 1861 in protest against the teachings of both Gurney and Hicks, and against the "modified and modernized" tendencies of Wilbur's followers. They were largely Philadelphia Quakers. This group has declined seriously; only one congregation is in existence today with ten members.

The two Philadelphia meetings, the Religious Society of Friends of Philadelphia and Vicinity (5,261 members) and the Race Street Yearly Meeting (11,750 members), are perhaps the most influential and authoritative of Quaker groups. The New England Yearly Meeting is the oldest, organized in 1661; Philadelphia Quaker bodies were established in 1681 and New York bodies in 1695. Other larger Quaker bodies with their approximate memberships are Indiana Yearly Meeting, 15,000; Western Yearly Meeting, held in the western part of Indiana, 13,000; North Carolina Yearly Meeting, 13,000; Kansas Yearly Meeting, 8,537; Iowa Yearly Meeting, 7,615; California Yearly Meeting, 6,400; Ohio Yearly Meeting, 5,714; Wilmington (Ohio) Yearly Meeting, 5,200; Oregon Yearly Meeting, 4,047; New England Yearly Meeting, 4,000; New York Yearly Meeting, 4,000; Nebraska Yearly Meeting, 2,000.

House of David

BENJAMIN PURNELL, who founded the House of David at Benton Harbor, Michigan, in 1903, claimed to be the seventh messenger prophesied by the book of Revelation; the other six, of whom Johanna Southcott (1792) was the first, had all been British. Purnell set up his Benton Harbor colony as a "commonwealth, according to apostolic plan" and was accepted there as the supreme ruler over all the community's spiritual and temporal matters. All who joined the colony put their earthly funds and possessions into the commonwealth treasury and contributed their work and services thenceforth to the cause. They lived in anticipation of the ultimate establishing of the kingdom of God on this earth. Purnell therefore called them Israelites and his movement an ingathering, because they were the direct lineal descendents of the twelve lost tribes of Israel, to be restored at the last days to their rightful places as judges and rulers in the kingdom of God.

Charges of dishonesty and immorality were brought against "King Benjamin" Purnell, and he died at the height of the scandal just before the supreme court of Michigan brought in a verdict in his favor; the movement, however, survived and continues on the original location. There are about 350 members at the immediate headquarters and other members in Australia, New Zealand, England, Ireland, Scotland, Africa, and all states in the union. The colony is financed by the sale of produce from the farms, dairies, vineyards, greenhouses, cold-storage and fruit-preserving factories, and other industries and shops of the members. They are strict vegetarians, and they never shave their heads or faces. Traveling baseball teams have brought them national publicity.

Immortality of the natural body is the bulwark of their belief, with certain interpretations of the Scriptures as proof. They find that automobiles, telephones, radios, and motion pictures are prophesied in the Bible as signs of the end of the evil powers and of Satan's kingdom. The custom of letting the hair grow long is based upon "what Jesus did," and because in the Bible man is the head of the woman and the heads of women must never be "uncovered" according to the Nazarene law.

The present church is controlled and directed by a board of directors with full authority. The community shows no signs of dwindling and disappearing as other such communities have and seems to enjoy a peaceful and prosperous existence.

Church of Illumination

MEMBERSHIP in this unusual body is made up of those "who are members in other churches and that vast number who have left churches prior to 1909 and since have been debris floating on a sea of unbelief and uncertainty." It is really a church-at-large, not a church of congregations numbering "several millions."

Its purpose is to harmonize the teachings of philosophy with the truths of religion. Much is made of the "Priesthood of Melchizedek," which dates "beyond the year 4255 B.C." and represents that small body of chosen seekers initiated into the inner mysteries of faith and divine law. This priesthood has come down from the days of Genesis, through Jesus, the Gnostics, the early Egyptians, Greeks, Indians, Persians, and so on to the present time, when it is found in the Church of Illumination.

The present Priesthood of Melchizedek (Church of Illumination) is directly descended from the Ancient Schools of the Mysteries via the Order of the Magi, which became one with the Fraternitas Rosae Crucis at the time when various groups merged under the new name. Its teachings are based upon demonstrable truths ... [and] harmonize with those of the first church of the Christian era, the Gnostic.

It is believed that all churches eventually will merge into one, in as much as they all have the same goal. Government is in the hands of a council of seven members. An assemblage is held annually, and in 1945 there were seven established churches with five thousand members.

Independent Churches

IT IS difficult, if not impossible, to classify properly all those churches in the United States calling themselves independent. Generally they may be identified as churches not controlled by any denominational or ecclesiastical organization, but even this does not hold in all cases. The following groupings are possible:

1. Churches called union, community, nondenominational, undenominational, or interdenominational. Community and nondenominational churches together constitute nearly one half of the number of so-called Independent churches.

2. Churches using a denominational name but working without denominational supervision.

3. Churches organized by individuals: holiness, evangelistic churches or movements, Gospel churches or halls, "storefront" churches, and so forth.

4. United churches of all types; Mark Dawber estimated a possible total of 2,500 such churches in 1940.

5. Federated Churches (already discussed; see page 90).

Many of these churches shift from one classification to another; one listed as United one year may be listed as Community (Methodist) the next. Free as they are of denominational control, they are as widely different in doctrine and polity as the preferences of the individuals and groups involved are different.

While there are as yet no accurate or official reports or statistics on it, the Community Church movement is definitely growing; churches bearing this name, often adding the word "Independent," are rapidly developing toward a United Church of the United States— if that name is appropriate. A National Council of Community Churches with two hundred congregations has been organized under the leadership of Roy Burkhart of the Community Church of Columbus, Ohio. A Biennial Council of Community Churches, made up of more than a hundred Negro congregations, merged in August, 1950, at Lake Forest, Illinois, with the national council in a new body known as the International Council of Community Churches. The International Council thus claims three hundred out of a possible three thousand autonomous, nondenominational community churches in the United States, with a potential membership of more than a million. It is a movement of real proportions and importance.

Independent Fundamental Churches of America

ORGANIZED IN 1930 at Cicero, Illinois, by representatives of various independent churches anxious to safeguard fundamentalist doctrine, this body has two types of membership—one for churches, the other for ministers, missionaries, and evangelists. About four hundred churches were listed in 1950, and one thousand ministers, missionaries, or evangelists. A full-time executive secretary has been installed at the headquarters in Chicago. The president of the body presides over an annual conference in which the members have voting power. An executive committee of eleven serves for four years, acting between meetings of the annual conference, which is an advisory body. The constituent churches are completely independent but are required to subscribe to the statement of faith of the organization. Approximately 65,000 lay members are represented in this organization.

International Church of the Foursquare Gospel

RISING OUT of the evangelistic work of "Sister" Aimee Semple McPherson, this church is a tribute to the organizing genius and striking methods of its founder. Born in Ontario in 1890, Mrs. McPherson was converted under the preaching of her first husband, Robert Semple, a Baptist evangelist. He died in China, and she returned to the United States in 1918 to tour the country in a series of gospel meetings which were spectacular even in war years. She settled in Los Angeles in 1918, building the famous Angelus Temple and founding the Echo Park Evangelistic Association, which included the L.I.F.E. Bible College (Lighthouse of International Foursquare Evangelism).

Adept at crowd psychology and a dramatic artist on the platform, Mrs. McPherson attracted thousands to her meetings and fascinated them with her clever use of pageantry, lighting effects, colorful costumes, and it is said, healing of the sick; her more irreverent critics felt that her meetings were more often spectacles than services. There was great interest in the sick and the poor; "more than a million" are said to have been fed by the Los Angeles organization.

The teaching of the sect is set forth in a twenty-one paragraph *Declaration of Faith* written by Mrs. McPherson. Strongly fundamentalistic, the sect is Adventist, perfectionist, and Trinitarian; the Bible is "true, immutable, steadfast, unchangeable as its author, the Lord Jehovah"; Spirit baptism follows conversion, and there is the gift of tongues and the power to heal in answer to believing prayer; there are the usual doctrines on the Atonement, the second coming of Christ "in clouds of glory," reward for the righteous at the judgment, and eternal punishment for the wicked. Baptism and the Lord's Supper are observed.

Mrs. McPherson was president of the church during her lifetime and was the ruling power and voice of the organization; the office was conferred upon her son at her death. A general assembly is held annually, in which the officers of the corporation, the board of directors or trustees, ministers, evangelists, and lay delegates are entitled to vote. The board of directors, five in number, manages the business of the church and appoints field supervisors in charge of the districts into which the 492 branch churches are divided. Each church is governed by a church council and contributes one offering a month to home and foreign missionary work. Foreign missionary stations are established in China, the Philippines, Belgian Congo, South Africa, Panama, Bolivia, and Puerto Rico, and Bible colleges have been established in northern China and in the Belgian Congo. An ordination and a missionary board examines, admits, and license all ministers, missionaries, evangelists, and other workers.

There are 66,611 members, and all are required to subscribe to the *Declaration of Faith*. The young people are organized into bands of Foursquare Crusaders. A church flag—red, yellow, blue, and purple with a red cross on a white background, bearing a superimposed "4"— is prominently displayed in the churches, rallies, and assemblies; a radio station K.F.S.G., broadcasts from Los Angeles

Italian Christian Church of North America

THIS CHURCH represents a merger of two former Italian denominations: the Italian Christian Churches of North America and the General Council of the Italian Pentecostal Assemblies of God. The former group, by far the larger, was founded in 1907 by Louis Francescon in Chicago as a "nondenominational and nonsectarian" union of independent Italian congregations; its work spread across the country and into Italy, Brazil, and Argentina. The Pentecostal Assemblies group was founded in 1904 by Rocco Santamaria and his father, John Santamaria, also in Chicago, gathering together about two hundred Italian missions and congregations.

The united church has its headquarters at Niagara Falls, New York, and lists about 23,000 members in 196 churches. No statement on the work or administration of this church is available. Doctrine is fundamentalist, stressing belief in the infallibility of the Scriptures, the Trinity, regeneration, justification, Spirit baptism, speaking in tongues, premillennialism, future rewards and punishments, and so forth. Baptism by immersion and the Lord's Supper are celebrated as sacraments.

Jehovah's Witnesses

THE PEOPLE called Jehovah's Witnesses deny that their movement is religious, maintain that the organized religious bodies of our times are "not of the Lord God and Christ but of their enemy, Satan," and acknowledge no human founder. Yet they have become, at least in point of public interest, an outstanding religious phenomenon in modern America.

They were not known as Jehovah's Witnesses until 1931, when the name was adopted at the suggestion of their president, Judge J. F. Rutherford; up to this time they were called Millennial Dawnists, International Bible Students, and, earlier, Russellites after the man who brought about their incorporation in 1884. Pastor Charles Taze Russell, their first president, is not acknowledged as founder but as general organizer; Judge Rutherford claimed that the Witnesses had been on earth as an organization for more than five thousand years and cited Isaiah 43:10-12, Hebrews 11, and John 18:37 to prove it.

Russell was never an ordained minister; he was a layman who, deeply influenced by Adventism, studied the Bible avidly and attracted huge crowds to hear him expound the Scriptures. The first formal organization of his followers came in Pittsburgh in 1872; his books, of which thirteen million are said to have been circulated, laid the foundations of the movement. Russell was president; to assist him, a board of directors was elected by the vote of all members who subscribed ten dollars or more to the support of the work.

Dying in 1916, Russell was succeeded as president by Judge Rutherford, who moved headquarters to Brooklyn in 1909 and in 1939 incorporated the body under its present name, the Watch Tower Bible and Tract Society. Rutherford was a Missouri lawyer who occasionally sat as a circuit-court judge. He wrote tirelessly; his books, pamphlets, and tracts supplanted those of Russell, and his neglect of some of Russell's teachings brought dissension. The development of a hierarchy and of highly authoritarian government also marked Rutherford's leadership. Three corporations eventually controlled the society: the Watch Tower Bible and Tract Society of Pennsylvania, the Watch Tower Bible and Tract Society of New York, and the International Bible Student's Association of England. The judge, however, was the actual ruling power.

Under the direction of these leaders at headquarters regional servants—they would be bishops in episcopal churches—six in number, are in charge of the six areas into which the country is divided. Under them are 154 zone servants or district superintendents. Local groups of Witnesses are not called churches but companies. They meet in Kingdom Halls under the leadership of a company servant (minister or pastor).

All members are required to give stated hours of time to witnessing or "publishing," depending upon their status. There are "publishers," or part-time workers, expected to give sixty hours per month to spreading Witness literature and playing phonograph recordings of Judge Rutherford's speeches house to house. "Pioneers" are full-time workers; "special pioneers" are asked to give 175 hours per month, and receive a monthly allowance of twenty-five dollars; general pioneers are expected to give 150 hours, and receive ten dollars per month. Many engage in other occupations to make a living. The literature they distribute pours like a flood from the presses in Brooklyn, turned out by Witnesses who receive ten dollars per month plus board and room for their services. In 1948, 181,071 "publishers" around the world distributed more than 20,000,000 books and booklets, 12,000,000 magazines, 18,000,000 tracts, and 218,000 Bibles.

In this literature, most of which was written by Judge Rutherford, is contained the teaching of the society. Its foundation is the idea of the Theocracy, or rule of God. The world in the beginning, according to the Witnesses, was under the theocratic rule of the Almighty; all was "happiness, peace and blessedness" then. But Satan (Lucifer) rebelled and became ruler of the world, and from that point on mankind has followed his evil lead. Then came Jesus,

as the prophets had predicted, to end Satan's rule; Jesus' rule began in 1914. In 1918, just as Rutherford was sentenced to prison for refusal to support the government in World War I, Christ "came to the temple of Jehovah." In 1922, when Rutherford reorganized the movement shattered by the war, Jesus, enthroned in the temple, began illuminating the prophesies and sending out his followers to preach. God is one, not three in one; the Trinity is denied. God is more judge and avenger than loving Father, more the God of the Old Testament than of the New. The Holy Ghost is not a person but the invisible "power of Jehovah" on earth. Jesus, the Son of God, is God's representative on earth, come to vindicate God's name, to redeem mankind, and to set up Jehovah's kingdom, or the Theocracy. He will do this after earth's last battle of Armageddon has been fought. Christ will lead the army of righteousness, composed of "the host of heaven, the holy angels," and completely annihilate the army of Satan. The righteous of earth will watch this struggle but will not participate. A righteous remnant will be left to rule the earth under "Christ, the King of the great Theocracy." The righteous will be resurrected to reign with him, but the wicked will not be resurrected; they shall reign for a thousand years, after which Satan will rise again and be finally and completely destroyed. Even the memory of the devil will be gone, and the righteous will rule forever after in peace and blessedness. Rutherford said, "Millions now living shall never die," which meant that Armageddon was close; the kingdom was at hand. He died in 1942, leaving guidance of the movement in the hands of the present president, Nathan H. Knorr, and Armageddon had not yet been fought. But the certainty of its imminence persists.

All this is based upon the Bible; Witnesses elaborately quote scriptural chapter and verse in proof of all their teaching. All other teachings and interpretations but their own are suspect and unreliable. They oppose all churches, ministers, and theologies, and are especially vehement in denunciation of the Roman Catholic Church.

Their opposition to many of the laws of the state has resulted in an unbelievable persecution—whippings, j a i l i n g, stoning, tarring and feathering, and the burning of their homes. Insisting that their first duty is to God and not to any state, they have refused to vote, to do jury duty, to salute the flag or allow their children to salute it in public schools. They are now supported in their refusal to salute the flag by a Supreme Court decision. They have refused to go to war, not because they are pacifists— considering Armageddon, they would seem to countenance some war and vio-

lence—but because their members in World War II were denied the 4-D classification in the draft, which would have given them exemption as ministers of religion. They also stand firmly on the ground that wars between nations demand allegiance to earthly rulers, and their only acknowledged allegiance is to God.

No membership records are kept, and no statistics are published. Local companies are generally small, 100 to 200, and there are said to be 3,056 such companies in this country; but estimates based on the staff and strength of these companies would be far from accurate. Some put their United States membership at 300,-000 and their world membership at 3,000,000.

JEWISH CONGREGATIONS

Jews arrived early in the American colonies; fleeing persecution in Europe, some were here before 1650. To escape the terror of the Portuguese Inquisition a small group of them found safety if not complete understanding in Peter Stuyvesant's New Amsterdam, where they established the first official congregation in North America, Sheerith Israel (Remnant of Israel) in 1655. Three years later there was a small group of Jews at Newport, Rhode Island. Jews came to Georgia with Oglethorpe and in 1733 organized a synagogue at Savannah. By 1850 there were seventy-seven Jewish congregations in twenty-one states and at the end of the century more than six hundred congregations of over a million Jews. Nearly five million American Jews today have a widely varying synagogue membership estimated at anywhere from a minimum of 1,500,000.

The historic sense of unity among the Jewish people soon demonstrated itself here as it had abroad. That unity had defied centuries of dispersion and persecution, and it now welded the followers of Judaism into one of the most influen-

tial religious groups in America. This is especially impressive when we consider the fact that Judaism has no central creed and no articles of faith. In *The Truth About the Pharisees* it has been described by R. T. Herford as "a detailed system of ethical practices by which its adherents consecrated their daily lives to the service of God. The cornerstone of Judaism was the *deed*, not the *dogma*."

There are, however, two twin pillars upon which Judaism rests. One is the teaching of the Old Testament, particularly of the Pentateuch, the Five Books of Moses. This is known in Judaism as the Torah. It is the revelation of God, divine in origin and containing the earliest written laws and traditions of the Jewish people. The other is the Talmud, which is a rabbinical commentary and enlargement of the Torah, an elaborate, discursive compendium containing the written and the oral law which guides the Jew in every phase of his living.

In Torah and Talmud are the Judaistic foundation principles of justice, purity, hope, thanksgiving, righteousness and love, freedom of the will, divine providence and human responsibility, repentance, prayer, and the resurrection of the dead. At the heart of it all lies the Hebrew concept of the oneness of God. Every day of his life the good Jew repeats the ancient biblical verse, "Hear, O Israel, the Lord is our God, the Lord is One." All other gods are to be shunned; there is but one creator of man and the world, holding the destiny of both in his almighty hands.

Man, created by this one God, is inherently good. There is no original sin, no instinctive evil or fundamental impurity in him; he is made in God's image and endowed with an intelligence which enables him to choose for himself between good and evil. He has and needs no mediator such as the Christians have in Christ; he approaches God directly. Men, Jews and Gentiles alike, attain immortality as the reward for righteous living.

Judaism looks forward to the perfection of man and to the establishment of a perfect divine kingdom of truth and righteousness upon this earth, the messianic era, in which all will be peace and bliss. To work toward this kingdom the Jews have been established of God as a deathless, unique people, a "kingdom of priests and a holy nation," and as the "Servant of the Lord."

Some of their laws provide for the great festivals of the Jewish year: Pesach, or Passover, in April, a memorial of the Jewish liberation from Egypt; Shabuoth, the Feast of Weeks, or Pentecost, in June commemorating the giving of the Ten Commandments to Moses; Sukkoth, or the Feast of Tabernacles or Booths, in October marking the years of Jewish wandering in the wilderness; the Feast of Lights, or Hanukkah, in December celebrating the purification of the temple by the Maccabees after its defilement by Antiochus Epiphanes; the Feast of Lots, or Purim, in March honoring the heroine Esther. Three principal minor fasts are observed: the Fast of Tebeth in January commemorating the siege of Jerusalem; the Fast of Tammuz in July observing the breach of Jerusalem's walls; and the Fast of Ab also in July memorializing the fall of the city and the destruction of the temple. The most important days in the Jewish religious calendar are the great fast of Yom Kippur, the Day of Atonement, in September closing the Ten Days of Penitence which begin with Rosh Hashana, or New Year's Day.

Other laws are kept as reminders of God's covenant with Israel; these include the laws of circumcision and Sabbath observance. Still others are held as marks of divine distinction and are kept to preserve the ideal of Israel as a chosen, separate people.

Within the local congregation there is full independence. There are no synods, assemblies, or hierarchies of leaders to control anything whatsoever in the synagogue. The Jews are loosely bound by the "rope of sand" of Jewish unity, with wide variation in custom and procedure. They have been influenced deeply by the many peoples and cultures with which they have come in contact, and have made adjustments accordingly. Because of differences in historical background over the centuries some congregations use a German-version Hebrew prayer book; others use a Spanish version. Some use English at various points in their services, such as the sermons, but all use Hebrew in their prayers. Sermons may be heard in English or Yiddish, a German dialect influenced by Hebrew. Traditional orthodox and conservative synagogues have no instrumental music in their services; the congregation worships with covered head, and the men and women sit separately. In reform temples these traditions are not observed.

At the head of the congregation stands the rabbi, trained in college and seminary and fully ordained. He is preacher and pastor. He officiates at marriages and grants divorce decrees in accordance with Jewish law after civil divorce has been granted by the state. He conducts funerals and generally supervises the burial of Jews as Jewish law requires. Congregations usually own their own cemeteries or organize cemetery societies; there are also many private cemetery or burial associations owned and controlled by Jewish benevolent groups. Orthodox rabbis are also charged with the supervision of slaughtering animals for food and with the distribution of kosher meat products in accordance with the Levitical dietary laws. Many congregations engage readers or cantors, but it is the rabbi who is the leader and authority on Jewish law and ritual.

There is no examination for synagogue membership, all Jews being readily accepted as congregants. However married women and unmarried children are not usually recognized as voting members. Men are almost always the corporate members. There are sometimes also pew holders, who contribute to and engage in the work of the synagogue but without the authority of corporate members. A third class of synagogue membership consists of those who merely pay for the use of a synagogue seat during the High Holidays. Corporate members are supposed to control all synagogue property and to guide congregational policy and activity, but the other members often participate on almost equal footing.

There are four divisions in American Judaism: Orthodox Judaism represented nationally by the Union of Orthodox Jewish Congregations of America, the Rabbinical Council of America, and the Union of Orthodox Rabbis of the United States and Canada, numerically by far the largest Jewish body in the United States; Reform Judaism with the Central Conference of American Rabbis and the Union of American Hebrew Congregations—the first national organization of synagogues in America, established in 1873—as spokesmen; Conservative Judaism organized in the United Synagogue of America and the Rabbinical Assembly of America; and Reconstruction Judaism, sponsored by the Jewish Reconstructionist Foundation organized in 1940. The first three of these national organizations are constituent members of the Synagogue Council of America.

No accurate survey of membership in these American Jewish congregations has ever been taken, and one probably cannot be taken. Estimates differ widely depending upon the methods and classifications employed. Those who hold that all members of the race are by nature and spiritual necessity also members of the synagogue identify the number of American Jews, 5,000,000, with American synagogue membership. This is the figure set in 1950 by the Jewish Statistical Bureau. Others estimate total synagogue membership as low as 1,500,000, or less than one third of the Jews in the United States. It is impossible to estimate the number of either members or synagogues with any accuracy at all, in as much as many of them never report to any national Jewish organization.

The multiplicity of Jewish national organizations in the United States is bewildering. The American Jewish Yearbook for 1950 lists them in the following categories: civic, defense, and political, 13; cultural, 25; overseas aid, 24; religious and educational, 53; social and mutual benefit, 60; social welfare, 24; Zionist and pro-Israel, 51. These are for the United States alone. There are many more in foreign countries, and the number in this country is increased by subsidiary organizations working under the above categories. Over 600 communities in this country have federations, welfare funds, and community councils working locally. There are 206 Jewish periodicals and newspapers in 30 states and the District of Columbia, and three Jewish news syndicates. *Liberal Judaism* is the monthly Reform organ; the bimonthly *Jewish Life* speaks for the Orthodox branch; *Conservative Judaism* is the quarterly printed voice of the Conservatives; and the fortnightly *Reconstructionist* speaks for Reconstructionism. Among the magazines of general interest are *Commentator, Menorah Journal*, the *Jewish Frontier*, and the *Jewish Spectator* and the *National Jewish Post*, a news weekly.

Education on all levels is a major Jewish enterprise. In 1935 it was estimated that Jewish education in the United States cost approximately $4,900,000. Children are enrolled in Sabbath schools, weekday schools, all-day schools, Yiddish schools, and released-time schools. In 1949 there was a total of 255,865 children in all weekday and Sabbath schools, but it was still estimated that not more than 75 per cent of available Jewish children were enrolled in Jewish schools.

Institutions of higher learning are largely limited to schools for the training of rabbis. The most important are the Rabbi Isaac Elehanan Theological Seminary in Yeshiva University in New York City (Orthodox); the Hebrew Union College in Cincinnati and the Jewish Institute of Religion in New York City (Reform institutions that were merged in 1948 into what is now called H.U.C.—J.I.R.); the Jewish Theological Seminary in New York City (Conservative); and the Beth Midrash l'Torah in Chicago (Orthodox). The Jewish Theological Seminary has a branch in Los Angeles called the University of Judaism. Dropsie College, "a postgraduate, nonsectarian institution of Semitic learning" in Philadelphia and the Yiddish Scientific Institute in New York City are the only two institutions of higher learning working independently of Jewish seminaries; Yeshiva University in New York City and Brandeis University in Waltham, Massachusetts, are the only Jewish colleges awarding a B.A. degree.

Jewish charity is amazingly efficient. The United Jewish Appeal in 1948 raised $150,000,000 for all purposes. This sum was divided between the United Palestine Appeal, the American Joint Distribution Committee, and the United Service for New Americans. The Joint Distribution Committee handled $70,-600,000 in cash and relief material in world-wide operations that year. The U.J.A. drove for $250,000,000 in 1949.

The American Jewish Committee is organized to protect the civil and religious rights of all Jews around the world. It offers legal assistance, seeks equality for Jews in economic, social, and educational opportunities, and gives protection from persecution and intolerance through the Joint Defense Appeal, in which it co-operates with the Anti-Defamation League of B'nai B'rith.

Among the Zionist societies the Zionist Organization of America is the largest and most powerful; it is in the United States the acknowledged spokesman in politics and public relations for the whole movement. Zionism is limited to no one of the four major religious groups; it has crossed the line everywhere. The only organized opposition to Zionism within American Jewry is found in the comparatively small Council for Judaism.

Two trends are noticeable in American Judaism. One is the trend toward a relaxation of strict or letter observance of the time-honored Jewish law; the other, in seeming opposition, is the tendency to consider the inner spiritual strength of Judaism as its only hope for the future. Under this latter drive American Jews know fewer and fewer divisions, more and more co-operation and unity.

Orthodox Judaism

ORTHODOX JUDAISM preserves the theology and traditions of Old World Jewry in the New World. It assigns equal authority to the written and the oral law and to the ancient Jewish codes embodied in the Torah and the Talmud and their commentaries. The Torah is of God, given to Moses. Moses is believed to have transmitted orally this great body of teaching to his successors, who transmitted it down to the time when it was first committed to writing. Orthodox Jews believe in the political rebirth of their nation, in the return of the Jew to Palestine to rebuild his temple on Mount Zion and to re-establish his ancient sacrificial ritual. They look forward to the personal coming of the Messiah, who is to be a descendant of David. The biblical dietary laws are strictly observed, and the traditional holy days and festivals are observed faithfully. The Hebrew language is used in their synagogue prayers, English in their sermons. They are the fundamentalists of Judaism.

Reform Judaism

REFORM JUDAISM is liberal Judaism, which sometimes comes close to liberal Christianity. It holds that there is divine authority only in the written law of the Old Testament; this is its main distinction from Orthodox Judaism. To the Reform Jew, however, revelation is not confined to the Old Testament; it is progressive. He limits himself to the practice of the ceremonial laws of the Pentateuch with the exception of those laws which, like the law of sacrifice, he regards as having no application or purpose in the present day. The sacrifices of the Mosaic era, he insists, were merely concessions to the customs of the times. In other words the Orthodox Jew accepts the entire body of oral and written law as sanctified by tradition; the Reform Jew has simplified the ritual and adapted it to modern needs. Unlike his Orthodox brothers he does not believe in the messianic restoration of the Jewish state and return to Jerusalem; he is abandoning belief in a personal Messiah, but he still holds to his faith in the coming of a messianic age. He does, however, support the return to Palestine under the Zionist movement, not so much on spiritual or Talmudic grounds as on the ground that Palestine offers a place of refuge for the persecuted Jews of Europe. He advocates the preservation in the new state of Israel of such Jewish values, customs, and traditions as have inspirational value.

Conservative Judaism

CONSERVATIVE JUDAISM holds middle ground between Orthodox and Reform, and seeks the preservation of the values and ideals of both. From Orthodoxy it takes its belief in the Torah, observance of the dietary laws, and the use of the Hebrew language; from Reform it takes its tendency to reconcile the ancient truths and practices with modern cultures, the application of up-to-date methods in education, the use of English sometimes in synagogue prayers, and the use of the family pew in the synagogue.

Reconstructionism

RECONSTRUCTIONISM under the sponsorship of the Jewish Reconstructionist Foundation, Incorporated, is too small and new a movement to be of much influence as yet. Under the aggressive leadership of Mordecai M. Kaplan it asks for a reorganization of all Jewish life. It is active in the struggle to establish a Jewish national home in Palestine, the broadening of Jewish education beyond instruction in language, ritual, and catechism, the reinterpretation of Judaism to bring it into harmony with modern thought, and the establishment of a world-wide co-operative Jewish society. It is the radical "left wing" of American Judaism.

Commandment Keepers, or Black Jews

THIS IS a Negro Jewish sect in New York's Harlem, following Orthodox Judaism. It was founded in 1919 by Rabbi Wentworth David Matthew, who claims 3,300 members in Harlem and an equal number in other congregations beyond that section. They teach that the Negroes are actually Hebrews originating in Ethiopia. They maintain a home for the aged and co-operate in various business enterprises with the white Jews of Harlem. Two other Jewish Negro groups, the House of Israel and the Moorish Science Temple, also operate in and around Harlem. They wear full beards and teach that Adam was a Negro, and that Negroes are the real Hebrews.

106

LATTER-DAY SAINTS, OR MORMONS

Kodesh Church of Immanuel

FORMED IN 1929 and incorporated in April, 1930, by the Rev. Frank Russell Killingsworth and 120 laymen, some of whom were former members of the African Methodist Episcopal Zion Church, this is an interracial group with 1,200 members, most of whom are Negroes. The seven churches of the group are located in Pennsylvania, Virginia, and the District of Columbia. Teachings are Wesleyan and Arminian, stressing entire sanctification by the baptism of the Holy Spirit; and premillennialism. Divine healing is practiced, but not to the exclusion of medicine.

As the church was founded for the purpose of "conserving and propagating sane, Bible holiness," the use of alcoholic liquors and tobacco is forbidden; pride in dress and behavior, Sabbath desecration, secret societies, dissolute dancing, and attendance at inferior and obscene theaters are denounced. Divorce is recognized only on the biblical ground of adultery. Water baptism is by the optional modes of sprinkling, pouring, or immersion.

The churches are under the charge of ministers and the oversight of supervising elders. Ministers are elected and ordained by annual assemblies to which they report. Supervising elders are elected and consecrated by the general assembly which meets quadrennially to enact all laws of the church. The work of the entire church, including the support of foreign missionaries, is maintained by tithes and freewill offerings.

LATTER-DAY SAINTS, OR MORMONS

*B*etter known as Mormons, the Latter-day Saints have had the most tempestuous history of any church body in the United States. Attacked by mobs and once invaded by United States Army troops, they built a religious empire in what was once a desert and established themselves as one of the outstanding religious groups of the nation.

Essentially a layman's movement in its origin, their church is rooted in the visions of Joseph Smith, who founded the movement in 1830 at Fayette, New York. Smith claimed to have experienced a series of heavenly visitations in which he was informed that all existing churches were in error, that the true gospel was yet to be restored, that it would be revealed to him, and that he was to re-establish the true Church on earth. He was led by an angel to discover certain golden plates or tablets buried in a hill called Cumorah near Manchester Village, left there by an ancient prophet and containing the sacred records of the ancient inhabitants of America and the true Word of God. According to the Mormons, America was originally settled by the Jaredites, one of the groups dispersed during the confusion of tongues at Babel; the American Indians were direct descendents of the Hebrews who came from Jerusalem in 600 B.C. Jesus himself visited this country after his resurrection.

With the aid of his heavenly helpers and Oliver Cowdery, a former schoolteacher, Smith translated the hieroglyphics on the golden tablets into the *Book of Mormon,* from which the name "Mormon" comes. This *Book of Mormon* is considered by the saints as equal with and "supporting but not supplanting" the Bible; with two other writings of Joseph Smith, the *Book of Doctrines and Covenants* and the *Pearl of Great Price,* it contains the foundation teachings of the church. The golden plates have disappeared; their authenticity has been challenged by non-Mormon scholars and as ardently defended by the Mormons, who offer the names of eleven other persons beside Smith who saw them. Smith and Cowdery had "the priesthood of Aaron" conferred upon them by a heavenly messenger, John the Baptist, who instructed them to baptize each other; later three other divine visitants, Peter, James, and John, bestowed upon them the "priesthood of Melchizedek" and gave them the keys of apostleship. This was in 1829, a year before the founding of the church with six charter members.

Opposition arose as the church gained strength, and the Mormons left New York in 1831 for Ohio, where headquarters were established at Kirtland. Another large Mormon center developed at Independence, Missouri, where they planned to build the ideal community with a temple at its heart. Friction with other settlers became so acute that the Mormons were expelled from Missouri; they settled at Nauvoo, Illinois. Violence followed them there and reached its peak with the murder of Joseph Smith and Hyrum Smith, the patriarchs of the church, in the jail at Carthage.

With Smith's death aggressive, young Brigham Young was elected president. A group of the defeated minority refused to accept his election or leadership and withdrew to form other Mormon churches. They objected on the ground that Young was not the legal successor to Smith, that control of the church belonged properly to the twelve apostles appointed by Smith, and that Young approved of the practice of polygamy, which had been responsible for much of their persecution. But Young held his office; he had the vote of the majority, and he also had the courage and the administrative ability necessary at that crucial period to save the church from extinction.

The saints were driven from Nauvoo in the dead of winter in February, 1846, and began their epic march to what is now Utah. In the valley of the Great Salt Lake they finally found safety, building there the famous tabernacle and temple at the heart of what was to become a world-wide Mormonism, and creating a self-existent community. Their community became the State of Utah in 1896.

Based upon the *Book of Mormon* and the Bible, which is accepted "as far as it is translated correctly," the faith of the Mormons is in most respects the faith to be found in any number of conservative, fundamentalist Protestant churches, plus the revelations of Joseph Smith. They believe in the three persons of the Trinity; that men will be punished for their own individual sins and not for the original sin of Adam. All mankind may be saved through the atonement of Christ and by obedience to the laws and ordinances of the gospel; these laws and ordinances include faith in Christ, repentance, baptism by immersion for the remission of sins, observance every Sunday of the Lord's Supper, the laying on of hands for the gift of the Holy Ghost, tongues and interpretation of tongues, visions, revelation, prophecy, and healing. There is a strong Adventism in this church. Christ will return to rule the earth from his capitals in Zion and Jerusalem, following the restoration of the Ten Tribes of Israel.

Revelation is not regarded as confined to either the Bible or the *Book of Mormon;* it continues in people living today —in the apostles, prophets, pastors, teachers, and evangelists of the modern Mormon Church. Baptism is necessary to salvation, and obedience to the priesthood is of first importance. Subjection to civil laws and rules is advocated, together with an insistence upon the right of the individual to worship according to the dictates of his conscience.

Two Mormon practices, baptism for the dead and sealing in marriage for eternity, are exclusive with their church. Baptism and salvation for the dead is based upon the conviction that those who died without a chance to hear or accept the gospel cannot possibly be condemned by a just and merciful God. The gospel must be preached to them after death; authority for this is found in I Peter 4:6: "For this cause was the gospel preached also to them that are dead." Baptism is considered as essential to the dead as to the living, though the rite will not finally save them; there must be faith and repentance for salvation. The ceremony is performed with a living person standing proxy for the dead.

Marriage in Mormonism has two forms: marriage for time and marriage for eternity, or celestial marriage. Marriage for time is for those considered unfit for the higher celestial marriage or for those who prefer it. Mormon women believed that there could be no salvation for them unless they were married. Thus plural marriages were accepted and encouraged. Some plural marriages were for both time and eternity, and had been practiced for some time before Joseph Smith's revelation on the practice was announced publicly by Brigham Young in 1852. Polygamy was abolished by national law in 1890, but some of the plural marriages contracted before that date were allowed to continue. Some of the dissenting Mormon churches held that it was never widely practiced or accepted and that Joseph Smith never approved or practiced it himself. Some Mormon women, however, may still be "sealed" with a dead man with the approval of the widow and the president of the church. As late as 1941 twenty Mormons, breaking the law of both church and state, were convicted of polygamy and sentenced to prison; but generally the practice of polygamy has been abandoned.

Organization and government of the church differ in detail among the six Mormon denominations but agree in essentials. It is based upon the two priesthoods: the higher priesthood of Melchizedek, which holds power of presidency and authority over the offices of the church, and whose officers include apostles, patriarchs, high priests, seventies (missionaries), elders, and bishops; and the lesser priesthood of Aaron, which guides the temporal affairs of the church through its priests, teachers, and deacons. The first council of the church is the First Presidency, made up of three high priests—the president and two counselors. Its authority is final and universal in

both spiritual and temporal affairs. The president of the church is "the mouthpiece of God"; through him come the laws of the church by direct revelation.

Next to the presidency stands the Council of the Twelve Apostles, chosen by the First Presidency to supervise the whole work of the church and to ordain all ministers. The apostles supervise the lesser patriarchs, who are usually evangelical ministers.

The church is divided into stakes (geographical divisions) which are composed of a number of wards corresponding to local churches or parishes. High priest, assisted by elders, are in charge of the stakes. Members of the Melchizedek priesthood hold authority under the direction of the presidency to officiate in all ordinances of the gospel. Seventies are composed of missionaries working under the direction of the twelve apostles; they are organized into quorums of seventy each, with seven presidents of equal rank presiding over each quorum. The twelve apostles and the seventies work principally outside the church organization; the patriarchs, high priests, and elders work within the framework of stakes, wards, and branches. The Aaronic priesthood is headed by a presiding bishopric of three under the supervision of the first presidency.

The church influences every phase of the living of every member; it supplies relief in illness or poverty, provides education, recreation, and employment. Such a program has inevitably resulted in deep loyalty in its membership. More than four thousand young Mormons go out two-by-two each year as missionaries without compensation, giving a year or more to the work of spreading the teaching of their church at home and abroad. In fact less than thirty-five persons in leadership positions in the church receive salaries. They do not win converts in any great numbers, but their missionary experience strengthens both them and their church, and offers a model of church service and zeal equalled in very few of the other larger churches in America.

A total of 1,106,018 Mormons in 2,731 churches in the United States are divided into six bodies.

Church of Jesus Christ of Latter-day Saints

WITH HEADQUARTERS at Salt Lake City this church is by far the largest numerically with 980,347 members and 2,066 churches in Utah and Idaho in 1949. It follows the governmental pattern already described. A general conference is held twice a year. The church is supported by the tithes of the membership; each convert is expected to contribute one tenth of his property at conversion and to give one tenth of his income thereafter.

The missionary effort of this church is one of the most consistent and vigorous to be found anywhere in America; at its centennial celebration in 1947 it was reported that in the preceding one hundred years 51,622 missionaries had been sent out, each at his own expense and most of them serving a full two years. There were 8,695 missionaries at work in home and foreign fields in 1949 among American Indians, or doing propaganda work, or serving in stations abroad in thirty-eight countries. There were twenty-one mission stations in North and South America and thirteen in Europe.

In education the Mormons have lifted Utah high among the states. They have four senior colleges and three junior colleges in Utah, which has the highest percentage of males and females in school among all the states. It stands fourth among the states in the percentage of income devoted to education. Utah's educational achievement is second to none in America and probably in the world.

The health and welfare programs of the church have given Utah a death rate of 519 per 1,000 members. This is lower than that of any group of people of the same size anywhere else in the world; it is the direct result of Mormon abstinence

from liquor, tobacco, and so forth, and of their welfare efforts. This church has 105 storehouses for community food and clothing, with an asset value of $2,289,-408; members maintain vegetable, seed, and wheat farms, orchards, a cotton plantation, dairies, sewing centers, fish canneries, soap factories, cattle, sheep, and hog farms, food processing plants, a vitamin pill factory, and several grain elevators. Most of the products of these industries are consumed at home, but nearly 15,000 relief packages were forwarded under a plan of European relief in 1946-47.

Reorganized Church of Jesus Christ of Latter-day Saints

THIS IS the second largest group in the Mormon Church with 144,094 members and 641 churches in 1950. It claims to be the legal and true successor of the church as it was founded by Joseph Smith and mentions an Ohio court decision in 1880 to substantiate its claim. The Reorganized Church rejected the leadership of Brigham Young—a rejection due primarily to Young's claim of the revelation on polygamy, which the Reorganized Church has always condemned, approving of only one marriage for either man or woman. It was organized at Beloit, Wisconsin, in 1852, and Joseph Smith, son of the founder, became its president in 1860.

The Reorganized Church had five basic principles: (1) the continuity of divine revelation; (2) the open canon of Scripture; (3) the restoration of Christ's Church on the New Testament plan; (4) the principle of stewardship in relation to life and property; (5) practical idealism in a Christian community in social, cultural, and economic life.

It is believed that there will be a "gathering to Zion" before Christ's return, and that the gathering will take place in Missouri, where headquarters of the Reorganized Church are located at Independence. There is strong emphasis upon tithing and mutual helpfulness or "social consciousness." Administration of the church is but slightly different from the Salt Lake church; the local churches are "branches," and the "Central Place," or Zion, is situated at Independence, Missouri. Foreign missionary stations are supported in the Society Islands, Australia, New Zealand, Hawaii, and Europe, with headquarters in England and the Netherlands. Graceland College at Lamoni, Iowa, has 550 students; there are two homes for the aged and one hospital.

Church of Christ (Temple Lot)

THIS CHURCH had 2,179 members in 56 churches in 1940; it was founded at Bloomington, Illinois, at the time of Joseph Smith's death. This dissenting body rejected the teachings of baptism for the dead, the elevation of men to the estate of gods following death, the doctrine of lineal right to office in the church, and the practice of polygamy. The group returned to Independence, Missouri, in 1867 and began raising funds for the purchase of a temple lot upon which was to be erected the temple of the Lord for the day of his return and the gathering of the ten lost tribes of Israel. The temple lot will be the center of the New Jerusalem, which will be "a movement of brotherhood and the turning point when the fullness of the gospel goes from the Gentiles to the Jews." The lot was lost to the Reorganized Church in a lawsuit in 1891-95, but the Temple Lot Church still believes that it is commissioned to build the temple there and in this generation.

A general bishopric under the guidance of a general conference administers the work of the church; the highest officers are found in the Quorum of the Twelve, and local bishops direct the temporal affairs of the local church "under supervision of the congregation."

Church of Jesus Christ (Bickertonites)

THIS GROUP was organized under the leadership of Sidney Rigdon, one of the pioneers of Mormonism. His followers refused to join the march to Utah under Brigham Young, denounced him and the twelve apostles for general wickedness (polygamy), and condemned the teachings of plurality of gods and baptism for the dead. They organized at Greenock, Pennsylvania, in 1862, claiming clear and divine succession of priesthood and authority.

Foot washing is practiced among the Bickertonites, and they salute each other with the holy kiss. Monogamy is required except in case of death. Members are required to obey all state and civil law, but there is strong opposition to participation in war. Headquarters are located at Monongahela, Pennsylvania, where the general conference as the supreme body of the church meets annually. A missionary work is conducted among the Indians of the United States and Canada; there are sixteen hundred members and twenty-nine churches.

Church of Jesus Christ (Cutlerites)

THIS CHURCH was organized in 1853 by Alpheus Cutler, who was the seventh in line of the original seven elders of the church under Joseph Smith. He and his followers believed that they were commissioned to build the Lord's temple at Nauvoo, Illinois. Cutler ordained new elders "to act in the lesser offices of the church." Community of property is practiced in this church, which consists of two congregations, one at Independence, Missouri, and the other at Clitherall, Minnesota, where headquarters have been established. There were twenty-four members and two churches in 1944.

Church of Jesus Christ (Strangites)

THIS GROUP claims that it is "the one and original Church of Christ of Latter-Day Saints" and that its founder, James J. Strang, is the only legal successor to church leadership with written credentials from Joseph Smith. Strang had many revelations, some of which were inscribed upon the "Plates of Laban" mentioned in the *Book of Mormon*. He was crowned "king" of his church in 1850 and was murdered in 1856 during a wave of anti-Mormonism in the Great Lakes region. Organized at Burlington, Wisconsin, in 1844, this church denied the Virgin Birth and the Atonement; Christ was made Saviour in their view solely by his resurrection from the dead. A presiding high priest is their "only high officer," and there are 4 churches with 123 members.

Liberal Catholic Church

TRACING ITS beginnings to the Old Catholic Church movement in Great Britain and Holland, and its orders to a valid apostolic succession running back to the Roman Catholic Church of Pope Urban VIII and even to the twelve apostles, the Liberal Catholic Church is liberal in the extreme. It aims at a combination of the traditional Catholic forms of worship with the utmost freedom of individual conscience and thought. It claims to be neither Roman Catholic nor Protestant, but "Catholic" in the broadest sense of the word. It was established during the reorganization of the British Old Catholic movement in 1915-16.

Theosophists were prominent in its early organization, and the principles of theosophy were blended with the more liberal principles of Christianity during the first years of the church. Conflict between the theosophists and those wishing to make it an unmistakably Christian church brought about a division with the majority of the members and clergy in America breaking with the world organization. Actually as a result of this division there are now two Liberal Catholic churches in the United States, one made up of the more theosophically-minded members and the other stressing the Christian elements. A parallel might be found in the Low Church and Anglo-Catholic divisions in the membership of the Protestant Episcopal Church. Members of the larger Liberal Catholic Church—with about two thousand members and thirteen churches—are determined to make it a definitely Christian church rather than a reflection of the Theosophical Society. They use the Nicene Creed in most of their churches, do not require their laymen to subscribe to any interpretation of creeds, scriptures, or tradition, and seek "not uniformity of belief but tolerance for all faiths and a readiness to worship together in a common ritual." All religions and all sacred scriptures are considered as divinely inspired.

The summary of doctrine of the Liberal Catholic Church holds the existence of God to be "infinite, eternal, transcendent and immanent." God manifests himself in the universe under a "triplicity" of Father, Son, and Holy Spirit. Christ "ever lives as a mighty spiritual Presence in the world, guiding and sustaining His people; sharing God's nature, he cannot cease to exist, is therefore eternal, and his future is one whose glory and splendour have no limit." Made in the image of God, man "is himself divine in essence —a Spark of the divine Fire," and his duty is to discern the divine light in himself and others. The world is the "theatre of an ordered Plan," and man's doings in physical incarnation "largely determine his experience after death in the intermediate world (or world of purgation) and the heavenly world." There is a communion of saints, or holy ones, who help mankind, and there is also a ministry of angels. Salvation is the gradual realization of man's oneness with God, an estate obtainable by all. Man is not punished in everlasting hell; together with the concept of a wrathful punishing God this is considered as irreconcilable with the idea of a loving Father.

The living Christ is present in the sacraments, of which there are seven: baptism, confirmation, the Holy Eucharist, Absolution, Holy Unction, holy matrimony, and holy orders. The liturgy follows closely that of the Anglican high mass, based upon that of the Roman Catholic Church. No images of the dead Christ are permitted in Liberal Catholic churches. Priests or bishops may or may not marry, and they exact no fee for the administration of the sacraments. Divine healing is emphasized, through "the revivifying power of the Holy Spirit, the grace of Absolution, the Sacred Oil for the Sick and the Sacrament of Holy Unction," but not to the exclusion of physicians or medicine.

American and Canadian headquarters are located in the Cathedral Church of St. Albans in Los Angeles. Bishops are in charge of regional areas, and the General Episcopal Synod is the chief administrative and legislative body.

Lithuanian National Reformed Church

ORGANIZED AT Scranton, Pennsylvania, in 1914 with the assistance of Bishop Francis Hodur, head of the Polish National Catholic Church of America, this is a small group of 3,325 members in Pennsylvania, Massachusetts, and Illinois. The Illinois (Chicago) churches were established under the jurisdiction of Archbishop Carmel Henry Carfora of the North American Old Roman Catholic Church but have since become independent.

Doctrine in this church is based upon the first four general councils of the church, and the Nicene-Constantinopolitan Creed is used. Liturgy is in the Lithuanian tongue; a synod exercises ecclesiastical authority over the local churches, of which there are six.

LUTHERANS

Lutheran was a nickname fastened upon the followers of Martin Luther by their enemies in the days of the Protestant Reformation; today it stands for something far more comprehensive. "It is clear," says Abdel R. Wentz, "that 'Lutheran' is a very inadequate name to give to a movement that is not limited to a person or an era but is as ecumenical and abiding as Christianity itself." Luther's teachings of justification by faith and of the universal priesthood of believers might be called the cornerstone of Protestantism.

The story of Luther's rebellion against the Roman Catholic Church is well-known history. His position was, briefly, that the Roman Catholic Church and papacy had no "divine right" in things spiritual, that the Scriptures and not the Roman Catholic priest or church had final authority over conscience. "Whatever is not against Scripture is for Scripture," said Luther, "and Scripture is for it." Men were forgiven and absolved of their sins, he believed, not by good works or imposed church rite, and especially not through the purchase of indulgences offered for sale by the Roman Catholic Church, but by man's action in turning from sin directly to God. Justification came through faith and not through ceremony, and faith was not subscription to the dictates of the church but "by the heart's utter trust in Christ." "The just shall live by faith" was the beginning and the end of his thought. He held the individual conscience to be responsible to God alone; he also held that the Bible was the clear, perfect, inspired, and authoritative Word of God and guide of man. God, conscience, and the Book—on these were Lutheranism founded.

In 1529 Luther wrote his Longer and Shorter Catechisms; a year later a statement of faith known as the Augsburg Confession was authored by his scholarly associate Philip Melanchthon; 1537 brought the Schmalkald articles of faith drawn up by Luther, Melanchthon, and other German reformers; and in 1580 the Formula of Concord was drawn up.

These documents in explanation of Luther's ideology and theology form the doctrinal basis of Lutheranism.

The Reformation resulted not in a united Protestantism but in a Protestantism with two branches: Evangelical Lutheranism with Luther and Melanchthon as leaders, and the Reformed Church or branch, led by Calvin, Zwingli, and John Knox. Evangelical Lutheranism spread from its birthplace in Germany to Poland, Russia, Lithuania, Czechoslovakia, Austria, Hungary, Yugoslavia, France, and Holland; it became in time the state church of Denmark, Norway, Sweden, Finland, Iceland, Estonia, and Latvia. It was mainly from Germany and Scandinavia that Lutheranism came to the United States.

A Lutheran Christmas service was held on Hudson Bay in 1619; the first European Lutherans to come here and stay permanently arrived on Manhattan Island from Holland in 1623. They had a congregation worshiping in New Amsterdam in 1648, but they did not enjoy full freedom in their worship until the English took over control of "New York" in 1664. The first independent colony of Lutherans was established by Swedes along the Delaware at Fort Christiana in the colony of New Sweden in 1638.

The New York Lutherans were largely Germans. German exiles from Salzburg settled in Georgia, where in 1736 they built the first orphanage in America. Lutherans from Württemberg settled in South Carolina. But the great influx came to Pennsylvania, where by the middle of the eighteenth century there were thirty thousand Lutherans, four fifths of them being German and one fifth Swedes. From Philadelphia they swept over New Jersey, Maryland, Virginia, and North Carolina.

Their first churches were small, often without pastors, and because only a minority of the immigrants joined the church, they were poor churches. The situation was relieved with the coming of Henry Melchoir Muhlenberg from the University of Halle to effect the first real organization of American Lutherans; in 1748 he organized pastors and congregations in Pennsylvania, New Jersey, New York, and Maryland into what came to be called the Ministerium of Pennsylvania; it was the first of many Lutheran synods in America. Other synods followed slowly: New York in 1786, North Carolina in 1803, Ohio in 1818, and Maryland, Virginia, and Tennessee in 1820. Each synod adjusted itself to its peculiar conditions of language, national background, previous ecclesiastical relationship with Luther and authorities abroad, and geographical location. The need for even further organization, aggravated by the ever-increasing immigration of Lutherans from Europe, resulted in the formation of a general synod in 1820; with that the last real bonds with European Lutheranism began to break, and American Lutheranism was increasingly on its own.

The general synod was obliged to extend its efforts farther and farther west as German, Swedish, Norwegian, Danish, Icelandic, and Finnish Lutherans came pouring into the new country. The Missouri Synod was formed in 1847. From 1850 to 1860 one million Germans arrived, and the majority of them were Lutherans; the German Iowa Synod was organized in 1854, and in the same year the Norwegian Lutheran Church was established. The Augustana Synod was created in 1860 to care for Swedes in the new West. By 1870 the Lutherans had the fourth largest Protestant church in the country with 400,000 members.

The Civil War brought the first serious break in the Lutheran ranks with the organization of the United Synod of the South in 1863; three years later a number of other synods led by the Ministerium of Pennsylvania withdrew from the general synod to form a general council. To increase the complexity, Lutheran immigrants arrived in larger and larger numbers; from 1870 to 1910 approximately 1,750,000 came from Sweden, Norway, and Denmark, and in those years the Lutheran church membership leaped from 50,000 to nearly 2,250,000. New Lutheran churches, colleges, seminaries, and publications were established from coast to coast.

Since 1910 there has been an almost constant effort toward the unification of Lutheran churches and agencies. Three of the large Norwegian bodies united in 1917 in the Norwegian Lutheran Church of America; some of the Midwest German synods merged in the Joint Synod of Wisconsin in 1918; the synods of Iowa, Ohio, and Buffalo merged in the American Lutheran Church in 1930. Largest of all was the union, or reunion, of the general synod, the general council, and the United Synod of the South into the United Lutheran Church in 1918. In addition to these, three national groupings were created for the sake of closer co-operation in the work of the churches: the Synodical Conference (1872), the National Lutheran Council (1918), and the American Lutheran Conference (1930). These are purely co-operative bodies with no legislative or administrative authority over the synods or congregations involved. The National Lutheran Council is especially effective in co-ordinating the work in welfare, American missions, student service, public relations, and ministry to the armed forces of eight participating churches: the United Lutheran Church in America, the Evangelical Lutheran Church in America, the American Lutheran Church, the Augustana Evangelical Lutheran Church, the Lutheran Free Church, the United Evangelical Lutheran Church, the Danish Lutheran Church of America, and the Suomi Synod. Perhaps the most co-operative effort in the history of American Lutheranism is found in Lutheran World Action, through which forty million dollars in goods and cash have been contributed in the past decade.

In spite of their organic division there is real unity among American Lutherans; it is a unity based more upon faith than upon organization. All Lutheran churches represent a single type of Protestant Christianity. Their faith is built upon Luther's principle of justification by faith alone in Jesus Christ; it centers in the gospel for fallen men. The Bible is the inspired Word of God and the infallible rule and standard of faith and practice. Lutherans confess their faith through the three general creeds of Christendom, the Apostles', Nicene, and Athanasian, which they believe to be in accordance with the Scriptures. They also believe that the unaltered Augsburg Confession is a correct exposition of the faith and doctrine of Evangelical Lutheranism. The apology of the Augsburg Confession, the two catechisms of Luther, the Schmalkald Articles, and the Formula of Concord are held to be a faithful development and interpretation of Evangelical Lutheranism and of the Bible.

The two sacraments of baptism and the Lord's Supper are not merely signs or memorials to the Lutheran but channels through which God bestows his forgiving and empowering grace upon men. The body and blood of Christ are believed to be present "in, with, and under" the bread and wine of the Supper, and are received sacramentally and supernaturally. Consubstantiation, transubstantiation, and impanation are rejected. Infants are baptized, and baptized persons are believed to receive the gift of regeneration from the Holy Ghost.

The congregation is the basic unit of Lutheran government. Independent, the government is usually administered by a church council consisting of the pastor and a number of elected lay officers, some of whom are called elders, some deacons, and some trustees. There is a growing tendency to call all lay officials deacons. Pastors are elected, called, or dismissed by the voting members of the congregation, but they may never depose a pastor from the ministry. As a rule ministers are ordained at the annual meetings of the synods; they are practically all trained in college and seminary; less than 10 per cent of them have had neither.

The synod is the next higher body above the congregation; it is composed of the pastors and lay representatives elected by the congregations and has only such authority as is granted by the synod constitution. In some other instances there are territorial districts or conferences instead of a synod, operating in the same manner and under the same restrictions; some of these may legislate, while others are for advisory or consultative purposes only.

The highest level of Lutheran government is found in the general body, which may be national or even international and which is called variously "church," "synod," or "conference." Some of these general bodies are legislative in nature, some consultative; they supervise the work in worship, education, publications, charity, and missions. Congregations have business meetings at least annually; constituent synods, districts, and conferences hold yearly conventions, and the general bodies meet annually, biennially, or triennially.

Worship is liturgical, centering on the altar and the pulpit. "No sect in Western Christendom outside the Church of Rome," said the late Lutheran Archbishop Nathan Söderblom of Sweden, "has accentuated in its doctrine the Real Presence and the mysterious communion of the sacrament as has our Evangelic Lutheran sect, although our faith repudiates any quasi-rational magical explanation of the virtue of the sacrament."

Non-Lutherans are often critical of the divisions among American Lutherans, but actually they are not so divided as they seem. It is true that there have been at one time or another no fewer than 150 different Lutheran bodies in this country, but movements toward consolidation, unification, and federation have now reduced the number to less than 20. Six of the bodies in the United States account for 5,729,155 members, or about 96 per cent of all Lutherans in North America. Three groups contain

99 per cent of them: 1,952,569 in the United Lutheran Church of America, 1,993,244 in the American Lutheran Conference, and 1,191,828 in the Synodical Conference. Nearly 4,000,000 Lutherans, or two thirds of the total North American membership, are in the National Lutheran Council.

Movements toward further unification within American Lutheranism are numerous; surely and steadily their forces are being combined. Even on the international front such movements are noticeable; delegates from Lutheran churches in twenty-two countries in 1923 formed a Lutheran World Convention, which became the Lutheran World Federation in 1947, for the purposes of relief and rehabilitation among Lutherans on a global scale.

Historically the Lutherans have shown a tendency to remain apart from the rest of Protestantism; in the United States they have consisted of churches founded by immigrant groups deeply conscious of their national and linguistic origins, conservative, confessional, and nonrevivalistic, and suspicious of anything that might tend to modify their Old World faith and traditions. But these traits seem to be vanishing as the older membership passes and an English-speaking generation takes over. The mother tongues of Lutheranism are still used occasionally, but English is predominant. One Lutheran body, the United Lutheran Church, has been listed as a consultative member of the Federal Council of the Churches of Christ in America. Three other bodies—the United Lutheran Church of America, the Augustana Lutheran Church, and the Danish Lutheran Church—plan to join the National Council of the Churches of Christ in the U.S.A. Four bodies—the United Lutheran Church, the American Lutheran Church, the Augustana Lutheran Church, and the Danish Evangelical Lutheran Church of America—participated in the organization of the World Council of Churches. Lutheran bodies participating in interdenominational organizations have always insisted upon the operation of two principles within those organizations: the evangelical principle that the churches in the association should be those confessing the deity and saviorhood of Jesus Christ and the representative principle that the organizations shall be made up of officially chosen representatives of the churches.

American Lutheran Conference

THIS IS the youngest federation of Lutheran synods and churches in the United States. Organized at Minneapolis in 1930, it includes the American Lutheran Church, the Augustana Evangelical Lutheran Church, the Evangelical Lutheran Church of America, the Lutheran Free Church, and the United Evangelical Lutheran Church in America. Each synod and church within this co-operative union is left quite free and sovereign; it is organized for mutual counsel and co-operation in the work of missions, education, Lutheran unity, social relations, young people's work, and so forth. Commissions and committees working under an executive committee function between the biennial meetings of the conference, which speaks for almost two million American Lutherans in the five constituent bodies.

American Lutheran Church

A PARTICIPATING member of the National Lutheran Council and the American Lutheran Conference, this church was organized in 1930 and represents a merger at Toledo, Ohio, of three synods: the Joint Synod of Ohio and Other States, organized in 1818; the Lutheran Synod of Buffalo, organized in 1845; and the Synod of Iowa and Other States, organized in 1854. Districts meet annually and the general body biennially. The work of the American Lutheran Church is divided into nine departments: American missions, foreign missions, higher education, parish education, social action, pensions and aid, youth, stewardship and finance, publication. It owns and operates three senior colleges, one junior college, and two theological seminaries. It co-operates with other Lutherans in maintaining another senior college and another seminary. It maintains a theological training school for workers among the Negroes and another for workers among the Mexicans. It administers 215 home mission stations and conducts foreign mission work in India and New Guinea, owns five welfare institutions, is related to three others, and recognizes 28 other church-recognized institutions and extrasynodical agencies. There were 714,556 baptized members in 2,010 churches on January 1, 1950.

Augustana Evangelical Lutheran Church

THIS BODY was organized originally by the Swedes who settled along the Delaware River. Two of their historic old churches—Holy Trinity (Old Swedes) Church in Wilmington, Delaware, and Gloria Dei Church in Philadelphia—have passed under the control of the Protestant Episcopal Church.

The great tide of Swedish immigration in the 1840's, however, produced a large number of Swedish Lutherans who remained "within the fold." The first congregation of these immigrants, which later became part of the Augustana Synod, was organized in New Sweden, Iowa, in 1848; the second was in Andover, Illinois, in 1850. The original synodical organization was called the synod of Northern Illinois, organized in 1851; the Swedes and Norwegians left this synod to form the Scandinavian Augustana Synod of North America in 1860. The word "Scandinavian" was dropped in 1894. This Augustana Synod withdrew from the General Council, declining to enter the merger of the General Synod, the General Council, and the United Synod of the South in the United Lutheran Church of America in 1918, but later it joined the American Lutheran Conference and the National Lutheran Council.

The synod meets annually as a general body, and is presided over by a president chosen quadrennially. There are thirteen conferences within the synod, one of which is in Canada and each of which meets annually. There are 290 home mission stations, and foreign mission projects are maintained in China, Africa, and India. The synod lists four colleges, two junior colleges, one theological seminary, one family service agency, eighteen homes for the aged, twelve child care and child placing agencies and institutions, and twelve hospitals and sanatoria. There were 439,231 members in 1949 in 1,126 churches from coast to coast with the greatest membership concentrations in Minnesota, Iowa, and Illinois.

Evangelical Lutheran Church

THIS CHURCH is the result if a merger in 1917 of three Lutheran bodies: the United Norwegian Church, the Norwegian Synod, and the Hauge Synod. It has joined the American Lutheran Conference and the National Lutheran Council, and in 1946 adopted the name Evangelical Lutheran Church.

Norwegians have been resident in the United States since before 1825; most of them have settled in the northern Mississippi Valley and the West. Coming from a country in which the church was a department of the government, they experienced much difficulty at first in organizing their church in the new land. Their confusion was evident in the fact that by 1887 they had six competing Norwegian synods. Three of these—the Hauge Synod, the United Norwegian Church, and the Norwegian Lutheran Evangelical Church—united to form the Evangelical Lutheran Church in 1917; this brought together about 2,500 congregations and 445,000 Norwegian Lutherans. In 1949 they had 757,352 members and 2,720 churches.

This church uses the liturgy of the Church of Norway with certain modifications made in adjustment to its American environment. A general convention meets biennially. The church is divided into nine districts, one of which lies in Canada. Nine district presidents, together with the president of the general body and a lay member elected from each of the nine districts, constitute a church council which rules on all questions referred to it by local churches or districts. The council supervises all educational institutions, examines ministerial candidates, and offers mediation in church disputes.

Boards are in direct charge of property, education, home and foreign missions, charities, publications, and pensions. The church has seven colleges, one junior college, one Bible Institute in Saskatchewan, one academy and one theological seminary, one family service agency, four rescue homes, two deaconess homes and hospitals, eight children's homes or placing agencies, and nineteen homes for the aged. It supports 122 foreign missionaries in South Africa, Latin America, China, and Madagascar.

Lutheran Free Church

THIS CHURCH was organized as the result of a dispute between the trustees of the Augsburg Theological Seminary in Minneapolis and the United Norwegian Church over the control of the seminary. Certain churches and ministers expelled from the United Norwegian Church organized as the Friends of Augsburg and carried on the work of a regular synod until they formally adopted the name Lutheran Free Church in 1897.

Strictly this is not a synod at all in the Lutheran sense but an association of independent Lutheran congregations. It is not an incorporated body, but it does incorporate the missions, schools, and charitable institutions under its management. An annual conference decides questions of business and policy, and receives reports from the institutions and agencies of the church. All voting members of all Lutheran Free churches are voting members of the annual conference, and all other Lutherans who are members of any Lutheran church are also entitled to vote upon declaring in writing that they are in agreement with the aims and purposes of the Free Church and willing to work for them. The body is a participating member of the National Lutheran Council.

The Lutheran Free Church supports seventy-two missions and has foreign missions in China and Madagascar. It has one college, one deaconess mother house and training school, one junior college, one theological seminary, two homes for the aged, two homes for children, one hospital, and a seaman's mission in Seattle. There were 54,608 members and 339 churches in 1949.

United Evangelical Lutheran Church

THIS IS a Danish body with 46,442 members in 180 churches in 1949. A Norwegian-Danish Conference was organized in the United States in 1870; in 1884 the Danish churches in this conference withdrew to organize their own Danish Evangelical Lutheran Church Association; in 1894 about three thousand members in the Danish Evangelical Church left that body to form the Danish Evangelical Lutheran Church in North America. In 1896 these two bodies, the Danish Church Association and the Danish Church in North America, were united in what is now the United Evangelical Lutheran Church.

This church subscribes to the confession of faith of the Lutheran Church of Denmark, the three creeds of Lutheranism, the Augsburg Confession, and Luther's Shorter Catechism. More closely organized than most Lutheran bodies, it has an annual meeting as the largest governing unit and authority, made up of ministers and lay representatives; the decisions of this annual meeting on all questions within its jurisdiction are final and absolute. A board of five trustees functions between the meetings.

District boards administer the work of forty-seven home missions stations under a National Board of Home Missions; foreign missions are found in Africa, India, Japan, and South America. There are one college, one theological seminary, two homes for the aged, and three children's homes. The church is a participating member of the National Lutheran Council.

Evangelical Synodical Conference of North America

THIS IS the most conservative of all Lutheran groups in America. It was organized in 1872 by a group of synods adhering closely to the conservative doctrine of seventeenth-century Lutheranism "to encourage and strengthen one another in faith and confession; to further unity in doctrine and practice and to remove whatever might threaten to disturb this unity; to co-operate in matters of mutual interest." It strongly opposed any co-operation with other churches. The conference includes the Lutheran Church (Missouri Synod), the Evangelical Lutheran Joint Synod of Wisconsin and Other States, the Slovak Evangelical Synod of America, the Norwegian Synod of the American Evangelical Lutheran Church, and the Negro Mission conducted jointly by these four synods. Delegate meetings, called a convention, are held biennially. The total membership reaches nearly two million.

The Negro Mission is one of the most important projects of the Synodical Conference. It is made up of 107 churches in Negro communities in 24 states and the District of Columbia with 15,001 members in 1949.

The conference also supervises the work of ninety-six home mission stations and the work of the Nigeria mission in Africa, where there are 119 churches and 19,576 members. There are seven junior colleges or academies, one four-year college, one theological seminary, six homes for the aged and twelve child care and child placing agencies and institutions, fourteen hospitals and sanatoria.

Lutheran Church (Missouri Synod)

THIS IS the largest single body within the Synodical Conference, with 1,569,364 members in 1949 and 4,212 churches, and it is the second largest Lutheran body in the United States. This synod was organized in 1847 with twelve congregations and twenty-two ministers under the name German Evangelical Lutheran Synod of Missouri, Ohio, and Other States. Under the constitution adopted at the time all the symbolical books of the Lutheran Church were considered to be "the pure and uncorrupted explanation of the Divine Word," and all mingling of the churches was disapproved.

The doctrinal standard of the Missouri Synod is strictly observed and enforced. That standard is found in the Bible as it was interpreted by the Formula of Concord of 1580, including a textbook commentary upon the three creeds of Lutheranism—the Apostles', Nicene, and Athanasian—and upon the six Lutheran confessions, the Augsburg Confession, the Schmalkald Articles, and the two catechisms of Luther. The synod has been unswerving in its allegiance to this conservative Lutheranism. What has been hailed as "the first great step" toward union of the Missouri Synod with the American Lutheran Church came at the 1950 convention of the Missouri Synod when that body approved a doctrinal agreement covering statements on God, faith, man, redemption, election, means of grace, justification, conversion, sanctification, the church, and so on. It is progress toward union, but authorities agree that such union will probably not take place in the immediate future. There are the usual Lutheran districts and district conventions, and the general convention meets triennially.

The Missouri Synod has 1,136 parochial schools and 4,300 Sunday schools. There are 1,000 congregations in home mission fields and a total of 330 foreign mission congregations in India, Japan, New Guinea, and the Philippines. The synod serves a total of 743 colleges and universities through its Student Service Commission with 23 full-time pastors; it has 9 hospitals, 11 homes for the aged and 17 homes for children, 1 tuberculosis sanatorium and 1 convalescent home, 8 colleges, 2 seminaries, 2 teachers' colleges, 1 collegiate institute, and 1 academy.

Joint Synod of Wisconsin and Other States

ORGANIZED IN 1850 under the name First German Lutheran Synod of Wisconsin, three synods—Wisconsin, Minnesota, and Michigan—united in 1892 to form the present organization. The synod is divided into eight districts reaching from Missouri to the Pacific Northwest. The districts meet in convention each even year, the joint synod in odd years, in gatherings at which pastors, teachers, and laymen are delegates. With 297,922 members and 833 churches in 1949 it is a constituent member of the Synodical Conference, carrying on within that body a home mission work among the Apache Indians of Arizona and among the Negroes of the South. It has one college, five junior colleges and academies, four homes for the aged, four children's homes, and nine hospitals and sanitoria.

Slovak Evangelical Lutheran Church

THIS CHURCH was established at Connellsville, Pennsylvania, in 1902. It works in close co-operation with the Missouri Synod. The membership, which is over 21,000, and churches, which number 66, are grouped in three districts—eastern, central, and western. Synodical meetings are held every two years. Contributions are made by the membership to the home and foreign missions work of the Missouri Synod and the Synodical Conference, although the Slovak Church has its own board of missions.

Norwegian Synod of the American Evangelical Lutheran Church

THIS SYNOD was formed in 1918 by a minority group which declined to join the union of the other Norwegian bodies in 1917; they "desired to continue to work along thoroughly conservative lines." The jurisdiction of the synod is entirely advisory; all synod resolutions are accepted or rejected by the local congregations. The officers and boards of the synod, however, direct the work of common interest, in so far as they do not interfere with congregational rights or prerogatives. It is a constituent member of the Synodical Conference.

The Norwegian Synod co-operates in the foreign missionary program of the Missouri Synod, contributing to work in China and India. It has thirty-one home mission stations in the United States, one preparatory school, and 9,587 members in 66 churches. Its pastors and teachers attend the schools of the Missouri and Wisconsin synods.

United Lutheran Church in America

THE LARGEST Lutheran Church in North America, this group has 1,950,569 members and 4,150 churches. It dates back to colonial times and the Ministerium of Pennsylvania. It was created in the 1918 merger of the General Synod, the General Council, and the United Synod of the South. While strongly devoted to the historic creeds and confessions of Lutheranism, it might be distinguished from other groups such as the Missouri Synod in its application of a more liberal and progressive interpretation and policies.

The *Common Service Book* of the Lutheran Church, arranged between 1877 and 1902, was adopted in 1918. This is used throughout the United Lutheran Church. A president, secretary, and treasurer were elected, and the body was incorporated under the laws of the state of New York. Conventions have met biennially since 1918, and the forty-five constituent synods merged in 1918 have been reduced to thirty-three. The body is a participating member of the National Lutheran Council.

Polity is less firm than might be expected in so large a body; forms of government and worship are considered of secondary importance, and each church and synod is independent in these matters. Hence synodical and congregational polity varies.

The fifteen boards of the three merging bodies were in time reduced to nine: executive foreign missions, home missions, parish education, higher education, social missions, publications, deaconess work, pensions, and relief. Through these boards the work of the church is conducted and 95 per cent of its benevolent funds administered. Beside these there are national supervisory boards or committees for the Women's Missionary Society, the Luther League of America, which is the young people's organization, the Lutheran Brotherhood, and the Lutheran Laymen's Movement for Stewardship. Other special work is conducted through numerous other committees or commissions and through the National Lutheran Council and the Lutheran World Federation. The delegated convention of the church, including one pastor and one layman for every ten pastoral charges, meets biennially, and a conference of the presidents of constituent synods also meets biennially as an advisory body on questions of policy and procedure. The judicial body is called the Commission of Adjudication.

The United Lutheran Church has 13 colleges, 9 theological seminaries, 1 junior college, 2 deaconess training schools. Its churches use 16 languages. It has 623 home mission congregations and over 2,200 congregations on foreign mission fields in Liberia, Argentina, British Guiana, China, India, and Japan. There are 23 family service agencies, 26 homes for the aged and infirm, 37 child care and child placing agencies and institutions, 14 hospitals in the United States and 1 in the Virgin Islands.

Church of the Lutheran Brethren in America

THIS IS an independent Norwegian body in Wisconsin, Minnesota, and North Dakota, organized in 1900. Its founders disapproved of the practices of other existent Norwegian Lutheran churches, mainly in matters concerning the admission of members, confirmation, and church discipline. It differs from other Lutheran groups in accepting as members only those who profess a personal experience of salvation.

Elders and deacons officiate in local congregations; elders are sometimes ordained as ministers while in other cases the pastors are candidates from theological seminaries. The church as a body is the supreme administrative unit, with a president, vice-president, secretary, and treasurer. Home missions are supervised by a board of thirteen members. There are twenty-eight foreign missionaries at work in China and the African Sudan. The church controls the Lutheran Bible School at Fergus Falls, Minnesota, and the Sarepts Old People's Home at Sauk Center, Minnesota. There are 3,088 members and 35 churches.

Evangelical Lutheran Church in America (Eielsen Synod)

ORGANIZED IN 1846, this was the first Norwegian synod in this country. It bears the name of its great leader, Elling Eielsen, a preacher who had been active in the revival movement inspired by Hans Nielsen Hauge in Norway earlier in the century. A difference of opinion over questions of doctrine and the admission of members in the Eielsen Synod in 1875 resulted in a revised constitution and a change of name to Hauge's Norwegian Evangelical Lutheran Synod. A small group with Eielsen clung to the old constitution and name, and reorganized, electing him as president.

This is the smallest existent Lutheran general body in the United States, with 1,350 members and 12 churches. All male members vote in the annual meeting of the synod, which acts through a board of trustees and a church council of seven members each. The trustees have charge of all church property while the council rules on doctrine and discipline. A home missions board under the guidance of the church council directs a work among the Indians of Wisconsin. There are no foreign missionary workers, but members contribute to the work abroad of other Lutheran churches. There are nine parochial schools.

Finnish Apostolic Lutheran Church of America

THIS CHURCH was originated by Finnish immigrants coming to this country in the middle years of the nineteenth century and settling in or around Calumet, Michigan. They worshiped at first in the Lutheran Church of Calumet under a Norwegian minister; differences between the two national groups led to the forming in 1872 of a separate Finnish congregation led by Salomon Korteniemi and called the Salomon Korteniemi Lutheran Society. The present name was adopted in 1929 upon the merger of this group with other Finnish congregations in Michigan, Minnesota, the Dakotas, Massachusetts, Oregon, Washington, and California. The new church was divided into two districts, eastern and western.

A scriptural Christian experience is required as a condition of membership. The sixty-five churches of the body are left quite free to govern themselves; each congregation has a vote in the annual convention. A board of trustees of nine members elected every three years at the convention in turn elects a president, vice-president, and secretary of the church. There were 14,511 members reported in 1949.

Finnish Evangelical Lutheran Church of America (Suomi Synod)

THIS CHURCH was organized at Calumet, Michigan, in 1890 with nine congregations participating. It is strictly a confessional church. The annual synodical convention, composed of ministers and delegates, administers the common work of the body with each congregation autonomous. The church constitution confers certain limited judicial and executive authority upon a permanent consistory made up of the president, vice-president, and notary of the convention; its members are elected quadrennially. There are seventy-four home mission congregations in the United States, a junior college, and a theological seminary. The church is represented in the National Lutheran Council and has no foreign missions of its own but contributes to the Foreign Missionary Society of Finland. In 1949 there were 29,001 members in 172 churches.

Finnish Evangelical Lutheran National Church of America

CREATED BY a dissenting group which withdrew from the Suomi Synod in 1898, this church organized independently at Rock Springs, Wyoming. Local churches send delegates to an annual meeting, which ordains ministers and acts in the calling of pastors to local churches and in their installation, and in the appointment of missionaries. A board of five trustees is elected at each annual meeting, and the president of the meeting as executive officer of the church or- dains and appoints ministers, pastors, and missionaries, and acts as general repre- sentative of the denomination. This church co-operates with the missionary work of the Synodical Conference in Nigeria; there were 6,559 members and 65 churches in 1947.

Icelandic Evangelical Lutheran Synod in North America

THIS IS a constituent synod of the United Lutheran Church with 7,111 baptized members in 42 congregations. Actually it is an international synod, organized in 1885 among Icelandic immigrants to the United States and Canada. It is strongest in Canada, with only 1,386 members in the United States in 1941. With the aid of the United Lutheran Church and the Norwegian Lutheran Church it has established the Jon Bjarnason Academy at Winnepeg, Manitoba, and Bethel, a home for the aged, at Gimli, Manitoba. It co- operates with the United Lutheran Church in foreign missionary work.

Danish Evangelical Lutheran Church in America

THIS CHURCH was organized by ministers sent from Denmark in 1872 under the name Kirkelig Missions Forening. In 1894 about 19 pastors, 37 congregations, and about 3,000 members withdrew from this body to form what is now the United Evangelical Lutheran Church, but 35 pastors, 53 congregations, and about 5,000 members remained to form the Danish Evangelical Lutheran Church in America, which in 1949 had 19,048 members and 80 churches. It is a partici- pating member of the National Lutheran Council.

Worship is in accordance with the service book and liturgy of the Danish People's Church in Denmark but some- what modified. Congregations, not pas- tors, arrange and approve all such modi- fications. Congregations meet annually in a convention to discuss matters brought before it by the board of direc- tors of five members elected every two years, who are authorized to carry out the resolutions of the convention. Two orphans' homes and two homes for the aged are supported, and there is a sea- men's mission in Brooklyn, New York. The church maintains five missionaries in India and owns a college and theologi- cal seminary at Des Moines, Iowa.

Protestant Conference (Lutheran)

THIS GROUP came into existence in Wis- consin in 1928 as a result of differences with the Wisconsin synod. It has been considered by some to be a highly controversial group, objecting to "mistaken dogmas current in the church" and seeking to correct "the spirit of self-righteousness and self-sufficiency" through a re-emphasis upon "the Gospel of Forgiveness of Sins through Our Blessed Saviour." The conference is reticent to release any statistical information; 3,253 members were reported in 22 churches in 1936.

Independent Lutheran Congregations

THESE ARE congregations with no direct synodical or national connections; their ministers are occasionally found listed in the ministeriums of various synods, but they pursue independent policies and work. The number of independent churches seems to be seriously declining; seventeen churches with over seven thousand members were listed in 1943 but only nine churches and fifteen hundred members in 1949.

Mayan Temple

INCORPORATED in 1928 and reporting 3,312 members in 13 churches or groups in 1947, the Mayan Temple is "a restoration of the pristine faith catholic, practiced by the Mayas in prehistoric America and common to all North and South America, prior to the coming of the white man." Followers seek to preserve the ceremonials of various Indian tribes, to keep a record of all Americans with Indian blood, and to restore to religion certain values lost across the ages— music, the dance, healing, education, culture, interest in material as well as spiritual welfare, and so forth. They have as their aim the practice of scientific religion and the logical understanding of life and its purpose. They believe in one God and that reincarnation and the continuity of life are both reasonable and in accord with science and scientific discovery. The Ancient and Mystical Order of Po-ahtun, composed of both clergy and laity, is reported as the chief administrative body of the Temple; a pontiff, abbot, and dean are also listed. Headquarters are in Brooklyn, New York.

MENNONITES

The first Mennonite congregation of historical record was organized at Zurich, Switzerland, in 1525; it consisted of Swiss Brethren, or *Täufer*, who disagreed with Ulrich Zwingli in his readiness to consent to a union of church and state. They also denied the scriptural validity of infant baptism and hence were labeled "Anabaptists," or "Re-Baptizers." Anabaptist congregations were organized in Holland by Obbe Philips as early as 1534; Philips baptized Menno Simons (1496-1561) in 1536.

Menno was a converted Roman Catholic priest; he organized more Anabaptist congregations in Holland, and his followers gave his name to the movement. Many of his Flemish adherents crossed the channel on the invitation of Henry VIII; from them came the British Baptists. In England as well as in Germany, Holland, and Switzerland they met opposition, largely because of their determined distrust of any union of church and state. An impressive martyr roll was created; it might have been much larger had it not been for the sudden haven offered in the American colony of William Penn. Thirteen families settled in Germantown, near Philadelphia, in 1683; eventually they established a Mennonite congregation there, although many of them had left the Mennonite fold and united with the Quakers before they left Crefeld, Germany. Mennonite immigrants from Germany and Switzerland spread over Pennsylvania, Ohio, Virginia, Indiana, Illinois, farther west, and into Canada. Thanks to their historic insistence upon nonresistance their colonial settlements were comparatively peaceful and prosperous.

The faith of these Mennonites was based upon a confession of faith signed at Dortrecht, Holland, in 1632. In eighteen articles the following doctrines were laid down: faith in God as creator; man's fall and restoration at the coming of Christ; Christ as the Son of God, redeeming men on the cross; obedience to Christ's law in the Gospel; the necessity of repentance and conversion for salvation; baptism as a public testimony of faith; the Lord's Supper as an expression of common union and fellowship; matrimony as permissible only among those "spiritually kindred"; obedience to and respect for civil government except in the use of armed force; exclusion from the church of those who sin willfully and their social ostracism for the protection of the faith of others in the church, and future rewards and punishments for the faithful and the wicked.

The Lord's Supper is served twice a year in almost all Mennonite congregations, and in most of them baptism is by pouring. Most of them observe the foot-washing ordinance in connection with the Supper, after which they salute each other with "the kiss of peace." The sexes are separated in the last two ceremonies. All Mennonites baptize only on confession of faith, refuse to take oaths before magistrates, oppose secret societies, and follow strictly the teachings of the New Testament. They have a strong intrachurch program of mutual aid, and a world-wide relief and eleemosynary service through an all-Mennonite relief organization called the Mennonite Central Committee.

The local congregation is more or less autonomous and authoritative, although in some instances appeals are taken to district or state conferences. The officers of the church are bishops (often called elders), ministers, and deacons (almoners). Many ministers are self-supporting, working in secular employments when not occupied with the work of the church. There are other appointed officers for Sunday school, young people's work, and so forth.

The Amish movement within the ranks of the Mennonites takes its name from Jacob Amman, an Alsatian Mennonite bishop of the late seventeenth century who insisted upon strict conformation to the confession of faith, especially in the matter of the ban, or expulsion of members. This literalism brought about a separation in Switzerland in 1693; about two hundred years later the divided bodies with the exception of three Amish groups, were reunited.

Amish immigrants to the United States concentrated early in Pennsylvania and moved from there into Ohio, Indiana, Illinois, Nebraska, and other western states; some went into Canada. They have today a common literature. Many of the Amish, distinguished by their severely plain clothing, are found in the Conservative Amish Church and the larger Old Order Amish Mennonite Church. They are still the "literalists" of the movement, clinging tenaciously to the "Pennsylvania Dutch" language and to the seventeenth-century culture of their Swiss-German forebears. They oppose automobiles, telephones, higher education, and so forth, but are recognized as very efficient farmers.

Mennonite Church

THIS IS the largest single group of Mennonites in this country with 56,746 members and 434 churches in 1949. It is the church founded by the Germantown immigrants in 1683. It holds firmly to the Dortrecht Confession of Faith, though with a mild interpretation of "shunning" expelled members, and is progressive in practice. A general conference meets every two years as an advisory body; deacons and ministers who are not elected delegates from the district and state conferences may debate but not vote; the bishops and other delegates from the district conferences render decisions by a majority vote. Three conferences of the former Amish Mennonite Church have been merged with district and state conferences of this c h u r c h. Church-wide, autonomous boards and committees are in charge of missionary, educational, publishing, and philanthropic work; they are not under the supervision of the general conference. Home Missions stress evangelistic work, and foreign missions are found in India, Africa, Japan, China, and South America. There are two colleges, several academies, one hospital, two nurses' training schools, three orphans' homes, and four homes for the aged.

General Conference of the Mennonite Church of North America

THIS CONFERENCE was organized at the instigation of several Iowa congregations who sought the uniting of all Mennonite bodies into one; the actual outcome was the formation of an additional body. They created the general conference in 1860, drawing into it many Russian and German congregations and the Central Mennonite Conference, a former Amish body.

This conference accepts most established Mennonite doctrine and practice, but it does not require its women to cover their heads during prayer or worship, nor does it uniformly consider foot washing as "a command of Christ." Musical instruments are employed in many of the churches. Governmental organization parallels that of the Mennonite Church, with local and district conferences, and a general conference meeting every three years. The general conference elects a board of nine trustees and appoints boards for home missions, foreign missions, and publications. This body of Mennonites stresses the autonomy of the local congregation even more than the Mennonite Church.

Home missionary effort consists chiefly of evangelistic work and supplying needy congregations with ministers. Foreign mission stations are located among the American Indians and in India and Japan. Two colleges and one junior college are supported; there are five homes for the aged, seven hospitals, three girls' homes, and a nurses' training school. It is the second largest American Mennonite group, with 45,200 members and 230 churches in 1947.

Church of God in Christ (Mennonite)

THIS CHURCH grew out of the preaching and labors of John Holdeman, a member of the Mennonite Church who became dissatisfied with what he thought was a lack of allegiance in that church to the principles laid down by Menno Simons, especially in its failure to enforce the ban. Holdeman completed his organization in Ohio in 1859. Since his death his followers have considerably relaxed the discipline based on his views. The Church of God in Christ is unique in refusing to take interest on money loaned; this is prohibited in its membership. There were three thousand members and thirty churches in 1945.

Evangelical Mennonite Church

FORMERLY THE Defenseless Mennonite Church of North America, this is a branch of the Amish Mennonite Church which left that body in 1860 under the leadership of Henry Egli, seeking a more positive emphasis upon conversion. Members work closely with the Evangelical Mennonite Brethren, supporting missionary work in Tennessee, an orphanage at Flanagan, Illinois, and the foreign missionary stations of the Belgian Congo Mission. There are 1,830 members in 18 churches.

Evangelical Mennonite Brethren

FORMERLY CALLED the Conference of Defenseless Mennonites of North America, this group lists fifteen hundred members n ten churches. It was established by Russian Mennonite immigrants 1873-74, nd supports missionaries in China and Africa in co-operation with the Mennonite Church, and has identical polity nd doctrine.

Conservative Amish Mennonite Church

WITH 3,679 members in 24 churches his is a small body subscribing to the Dortrecht Confession of Faith; its first general conference was held at Pigeon, Michigan, in 1910. It separated gradually rom the Old Order Amish, installing such innovation as meetinghouses, Sunday schools, evening and "continued" meetings, and the use of English rather than German in worship.

Hutterian Brethren

THESE ARE the modern disciples of Jacob Huter, a sixteenth-century Anabaptist minister who advocated communal ownership of property. Many of them came from Russia about 1874; most of them today are of German ancestry and use the German tongue in their homes and churches. Aside from the "common property" idea they are quite similar to the Old Order Amish. They put strong emphasis upon elementary education; every community has its common school in which the Bible is paramount, and there is said to be no illiteracy among them. They have eight colonies in the United States and others in Canada. In 1949 they reported 1,255 members and 15 churches in the United States.

Krimmer Mennonite Brethren Conference

MADE UP largely of descendants of Russian immigrants, this group was founded in the Crimea by Jacob A. Wiebe in 1869. It has an unusual method of baptism, immersing candidates for membership backward, like the Baptists, instead of forward, as is the custom in most

Mennonite churches. Continued efforts have been made to unite this branch with the Mennonite Brethren Church. The conference has a home missionay work among the Negroes of North Carolina and foreign missions in Mongolia and China. There are two colleges, one academy, one hospital, one home for the aged, and 1,408 members in 9 churches.

United Missionary Church

UP TO 1947 this church was called the Mennonite Brethren in Christ. It experienced several changes in name, starting with Evangelical Mennonites, a name which explains much of their doctrine and polity. Members do a widespread work in evangelism, stressing holiness. Their articles of faith include three diversions from the Dortrecht Confession in statements on entire sanctification, justification, and regeneration, divine healing, and the millennium. Baptism is by immersion; church government is more on a Methodist pattern than on a Mennonite; episcopal authority is, however, in the hands not of individuals but of an executive committee. As in the Methodist Church there are local, quarterly, and annual conferences and a quadrennial general conference. The general conference rules on church discipline and order, and appoints the executive committee, which functions between sessions of the conference, and other denominational officers.

Home missions are highly evangelistic; foreign missions are found in China, India, the Sudan, Armenia, and Chile. There were 10,776 members in 1949.

Mennonite Brethren Church of North America

RUSSIAN IN background, this church stems from a Mennonite Brethren church organized on the Molotschna River in Russia by a Mennonite group seeking a rigid enforcement of the ban and closer attention to prayer and Bible study. Small bodies of these Russians reached

America in 1874, spreading through the Midwest to the Pacific coast and into Canada.

A general conference meets triennially as the chief administrative body, gathering delegates from five district conferences. District conferences supervise a large work in evangelism; home missions are found among the Indians and Mexicans of Oklahoma, and foreign missions are maintained in India, China, and Africa. There were 18,410 members and 145 churches in 1949.

Mennonite Kleine Gemeinde (Little Congregation)

BORN IN 1812 in a split among the Mennonites in Russia; the little congregations stood for a stricter enforcement of discipline. Several of them were established in the United States in the 1870's. Their United States membership by 1936 had declined to 275 in 2 local churches; majority of the Mennonite Kleine Gemeinde group has settled in Canada.

Old Order Amish Mennonite Church

ORGANIZED ABOUT 1865, this church adheres strictly to the older forms of worship and attire, using hooks and eyes instead of buttons on coats and vests, worshiping as a group in private homes, and having no conferences. Members do not believe in conferences, missions, or benevolent institutions and have aroused attention by their adamant opposition to centralized schools. Some of them, however, contribute to the missions and charities of the Mennonite Church. There were 14,364 members and 156 churches in 1949.

Old Order Mennonite Church (Wisler)

THIS CHURCH was named for the first Mennonite bishop in Indiana, Jacob Wisler, who led a separation from the Mennonite Church in 1870. Those who separated did so in protest against the use of English in the services and Sunday schools of the church. Joined in 1886, 1893, and 1901 by groups with similar ideas from Canada, Pennsylvania, and Virginia, they still maintain themselves on the bases of these protests. Each section of the church has its own district conference; there are no benevolent or missionary enterprises, but some members contribute to the work of the Mennonite Church in those fields. There are 3,304 members and 30 churches.

Reformed Mennonite Church

THIS CHURCH represents a protest against the established Mennonite churches as "corrupt and dead bodies," and the stricter enforcement of Mennonite discipline, led by Francis Herr and his son John Herr in Lancaster County, Pennsylvania, in 1812. The Reformed Church has no written discipline but is rigid in enforcing the ban on members who violate or neglect what might be called their "unwritten" discipline. It adheres rigorously to the principle of nonresistance, has no missionary or educational work, and reports a thousand members in twenty-seven churches. This is the group described in the novel *Tillie, a Mennonite Maid.*

Stauffer Mennonite Church

THIS BODY has only 2 churches and 161 members; it was organized by Jacob Stauffer at Lancaster, Pennsylvania, following a disciplinary dispute in the Groffdale, Pennsylvania, congregation between 1840-50. It is an extremely conservative church using the German language and with no educational, missionary, or benevolent work. A body known as the Weaver Mennonites left the church soon after its organization.

METHODISTS

*E*ngland's famed old Oxford University has been called "the cradle of lost causes," but at least one cause was born there which was not lost. This was Methodism; known and ridiculed at Oxford in 1729, it claims today over eleven million adherents in the United States and nearly fifteen million around the world. The influence of Methodism is even more impressive than its numbers.

In 1729 the Oxford Methodists (also dubbed "Bible Bigots," "Bible Moths," and the "Holy Club") were a tiny group of students who gave stated time to prayer and Bible reading; prominent among them were John and Charles Wesley and George Whitefield. They were methodically religious, talking of the necessity of being justified before they could be sanctified and of the need of holiness in human living, reading and discussing William Law's *A Serious Call to a Devout and Holy Life* and *A Treatise on Christian Perfection.* The two Wesleys were sons of a clergyman of the Church of England; with the other members of the Holy Club they stood their ground against jeering students and went out to preach and pray with the poor and desperate commoners of England—prisoners in jail, paupers in hovels, bitter and nearly hopeless "underdogs of a British society that was perilously close to moral and spiritual collapse." Methodism started on a campus and reached for the masses.

The Wesleys came to Georgia in 1736. Charles came as secretary to General Oglethorpe, and John was sent by the Society for the Propagation of the Gospel as a missionary to the Indians. It was an unsuccessful and unhappy two years for John Wesley with but one bright spot; on shipboard en route to the colonies he met a group of Moravians and became deeply impressed by their piety and humble Christian living. Later when he returned to London, he went one night to meet with a religious society in Aldersgate Street, heard the preacher read Luther's preface to the Epistle to the Romans and felt his heart "strangely warmed" as the meaning of the reformer's doctrine of "justification by faith" sank into his soul. It was the evangelistic spark that energized his life and started the revival flame of the Wesleyan revival in England. From the pious Moravians via Wesley came the warmhearted emphases upon conversion and holiness which are still the central themes of Methodism.

Whitefield and the Wesleys were too much afire to remain within the staid Church of England. When its doors were closed to them, they took to the open air, John preaching and Charles writing the hymns of the revival in streets, barns, and private homes and in the mining pits of Cornwall, preaching repentance, regeneration, turning from sin and the wrath to come, justification, holiness, and sanctification. The upper classes laughed, and the lower classes listened to the first words of hope they had heard in many a year. Converts came thick and fast; it became necessary to organize them into societies. The first Methodist society was attached to a Moravian congregation in Fetter Lane, London, in 1739 and later moved to its own quarters in an old abandoned government building known as the Foundry, where the first self-sustaining Methodist society in London was organized in 1740.

Between 1739 and 1744 the organizational elements of Methodism were instituted; we read of a "circuit system" and of an "itinerant ministry," of class meetings and class leaders, of lay preachers and annual conferences. There was a phenomenal growth in membership; more than 26,000 Methodists were worshiping in England, Ireland, Scotland, and Wales in 1767. Their impact upon British society was startling; the crudities and barbarisms of the times were alleviated and a "French revolution" averted. It was primarily a lay movement.

Wesley did his best to keep the movement within the Church of England; an Evangelical Party grew within the church, but the greater numbers recruited from among the unchurched made a separate organization imperative. In 1739 Wesley drew up a set of general rules which are still held by modern Methodists as an ideal delineation of Bible rules and conduct. A Deed of Declaration in 1784 gave legal status to the yearly Methodist conference. But John Wesley was dead in 1790 before Methodism in England had the name of a recognized church, the Wesleyan Methodist Connection.

Meanwhile the movement had invaded the American colonies. Wesley had begun to send out leaders; the first of them were Joseph Pilmore and Richard Boardman. Philip Embury, an Irish lay leader, encouraged by his cousin Barbara Heck, preached in New York and inspired the organization about 1766 of the first Methodist society overseas. By 1769 the New York Methodists had built Wesley Chapel, now known as John Street Methodist Church. To the south Captain Thomas Webb, a veteran of Braddock's ill-fated army, established societies in Philadelphia, and Robert Strawbridge started a revival in Maryland and built a log-cabin church at Sam's Creek, Devereux Jarratt, a transplanted evangelical Anglican minister, led a revival in Virginia which won thousands. The true center of Methodism in those days did indeed lie in the South; out of 3,148 Methodists in the colonies in 1735 about 2,384 lived south of Mason and Dixon's Line. Wesley, aware of the rapid spread of the movement in America, sent emissaries to take charge, among them Francis Asbury and his successor, Thomas Rankin, the latter as first full-fledged "superintendent of the entire work of Methodism in America." Rankin presided over the first conference in America, called at Philadelphia in 1773 and attended by ten ministers.

There were about 1,160 Methodists represented in the conference of 1773;

when the Liberty Bell rang in 1776, there were less than 7,000 in all the colonies and they seemed doomed to disappear a quickly as they had been gathered. The majority of their preachers had come from England and were incurable British; they were so roughly handled by the patriots that by 1779 nearly every one of them had fled either to Canada or home to England. Wesley's pro-British attitude also roused resentment, and Francis Asbury working almost single-handed had a difficult time keeping some of the churches alive. But a miracle happened; of all the religious groups in the colonies the Methodists alone actually seemed to prosper during the revolution. When the surrender came at Yorktown, their membership had grown to fourteen thousand and there were nearly eighty preachers. They were, after Yorktown, an American church, free of both England and the Church of England. Wesley accepted the inevitable; he ordained ministers for the colonies and appointed Asbury and Thomas Coke as superintendents or bishops.

Coke brought with him from England certain instructions from Wesley, a service book and hymnal, and authority to proceed with the organization. A "Christmas Conference" held at Baltimore in December of 1784 organized the Methodist Episcopal Church, elected Coke and Asbury as superintendents (later called bishops), and adopted the Sunday Service (an abridgement of the *Book of Common Prayer*) and articles of Religion as written by John Wesley, adding another article that as good patriots Methodists should vow allegiance to the United States government. The first general conference of the new church was held in 1792, made up solely of ministers; it was not until 1872 that laymen were admitted to what had become by that time a quadrennial general conference. Membership soared; from 37 circuits and 14,000 members at the close of the revolution there came a membership of 1,324,000 by the middle of the following century.

Methodism not only swept through the cities; it developed an amazing strength in small towns and rural areas. Everywhere there were circuit riders—ministers on horseback riding the expanding frontier and preaching in mountain cabins, prairie churches, schoolhouses, and camp meetings of free grace and individual responsibility and the need of conversion and regeneration. Their itinerant ministry was perfectly adapted to the democratic society of the frontier. The Methodist Book Concern was established in 1789, putting into the saddlebags of the circuit rider a religious literature which followed the march of American empire south and west. The camp meeting, born among the Presbyterians though not always carried on by them, was adopted by the Methodists and exploited to the limit; its revivalistic flavor and method were made to order for the followers of Wesley and Whitefield. There are still camp meetings in Methodism.

All was not peaceful, however, among all the Methodists; divisions came. Objecting, like good democrats, to what they considered abuses of the episcopal system, several bodies broke away: the Republican Methodists, later called the Christian Church, withdrew in Virginia; Methodist Protestants seceded in 1830. Between 1813 and 1817 large Negro groups formed independent churches: the African Methodist Church; the Union Church of Africans, now the Union American Methodist Episcopal Church; and the African Methodist Episcopal Zion Church. In 1844 came the most devastating split of all, the bisecting of the Methodist Episcopal Church into two churches, the Methodist Episcopal Church, the northern body, and the Methodist Episcopal Church, South.

The cause of this major split was of course slavery. Bishop Andrew, a Georgian, owned slaves through inheritance, and his wife was also a slaveholder. It was not possible for him or his wife to free their slaves under the laws of Geor-

gia. The general conference of 1844, held in New York City, ordered him to desist from the exercise of his office so long as he remained a slaveholder. Incensed, the southern delegates rebelled, a provisional plan of separation was formulated, and the southerners went home to organize their own church in 1845. It was a split that concerned neither doctrine nor polity; it was purely political and social, and it was a wound that waited until 1939 for healing; in that year the Methodist Episcopal Church, the Methodist Episcopal Church, South, and the Methodist Protestant Church were reunited at Kansas City, Missouri.

The uniting conference of 1939 adopted a new constitution in three sections: the Articles of Religion drawn up by John Wesley and based on the Thirty-nine Articles of Religion of the Church of England; the General Rules covering the conduct of church members and the duties of church officials; and the Articles of Organization and Government outlining the organization and conduct of conferences and local churches. This constitution cannot be changed by any general conference unless and until every annual conference has acted on the changes proposed.

In matters of faith there has been very little occasion for confusion or difference among Methodists; heresy trials and doctrinal quarrels have been noticeably absent. Historically they have never built theological fences or walls to keep anyone out; they have stressed the great foundation beliefs of Protestantism and offered common ground acceptable to those uninterested in theological trivialities. Some of the churches repeat the Apostles' Creed in their worship, but not all of them, though the discipline of the church provides for its use in formal worship. Their theology is Arminian, as interpreted by Wesley in his sermons, his notes on the New Testament, and his Articles of Religion.

They preach and teach doctrines of the Trinity, the natural sinfulness of mankind, man's fall and need of conversion and repentance, freedom of the will, justification by faith, sanctification and holiness, future rewards and punishments, the sufficiency of the Scriptures for salvation, perfection and the enabling grace of God. Two sacraments, baptism and the Lord's Supper, are observed; baptism is administered to both infants and adults, usually by sprinkling. Membership, full or probationary, is based upon confession of faith or by letter of transfer from other evangelical churches; admission of children to membership is usually limited to those thirteen years of age or over, though in the South the age may be two or three years younger. There is wide freedom in the interpretation and practice of all doctrine; liberals and conservatives work in close harmony.

The local churches in Methodism probably enjoy less freedom than most Protestant churches; they are called charges, to which pastors are appointed by the bishop at the annual conference. Official boards are made up of stewards and trustees and other church officers. Trustees manage the property interests of the church; stewards handle finances and generally guide the spiritual work.

Quarterly, annual, and general conferences prevail in most Methodist bodies; while Methodist government is popularly called episcopal, it is largely government by this series of conferences. The quarterly conference meets in the local charge or on the circuit with the district superintendent presiding; it fixes the salary of the pastor, sets the budget, elects the church officers, and sends delegates to the annual conference, where it seems advisable, as it usually does in large or "station" charges. The quarterly conference may delegate to the official board of the local church responsibility for many of these duties. Some areas have district conferences between the quarterly and the annual conferences, but it is not a universal arrangement in the church. Annual conferences cover defined geographical areas, ordain and admit ministers to the

ministry, vote on constitutional questions, supervise pensions and relief through act of the bishop exchange pastors with other annual conferences, and every fourth year elect lay and ministerial delegates to the general conference The general conference is the lawmaking body of the church, meeting quadrennially; the bishops preside, and the work of the conference is done largely in committees, whose reports when adopted by the general conference become Methodist law.

Worship and liturgy are based upon the English prayer book with widespread modifications. The language of the prayer book is much in evidence in the sacraments of the Methodist churches. In many forms of worship, however, each congregation is free to use or change the accepted pattern as it sees fit.

There are 19 separate Methodist bodies in the United States of which The Methodist Church is numerically the strongest with 8,792,569 members and 40,472 churches in 1949.

Methodist Church

THIS GROUP includes the three branches united at Kansas City in the general conference of 1939: the Methodist Episcopal Church, the northern body; the Methodist Episcopal Church, South; and the Methodist Protestant Church. The history of the Methodist Episcopal Church has already been outlined. The Methodist Episcopal Church, South, was organized at Louisville, Kentucky, in 1845 and held its first general conference a year later at Petersburg, Virginia, under the presidency of Bishops James O. Andrew and Joshua Soule. The southern church brought to the 1939 merger three universities, twenty-six colleges, twenty-two junior colleges, and twenty secondary schools, and a membership of more than three million. The Methodist Protestant Church was organized in revolt against the rule of the clergy in the Methodist Episcopal Church and the exclusion of laymen from its councils; it was formally organized in 1830 at Baltimore with about five thousand members. There were over fifty thousand members in the Methodist Protestant Church in 1939, five educational institutions, and foreign missions in China, India, and Japan.

The polity of the Methodist Church follows the general polity of all Methodism. There are 107 annual conferences in the United States with an average of 213 pastoral charges. With the union of the three bodies at Kansas City in 1939 a system of jurisdictional conferences was added; these meet every four years after the general conference has adjourned, to elect the bishops of the denomination and the representatives of the larger boards and commissions. In lands outside continental United States central conferences correspond somewhat to the jurisdictional conferences. They meet quadrennially, and when authorized to do so may elect their own bishops. The bishops of the jurisdictional and central conferences collectively are called the College of Bishops.

The general conference is the lawmaking body of the Methodist Church; it consists of not less than six hundred and not more than eight hundred delegates, half laymen and half ministers elected on a proportional basis by the annual conferences. A judicial council has been created to determine the constitutionality of any act of the general conference which may be appealed, and to hear and determine any appeal from a bishop's decision on a question of law in any district, annual, central, or jurisdictional conference. It is made up of five ministerial and four lay members, and has become so important that it is often called the "Supreme Court of the Methodist Church." Its decisions are final.

Bishops are elected for life, with retirement set at seventy-two; there are sixty-seven of them in the United States and abroad in charge of the areas of the church, such as the New York Area, the Denver Area, and so forth. Together they constitute the council of bishops, which meets at least once a year and usually twice a year "for the general oversight and promotion of the temporal and spiritual affairs of the entire Church." This is the chief executive body of the Methodist Church, bound only by the rules of the general conference and the fixed pattern of the episcopacy.

The work of the Methodist Church is "big business." It holds property valued in excess of $1,000,000,000; in 1949 it received and spent for all purposes nearly $200,000,000. It has spread over 50 countries; 16 of its bishops administer overseas areas. Nearly 6,000,000 students are enrolled in its Sunday schools; 125 educational institutions have been founded or fostered by this one church, including 9 universities, 68 colleges, and 10 graduate schools of theology; 360 additional schools and colleges are located abroad. There are 70 hospitals treating 1,000,000 patients a year in the United States alone. The Methodist Publishing House is the oldest and largest religious publishing concern in the world; and the *Christian Advocate*, the official church magazine, is the world's most widely circulated denominational weekly. The 21 boards, bureaus, and committees of this church administer a global and growing work. The May 10, 1949, issue of *Newsweek* has said that "Methodist strength lies not so much in figures as in the vitality of the Church itself. . . . [Its members] emphasize brotherhood and friendliness in their religion. Unhampered by a strict theology, they lead with their hearts instead of their heads." With an evangelistic passion for conversion and righteous living in the individual, on one hand, and a social passion matched by few other Protestant bodies, on the other, the Methodist Church has had an ennobling effect upon the individual and upon society which cannot be read in its statistics.

African Methodist Episcopal Church

WITH 1,066,301 members and 7,408 churches in 1949 this is the second largest Methodist group in the United States. Its genesis lies in the withdrawal in 1787 of a group of Negro Methodists from the Methodist Episcopal Church in Philadelphia; their objection was directed largely against practices of discrimination. They built a chapel and ordained a Negro preacher through the assistance of Bishop William White of the Protestant Episcopal Church. In 1793 Bishop Francis Asbury dedicated Bethel Church in Philadelphia, a church whose members prohibited any white brother from "electing or being elected into any office among [them], save that of a preacher or public speaker." In 1799 Bishop Asbury also ordained Richard Allen to preach. Other similar Methodist Negro bodies were formed; the African Methodist Episcopal Church was formally organized in 1816. It was a church confined in the years preceding the Civil War to the northern states; following the war its membership increased rapidly in the South, and today it is represented in nearly every state in the union.

Both doctrine and polity follow that of other Methodist bodies. General boards are constituted by nomination of the bishops, of which there are seventeen appointed at the general conference. The general conference also examines all judicial power and prerogatives. Each department of church work is supervised by a board of eighteen members, one for each episcopal district. The church has a widespread home and foreign missionary program, seventeen educational institutions, and six periodicals.

African Methodist Episcopal Zion Church

THIS CHURCH dates from 1796, when its first organization was instituted by a group of Negro members protesting discrimination in the John Street Church in New York City. Their first church, built in 1800, was called Zion, and the word was later made part of the denominational name. The first annual conference of the body was held in this church in 1821 with six Negro Methodist churches in New Haven, Philadelphia, and Newark, New Jersey, represented by nineteen preachers and presided over by the Rev. William Phoebus of the white Methodist Episcopal Church. James Varrick, one of the John Street dissenters, was elected their first bishop at this conference. The name African Methodist Episcopal Zion Church was approved in 1848.

This church spread quickly over the northern states; by the time of the general conference of 1880 there were fifteen annual conferences in the South. Livingstone College at Salisbury, North Carolina, the largest educational institution of the church, was established by that conference. Departments of missions, education, and publications were established in 1892; later came administrative boards to direct work in church extension, evangelism, finance, ministerial relief, and so forth. Home missions are supported in Louisiana, Mississippi, and in several states beyond the Mississippi, principally in Oklahoma. Foreign missionaries are found in Liberia, the Gold Coast colony, West Africa, South America and the West Indies. There were 6 educational institutions and 520,175 members in 2,096 churches in 1949.

African Union Methodist Protestant Church

A NEGRO body organized in 1866; this is a union of two former churches known as the African Union Church and the First Colored Methodist Protestant Church. Doctrine is in accord with most of Methodism, but there are differences in polity; there are no bishops and no offices higher than that of elder. Ministers and laymen have equal power in annual and general conferences. There is no foreign missionary program; home missions are maintained by a group of women known as the Grand Body. A general board, with a president, secretary, and treasurer directs the denominational effort, including that of the board of education; the board meets annually and the general conference quadrennially. There were 2,504 members and 41 churches in 1949.

Apostolic Methodist Church

THIS IS the smallest Methodist church in the United States, reporting only thirty-one members in two churches in 1936. It was organized in 1932 in protest against the modernist tendencies of Methodism and "to emphasize the Bible as the free and complete Word of God." It rejects the episcopal office as unscriptural and has what it calls a "federated congregationalist" government. A pastor elder is the chief church officer.

Colored Methodist Episcopal Church

THIS CHURCH was established in 1870 in the South in an amicable agreement between white and Negro members of the Methodist Episcopal Church, South. There were at the time between 225,000 and 250,000 Negro slave members in the Methodist Episcopal Church, South; with the Emancipation Proclamation all but 80,000 of these joined the two independent Negro Methodist bodies which had left the Methodist Episcopal Church, South, to join the northern church. When the general conference of the Methodist Episcopal Church, South, met at New Orleans in 1866, a commission from the Negro membership asked for separation into a church of their own. The request was granted, and in 1870 the organization of the Colored Methodist Episcopal Church was realized.

Its doctrine is the doctrine of the parent church; this church adds a local church conference to the quarterly, district, annual, and general conferences.

Each departmental board is presided over by a bishop assigned as chairman by the College of Bishops; the general secretaries of the departments are elected every four years by the general conference. There were 381,000 members, 4,300 churches, and 5 colleges in 1949.

Congregational Methodist Church

THIS CHURCH was constituted in Georgia in 1852 by a group that withdrew from the Methodist Episcopal Church, South, in objection to certain features of the episcopacy and the itinerancy. Two thirds of its membership withdrew to join the Congregational Church in 1887-88.

Local pastors are called by the local churches; district conferences grant licenses and ordain ministers and review local reports. District, annual, and general conferences are all considered as church courts, ruling on violations of church law, citing offending laymen or ministers, and holding the power of expulsion over unworthy members. There is a restricted home and foreign missionary program. In 1949 11,187 members were listed in 160 churches.

Congregational Methodist Church of America, Inc.

THIS CHURCH was organized in 1852 at Forsyth, Georgia. In 1936 it reported 5,857 members enrolled in 131 churches. It was incorporated at Anniston, Alabama, in 1937. No statements on the work of this church have been available.

Free Methodist Church of North America

THIS IS perhaps the most strictly fundamentalist group in American Methodism. Its founder was the Rev. B. T. Roberts, who with his associates objected to what was called "new-school Methodism," which they considered destructive to the Wesleyan standards of the church. They were "read out" of their churches and organized the Free Methodist Church at Pekin, New York, in 1860. The Genesee Conference, of which Roberts had been a member, restored his credentials to his son in 1910, but no reunion of the new body with the Methodist Church has yet been effected.

Doctrinally this body seeks a return to primitive Wesleyan teaching; it emphasizes the virgin birth and deity of Jesus, and his vicarious atonement and resurrection. No one may be received into its membership without an experience of confession and forgiveness of sin, and the experience of entire sanctification is sought in all members. Strict adherence to the general rules of Methodism is demanded, membership in secret societies is forbidden, and instrumental music and choirs are excluded. There were 49,104 members and 1,194 churches in 1949; foreign missions in Africa, China, India, Japan, and the Dominican Republic; 2 colleges, 7 seminaries, and 3 philanthropic institutions. Headquarters have been established at Winona Lake, Indiana. The church has a general conference and four bishops.

Holiness Methodist Church

ORGANIZED IN North Carolina in 1900, this church was formerly known as the Lumber Mission Conference of the Holiness Methodist Church and later as the Lumber River Annual Conference of the Holiness Methodist Church. Established to bring new emphasis to home missions and scriptural holiness, it stresses the doctrines of the atonement, the witness of the spirit, and "holiness in heart and life." Attendance at class meetings is required. There is no itinerant ministry as in most Methodist bodies; pastorates are not limited. The whole church meets each year in annual conference presided over by a bishop. There are 780 members and 8 churches.

Independent African Methodist Episcopal Church

THIS GROUP was formed in 1907 at Jacksonville, Florida, by twelve elders who withdrew from the African Methodist Episcopal Church following disputes with the district superintendents of that church. A new book of discipline, doctrine, and laws was drawn up; the *Book of Discipline* may be revised by the quadrennial general conference, but the twenty-five articles of religion it contains remain unchanged. There are quarterly, annual, and general conferences. The annual conference ordains ministers as deacons, and the general conference ordains elders and bishops. In 1940 there were a thousand members in twelve churches.

New Congregational Methodist Church

THIS CHURCH originated in an administrative quarrel in the Georgia conference of the Methodist Episcopal Church, South, over the consolidation of several small churches in the southern section of the state, and New Congregational Methodist Church was organized in 1881 on the plan of the Congregational Methodist Church. It offers a combination of Methodist doctrine and Congregational polity; congregations call and elect their own pastors; there are the usual local, district, and general conferences. The membership is confined principally to Georgia and Florida; in 1936 there were 1,449 members in 25 churches. Foot washing has been introduced in this group.

Primitive Methodist Church

THIS CHURCH had its initial organization in England. Lorenzo Dow, an American camp-meeting revivalist, went to England early in the nineteenth century to hold a series of camp meetings which resulted in the formation of a number of societies among his converts. Refused admission to the Wesleyan Connection, they formed the Primitive Methodist Church in 1812. The early Primitive bodies in this country were grouped in 1925-29 into eastern and western conferences. The early Wesleyan doctrines of redemption, repentance, justification, sanctification, and so forth, are held in this church. There are no bishops or district superintendents; denominational officers are the president, vice-president, secretary, and treasurer. There are annual conferences and a quadrennial general conference. Ministers, who have no time limit set upon their pastorates, are invited by the local churches, who designate their first, second, and third choices and extend their invitations in that order. All invited pastors are assigned to charges by the annual conference, and no ministerial candidates are received unless there are churches open for them. Work in education and missions is directed by the general conference; foreign missionaries are stationed in Guatemala. There were 11,963 members and 88 churches in 1949.

Reformed Methodist Church

THIS CHURCH was organized in 1814 by a group of Vermont laymen who had become dissatisfied with the episcopal form of government in the Methodist Episcopal Church. They formed six conferences, but large losses in their adherents from 1844 to the end of the century reduced the conferences to two. There were 326 members in 13 churches in 1944. Holiness teaching is prominent in this church. The Methodist system of conferences prevails, and two boards direct work in missions at home and in the British West Indies. There is an active annual camp meeting held near Binghampton, New York.

Reformed Methodist Union Episcopal Church

THIS CHURCH originated at Charleston, South Carolina, in 1885, in a withdrawal from the African Methodist Episcopal Church; the immediate cause of the division was a dispute over the election of ministerial candidates to the general conference. Intended at first as a nonepiscopal church, the body adopted the complete polity of the Methodist Episcopal Church in the general conferences of 1896 and 1916. Class meetings and love feasts are featured in the local congregation; there were 1,025 members and 22 churches in 1946.

Reformed Zion Union Apostolic Church

THIS CHURCH was organized at Boydton, Virginia, in 1869 by Elder James R. Howell, a minister of the African Methodist Zion Church in New York, in protest against white discrimination and against the ecclesiasticism of other Negro Methodist churches. This was originally known as the Zion Union Apostolic Church; internal friction completely disrupted the body by 1874, and in 1881-82 it was completely reorganized under the present name. There are no basic departures from standard Methodist doctrine or polity except that only one ordination, that of elder, is required of its ministers. There were twenty thousand members and fifty-two churches in 1949.

Southern Methodist Church

THIS GROUP is a continuation of the old Methodist Episcopal Church, South. Its 5,325 members and 42 churches declined to take part in the merger of the three largest Methodist bodies in 1939; actually they were organized as the Southern Methodist Church in 1938. All the essential elements of Methodist faith and government are preserved in this church. Headquarters are located at Atlanta, Georgia, where the denominational periodical, the *Southern Methodist Layman*, is published.

Union American Methodist Episcopal Church

THIS WAS one of the first Negro bodies to establish an independent church. Members left the Asbury Methodist Church in Wilmington, Delaware, in 1805. They worshiped out of doors and in private homes until 1813, when they built their first church and incorporated under the title Union Church of Africans; the change to the present name was made in 1852. Deflections of membership in 1850 were responsible for the formation of still another body, the African Union Church. General, annual, district, and quarterly conferences are held; general conferences are called only to consider proposed changes in name, law, or polity. There were 2 educational institutions, 9,369 members, and 71 churches in 1936.

Wesleyan Methodist Church of America

THIS CHURCH represented at the time of its founding in 1843 a protest against slavery and the episcopacy which predated by one year the historic division of the Methodist Episcopal Church and the Methodist Episcopal Church, South. With the slavery issue settled by the Civil War other differences of a spiritual or reform character—entire sanctification and opposition to the liquor traffic—seemed important enough to continue the separate existence of the Wesleyan Methodist Church.

The original Wesleyan doctrines, especially those dealing with sanctification, are all-important in this church; otherwise it is in accord with accepted Methodist belief and procedure. Candidates for membership are required to disavow the use, sale, or manufacture of tobacco and alcoholic beverages, and are requested to shun all secret societies. Active home missionary work is conducted among the Indians and in the South, and in 1936 twelve missionary conferences were listed. Foreign missionaries are found in Africa, India, and Japan. There were 4 schools and 34,202 members in 893 churches in 1949.

MORAVIANS

In a sense the Moravian Church had its first apostles in Cyril and Methodius, who were missionaries among the Slavs in the ninth century; as early as this Moravians and Bohemians in old Czechoslovakia were struggling for political and religious freedom. Later they followed John Hus, martyred in 1415, and Jerome of Prague, martyred in 1416. Their first association was formed in Bohemia in 1457. At the beginning of the Reformation there were more than 400 Brethren or Moravian churches with about 175,000 members.

As a church they opposed the corruption of the Roman Catholic Church and stressed purity of morals, apostolic discipline, and true scriptural teaching. For a time they inclined toward a very literal interpretation of the Sermon on the Mount and denounced war, the taking of oaths, and all unions of church and state. They called themselves *Jednota Bratraska*, the Church (or Communion) of Brethren; this is the correct translation of their later term *Unitas Fratrum*. They accepted the Apostles' Creed, rejected the purgatory and worship of the saints of the Roman Catholic Church as well as its authority, practiced infant baptism and confirmation, and put conduct above doctrine.

The Thirty Years' War all but annihilated their first societies; persecution drove them into Hungary, Holland, Poland, and Saxony. A small band found refuge on the estate of Nicholas Louis, Count of Zinzendorf, in Saxony, where they built the town of Herrnhut (1722-27). Zinzendorf was a Pietist and a

Lutheran, and he became so influential among the Moravians that they used for a time the Augsburg Confession of Faith of Lutheran Saxony. They adopted the name *Unitas Fratrum* from their ancient church and in 1735 again established the episcopacy which had been preserved through John Amos Comenius and his son-in-law Jablonsky. The *Unitas Fratrum* came to be popularly known as the Moravian Church because the leaders of the renewal had come from Moravia.

Moravian Church in America (Unitas Fratrum)

THIS CHURCH was established when a group of the brethren from Germany came to Georgia in 1734. John Wesley was a passenger on the same ship with them, and this was the beginning of his important relations with the Moravians. Political disturbances in Georgia soon disrupted their colony, and a group accompanied George Whitefield to Pennsylvania, where they settled in 1740. Three uniquely and exclusively Moravian towns grew swiftly in Pennsylvania at Bethlehem, Nazareth, and Lititz, based on the communities in Germany, Holland, and England. They remained exclusively Moravian until the middle years of the nineteenth century.

Zinzendorf came to America in 1741, attempted to merge all the colonial Germans into one body, and failed. He stayed on, however, to help with the establishment of Bethlehem and Nazareth and to lay the foundations of the Moravian missionary work among the Indians. By 1775 there were 2,500 Moravians in Pennsylvania alone.

The Moravians have no doctrine peculiar to them; they are broadly evangelical, insisting upon a principle of "in essentials unity, in nonessentials liberty, and in all things charity." Their scriptural interpretations agree substantially with the Apostles' Creed, the Westminster and Augsburg Confessions, and the Thirty-Nine Articles of Religion of the Church of England. They hold the Scriptures to be the inspired Word of God and an adequate rule of faith and practice, and they have doctrines dealing with the total depravity of man, the real Godhead and the real humanity of Christ, justification and redemption through the sacrifice of Christ, the work of the Holy Spirit, good works as the fruits of the Spirit, the fellowship of all believers, the second coming of Christ, and the resurrection of the dead to life and judgment. Their main doctrinal emphasis may be said to be upon the love of God manifested in the redemptive life and death of Jesus, the inner testimony of the Spirit, and Christian conduct in everyday affairs.

The sacrament of infant baptism by sprinkling is practiced, through which children become noncommunicant members until confirmation. There were 46,327 members in 149 churches in 1949. Members are admitted by vote of the congregational board of elders. The Lord's Supper is celebrated at least six times a year, and the old custom of the love feast is preserved. A variety of liturgies is used in worship; the church is notable for one especially beautiful outdoor service held at Easter.

The Moravian Church is divided in the United States into two provinces, northern and southern, and works under a modified episcopacy. Congregations are grouped into provincial and district synods; internationally they are joined in a "unity" with a general synod meeting as a world body every ten years. The highest administrative body in each American province is the provincial synod, composed of ministers and laymen and meeting every five years; it directs missionary, educational, and publishing work, and elects a provincial elders' conference, or executive board, which functions between synod meetings. Bishops are elected by provincial and general synods. They are spiritual, but not administrative, leaders in the church.

Missionary work has always been a first concern of the Moravians; with a comparatively small membership they conducted the most efficient missionary work among the Indians of any of the early colonial churches. The world-wide Moravian Church now supports work in thirteen foreign missionary fields, including North, Central, and South America, Africa, Tibet, and Palestine. A home missions work among the Eskimos of Alaska has been carried on since 1885. There are five schools of higher education, the oldest of which is the Moravian Seminary and College for Women at Bethlehem, Pennsylvania, founded in 1742.

Evangelical Unity of Bohemian-Moravian Brethren

THIS GROUP originated among Czech and Moravian immigrants arriving in Texas about 1850. In 1864 they organized as the Bohemian and Moravian Brethren and in 1903 as the Evangelical Union of Bohemian Brethren. A number of Iowa churches united with the Evangelical Union in 1919, and the present name was adopted. There are few departures from the doctrine and polity of the Moravian Church in America (*Unitas Fratrum*) except that the synod meets every two years. The church has no colleges or seminaries. In 1947 it reported about five thousand members and thirty-two churches confined to Texas.

Bohemian and Moravian Brethren

CONSISTING of 2 churches and 208 members, this group was founded in Iowa between 1858 and 1895. It has no connection with other Moravian churches but maintains "friendly relations" with the Presbyterian and Reformed Bohemian churches of the East and Northwest in educational and missionary work. Members accept the Helvetic and Westminster confessions and use the Heidelberg and Westminster catechisms. Polity is Presbyterian with local church government in the hands of boards of elders and trustees.

National David Spiritual Temple of Christ Church Union, Inc., U.S.A.

THIS IS a body founded in 1932 by David William Short, a former minister of the Missionary Baptist Church. Short wished to "proclaim the Orthodox Christian spiritual faith"; he was convinced that no man had the right or spiritual power "to make laws, rules, or doctrines for the real church founded by Jesus Christ," and that the denominational churches had been founded in error and in disregard of the apostolic example. He held wisdom, knowledge, faith, healing, miracles, prophecy, discerning of spirits, and divers kinds of tongues to be spiritual gifts, and that all races should be accepted in the true Church.

The members of this church consider themselves as the true and original church of Christ and not just another denomination. They rely entirely upon the Holy Ghost for inspiration and direction. Their church organization consists of pastors, prophets, prophetesses, divine healers, deacons, mothers, choir members, missionaries, altar boys, and altar girls. Bishop Short is the chief governing officer; a national executive board holds a national annual assembly. A restricted home missionary work is conducted in hospitals, and a nursing home is supported. A monthly newspaper, the *Christian Spiritual Voice*, is published at Kansas City, Kansas. Bishop Short is also founder, president, and mentor of the St. David Orthodox Christian Spiritual Seminary, which was dedicated in 1949 at Des Moines, Iowa. In 1949 this church reported 40,565 members in 56 congregations.

New Apostolic Church of North America

THE New Apostolic Church of North America is a variant or schism of the Catholic Apostolic Church movement in England. It claims common origin with the Catholic Apostolic Church in the appointment of an apostle in the parent body in 1832. Debate arose in 1860 over the appointment of new apostles to fill vacancies left by death; insisting that there must always be twelve apostles at the head of the true Church, Bishop Schwarz of Hamburg was excommunicated from the Catholic Apostolic Church in 1862 for proposing the election of new apostles. A priest named Preuss was elected to the office of apostle "through the spirit of prophecy" to lead the dissenting body, and Bishop Schwarz served under him until his own elevation to the apostolic office.

Under Preuss and Schwarz the New Apostolic Church spread from Europe to America, where today it is organized into apostle's districts, bishop's districts, and elder's districts. Each church has a rector and one or more assistants (priests, deacons, and so forth) who serve usually without remuneration. All ministers and other "office bearers" are selected by the apostleship. The American church is a constituent part of the international organization supervised by Chief Apostle Herman Niehaus in Germany.

Just as the true Chrurch must be governed on the scriptural pattern by twelve apostles, members of this church believe that only the apostles have received from Christ the commission and power to forgive sin. The New Apostolic Church accepts the Apostles' Creed and stresses the authority and inspiration of the Bible, the apostolic ordinance of the laying on of hands, the necessity of gifts of the Holy Spirit (which include prophecy, visions, dreams, divers tongues, songs of praise, wisdom, discrimination of spirits, the power of healing and performing wonders), tithing, and the speedy, personal, premillennial return of Christ. Three "Means of Grace" are found in three sacraments: baptism (including children), Holy Communion, and Holy Sealing (the dispensing and reception of the Holy Spirit). Work "along broader interior and missionary lines" is conducted in the United States and Canada. There are 6,888 members in 73 churches in the United States, and about 500,000 in 3,500 branches in the international organization.

OLD CATHOLIC CHURCHES

Old Catholic churches in the United States are outgrowths but not connected branches of the Old Catholic movement and churches of Europe. The European bodies originated in a protest against the dogma of papal infallibility promulgated by the Vatican in 1870. This revolt, especially strong in Switzerland and Holland, did not break with Roman Catholic doctrine, creeds, customs, or liturgy; it was also most anxious to preserve the orders and apostolic succession of its priests and bishops, in as much as they considered apostolic succession as the foundation of a valid Christian ministry.

Much confusion has resulted in conflicting claims of succession and validity of orders, especially in America. All Old Catholic bodies in this country were at one time or another connected with European bodies, but that is not true today. None of the leaders of American Old Catholic churches are recognized in orders or succession by the European churches or authorities, and most American groups have severed their connections with churches abroad.

Old Catholic missionaries were in America soon after 1870, establishing scattered churches. Father Joseph Réné

Vilatte, a French priest ordained by the Old Catholics of Switzerland, attempted to organize these drifting congregatios and at once became the storm center of the rising confusion. Vilatte himself vacillated between rival bodies; he studied in a Presbyterian college at Montreal and twice returned to submit to the Roman Catholic Church, dying at last in a French monastery. Vigorously opposed within his own church and by American Protestant Episcopalians, whose ranks he refused to join, he went to Switzerland in 1885 for ordination as an Old Catholic bishop and was finally consecrated as an archbishop by Archbishop Alvarez of Ceylon, who claimed orders through the Syro-Jacobite Church of Malabar. He then returned to America to found the American Catholic Church.

Separated and competing as they are, the Old Catholics in the United States nevertheless have a firm common doctrinal basis. This doctrine is more Eastern Catholic than Western. They accept the seven ecumenical councils of the church held before the division into Eastern and Western bodies in 1505; they reject the filioque clause of the Nicene Creed as well as the dogma of papal supremacy and infallibility, clerical celibacy, and all union of church and state. Modified forms of Eastern and Roman Catholic rituals are used, generally in the language of the membership of the church.

There are four main divisions of Old Catholic churches in the United States with an approximate total of ninety thousand members in ninety-one churches.

American Catholic Church

THIS CHURCH was established by Father Vilatte, as already described, in Chicago. Before returning to the Roman Catholic Church, Vilatte consecrated Bishop F. E. J. Floyd, a former Protestant Episcopal priest, who assumed the primacy and title of archbishop in the reorganized church. It is a small body, seriously affected by withdrawals from its membership, which is now reported at 4,023 in 29 churches. Faith and polity are the general faith and polity of Old Catholic groups, with an archbishop, two auxiliary bishops, a titular bishop, and several priests.

American Catholic Church, Archdiocese of New York

THIS CHURCH was organized by its present archbishop and primate, the Most Rev. James Francis Augustine Lashley, in 1927 and incorporated in 1932. Its orders are derived from the Syrian Church of Antioch through Father Vilatte, and had a membership of 8,435 in 20 churches in 1947, all of which are located in New York City and Brooklyn. Roman Catholic forms of ordination and consecration are followed in the investing of holy orders.

North American Old Roman Catholic Church

THE LARGEST Old Catholic body in the United States, this church had 78,000 members and 29 churches in 1949. It was incorporated in 1917. Archbishop Carmel H. Carfora, elected in 1919 and made primate in 1922, derives his orders and ordination through the Old Catholic Church in England. Various independent congregations have united with this body from time to time, giving it its present impressive strength. Church officers, including archbishops, bishops, general vicars, priests, and delegates, are elected by the local congregations and confirmed by the primate; each foreign group of churches has a bishop of its own nationality. There is a theological seminary in Chicago and several homes for religious orders, aged priests, and needy laymen. The primate is supreme in authority, and a general synod meets annually. The church is identical with the Roman Catholic Church in worship and doctrine, acknowledging the "supremacy of the successor to St. Peter," but with masses held in the vernacular of the people. The clergy are allowed to marry. This church was received into union with the Eastern Orthodox Church by the Archbishop of Beirut in 1911 and by the Orthodox Patriarch of Alexandria in 1912.

Old Catholic Church in America

DERIVING ITS episcopate from the Old Roman Catholic Church of Holland and from the Eastern Orthodox Church, this body represents the Old Catholic churches of Poland, Lithuania, France, Morocco, Central America, and Yugoslavia. It accepts the decrees of the seven ecumenical councils, holds mass in English, permits its priests to marry before ordination, and employs the rituals, slightly modified, of both Roman Catholic and Eastern Orthodox churches. There were 6,274 members in 28 churches in 1940.

PENTECOSTAL BODIES

Pentecostalism is a most inclusive term applied to a large number of revivalistic American sects, assemblies, and churches. Many of them have come out of either Methodist or Baptist backgrounds, and the term itself explains much of their nature; they are primarily concerned with perfection, holiness, and the Pentecostal experience.

They offer statements of faith which are often long and involved and highly repetitious, but through which may be traced certain common strains and elements. Most of them believe in the Trinity, original sin, man's salvation through the atoning blood of Christ, the virgin birth and deity of Jesus, the divine inspiration and literal infallibility of the Scriptures, manifestations and "blessings" of the working of the Holy Spirit often running into excessive emotionalism—shouting, trances, jerking, hand clapping, "tongue talking," and so forth —the fiery Pentecostal baptism of the Spirit, premillennialism, and future rewards and punishments. Two sacraments are found in most of their sects—baptism, usually by immersion, and the Lord's Supper; foot washing is frequently observed in connection with the Supper. Many Pentecostals practice divine healing, and speaking in tongues is widespread.

Ultrafundamentalistic, varying in size from small group meetings to huge mass meetings, and working independently of any recognized denominational organization, Pentecostalists are found in every state in the Union with their greatest strength in the South, West, and Middle West. They use a great variety of names; only those including the word "Pentecostal" are included here, and they are comparatively small sects. The majority of American Pentecostalists may be found in the Tomlinson groups of the Church of God and their offshoots. No accurate count of their total membership is possible, in as much as many groups never offer statistics of any kind.

Pentecostal Holiness Church

THIS CHURCH was organized in 1898 at Anderson, South Carolina, by a number of Pentecostal associations which at the time used the name Fire-Baptized Holiness Church. A year later another group organized as the Pentecostal Holiness Church; the two bodies united in 1911 at Falcon, North Carolina, under the latter name. A third body, the Tabernacle Pentecostal Church, joined them in 1915. There were 30,154 members in 826 churches in 1949.

The theological standards of Methodism prevail in the Pentecostal Holiness Church with certain modifications; it accepts the premillennial teaching of the Second Coming and believes that provision was made in the Atonement for the healing of the body. Divine healing is practiced but not to the exclusion of medicine. Three works of grace are stressed by this church as all-important: justification by faith, sanctification, and Spirit baptism attested by speaking in other tongues. Services are often characterized by "joyous demonstrations."

Polity is also Methodistic; there are annual conferences and a quadrennial general conference which elects two general superintendents (bishops) to hold office for four years only. The general conference also elects a general secretary and a general treasurer for the church, a general board of six members to supervise the work of the church, and an educational board. There are seventeen annual conferences in the United States and one in Canada; foreign missions are found in China, India, South Africa, South America, the Hawaiian Islands, and Mexico. There is a junior college at Franklin Springs, Georgia.

Pentecostal Fire-Baptized Holiness Church

THIS CHURCH was organized by a small group who declined to continue in the union of the Fire-Baptized Holiness Church and the Pentecostal Holiness Church in 1911; their objection had to do mainly with matters of discipline in the wearing of ornaments and elaborate dress. They withdrew from the union in 1918 and were joined in 1920 by the Pentecostal Freewill Baptist Church.

Members of this church are forbidden to buy or sell, or to engage in any labor or business for which they may receive "pecuniary remuneration." They are also forbidden "filthiness of speech, foolish talking or jesting, slang, attendance at fairs, swimming pools or shows of any kind, the use of jewelry, gold, feathers, flowers, costly apparel, neckties," and so forth.

The sect is strongly premillennialist and perfectionist; "joyous demonstrations" are prominent, finding expression in hand clapping, crying, and shouting. State conventions support convention evangelists, and there is a general convention which elects a seven-member board of missions. Foreign missions are supported in India, and there is an orphans' home at Toccoa, Georgia. There are 1,444 members, and 74 churches.

Church of God in Christ (Pentecostal)

THIS IS a small body with 210 members in 9 churches in 1936. It was founded in the early 1930's and is under the supervision of a bishop who has headquarters at Bluefield, West Virginia. Local churches are reported to have been established in Michigan, West Virginia, Illinois, Ohio, Tennessee, Texas, and Alabama.

International Pentecostal Assemblies

THIS BODY is the successor to the Association of Pentecostal Assemblies founded in 1921 and the National and International Pentecostal Missionary Union founded in 1914. Doctrine follows the usual Pentecostal standards: the sick are anointed with oil and healed by prayer, foot washing is optional, and there is strong opposition to participation in war. The last membership report, in 1936, listed 6,333 members in 98 churches under the general supervision of an official board which directed the activities of the church in 23 states at home and on several foreign mission fields. The entire work is supported by tithing of the membership.

Pentecostal Assemblies of the World

THIS WAS an interracial body at the time of its organization in 1914; the white members withdrew in 1924 to form the Pentecostal Church, Incorporated, which in turn became a constituent body of the United Pentecostal Church in 1945. Origin is traced "directly back to Pentecost, A.D. 33." Doctrine reveals no important departure from that of Pentecostalism in general. Secret societies are opposed, as are church festivals and collecting money on the streets; the wearing of jewelry, attractive hosiery, bobbed hair, bright ties, low-necked dresses, and so forth, is forbidden. Divorce is not permitted when both man and wife have had "the baptism of the Holy Ghost," but when the unbeliever in a marriage contract procures a divorce, the believer may remarry.

Organization is similar to that of the Methodist Church; a general assembly meets annually under a presiding bishop; there are a secretary-treasurer for foreign missions, a committee of three on evangelism, and a board of twenty-four district elders. An executive board composed of bishops is elected each year by the ministerial members of the assembly. Local assemblies are presided over by district elders. There is evangelistic work conducted in the United States and in several missions abroad. In 1936 there were 5,713 members in 87 churches.

Pentecostal Church of God in America

THIS CHURCH was organized at Chicago in 1919, incorporated in Missouri in 1936, and held its first national convention in 1940—the words "in America" being added to its name to distinguish it from another Kansas City body bearing a similar name. It is typically Pentecostal in faith, with immersion, Spirit baptism, speaking in tongues, foot washing, divine healing, and so forth. In the United States 60,000 members were reported in 580 churches in 1949. Officers include a moderator, secretary-treasurer, missionary secretary-treasurer, general field presbyters, and district superintendents. A general convention meets annually. Several missionary stations are supported abroad.

United Pentecostal Church, Inc.

THIS CHURCH is made up of a union of two previous Pentecostal bodies merged in 1945; the Pentecostal Assemblies of Jesus Christ and the Pentecostal Church, Incorporated. The first body was the result of a merger of several groups which refused to enter the general council of the Assemblies of God, and the latter consisted of the white members who withdrew from the Pentecostal Assemblies of the World when it ceased to be an interracial body in 1924. Identical in doctrine and similar in polity to the Pentecostal Assemblies of the World and taking much of its phraseology and ideology from that group, it had 19,136 members and 1,075 churches in the United States in 1949. A general conference meets annually.

Calvary Pentecostal Church, Inc.

THIS CHURCH was founded at Olympia, Washington, in 1931 by a group of ministers who saw evidence of a "sad departure" from the interest and fruits of the Pentecostal revival which had been evident in America a few years before. They sought a ministerial fellowship rather than a separate denomination, and freedom from the sectarian spirit. The body was incorporated in 1932, and a home and foreign missionary society was incorporated in the same year. Home missions work today consists mainly of evangelistic work, relief to weak churches, and the establishment of new churches. Foreign missions are supported in India and Brazil. A general superintendent and executive presbytery board administer the work of the church; the general body meets in convention annually or semiannually. Seminary, college, or even Bible-school education is considered beneficial but no requisite for the ministers of this church. Ministers include both men and women; those who give evidence of having heard the call of God to preach are qualified by ordination. Membership was reported at twenty thousand in thirty-five churches in 1949.

Pilgrim Holiness Church

THE Rev. Martin Wells Knapp, a Methodist minister, organized the International Apostolic Holiness Union in 1897 in his home at Cincinnati, Ohio, to encourage the preaching of the original Wesleyan doctrines of holiness, premillennialism, divine healing, and a return to "apostolic practices, methods, power, and success." His intention was to form a union of Holiness and Pentecostal groups in agreement with his ideas, but eventually through a rather bewildering series of mergers the proposed union became a full-fledged denomination. The bodies joining his union were the Holiness Christian Church; the Pentecostal Rescue Mission of Binghamton, New York; the Pilgrim Church of California; the Pentecostal Brethren in Christ in Ohio; the People's Mission Church of Colorado, and numerous other small bodies. These, united in the Pilgrim Holiness Church, now have a strength of 40,661 members in 1,075 churches. Eight hundred twenty of these churches with 30,079 members are in the United States and Canada, and 255 churches with 10,582 members are in foreign lands. There are churches in 36 states and the province of Ontario in Canada.

The Pilgrim Holiness Church is close to the Church of the Nazarene in both doctrine and polity, although doctrine is described as Arminian and Methodist and government as "a combination of Episcopal and Congregational forms." Theologically it is conservative, stressing the Trinity, the new birth, entire sanctification, divine healing, premillennialism, and the inspiration and infallibility of the Scriptures. Baptism, the mode of which is optional, and the Lord's Supper are accepted as sacraments. Members are admitted on confession of faith following appearances before an advisory board and the church congregation. Both men and women are accepted as ministers.

Local churches are governed by a church board composed of the pastor, elders, deacons, and other church officers; women may be elected deaconesses. District organizations meet annually, made up of ministers and laymen; they elect district councils which hold authority over the ministers and churches of their various districts. A general conference meets every four years and elects a general superintendent; assistant superintendents; secretary, treasurer; secretaries for foreign missions, church extension, Sunday school, and youth work; and an editor. Home missionaries work largely in the South and among the Indians of Ontario, Canada; foreign missions are found in Africa, India, Mexico, the Philippines, South America, and the West Indies. There are six theological institutions and several secondary schools.

Polish National Catholic Church

ORGANIZED AT Scranton, Pennsylvania, on March 14, 1897, the Polish National Catholic Church was born in resentment against certain resolutions passed by the Roman Catholic Council of Baltimore in 1884. These resolutions seemed to the dissenting Polish congregations to give the Roman hierarchy of the Roman Catholic Church an unwarranted religious, political, and social power, and to permit "an unlawful encroachment upon ownership of Church property and to pave the way for the political exploitation of the Polish people." Resentment smoldered gradually into open revolt and resulted in the founding of the independent Polish body. This is the only body of any considerable size to break away from the Roman Catholic Church in this country, but there are other groups among Slovaks, Lithuanians, Ruthenians, and Hungarians which have also broken away; several of the Slovak and Lithuanian parishes have merged with the Polish National Catholic Church.

A constitution for the new church was adopted by the Scranton parish on March 21, 1897, claiming for the Polish people the right to control all churches built and maintained by them, to administer such church property through a committee chosen by their own parish, and to choose their own pastors.

The first synod was held at Scranton in September of 1904 with 147 clerical and lay delegates representing parishes in Pennsylvania, Maryland, Massachusetts, Connecticut, and New Jersey. The Rev. Francis Hodur, the dominant figure in the church, was chosen bishop-elect, Latin service books were ordered translated into Polish, and a theological seminary was established at Scranton. Bishop-elect Hodur was consecrated bishop in 1907 at Utrecht, Holland, by three bishops of the Old Catholic Church.

The doctrine of the National Church is founded upon the Scriptures, the holy traditions, and the four ecumenical synods of the undivided church. This doctrine is expanded in the Credo, which includes statements of belief in the Trinity, the Holy Spirit as man's source of grace, power, and peace, the necessity of the spiritual unity of all believers, the church as teacher and confessor, the equality of all people as the common children of God, immortality and the future justice and judgment of God. A statement of the Eleven Great Principles further expands the teachings of the Credo. The doctrine of eternal damnation is rejected.

Seven sacraments are practiced, with baptism and confirmation being recognized as one sacrament. The Word of God "heard and preached" is proclaimed a sacrament; two forms of confession are in general use—a private or "ear" confession and a general public confession for adults only.

The general synod is the highest authority in the government of the church; it meets every ten years except for such special sessions as may be considered necessary, and is composed of bishops (of which there are now seven), clergy, and lay delegates from each parish. Administrative power rests with the prime bishop, Hodur, and the church council, which meets twice annually and is composed of all the bishops, five clergy, and five lay delegates elected by the general synod. In like manner the authority of the diocese is vested in the diocesan synod, which meets every five years. Each parish is governed by an elected board of trustees. There are 4 dioceses in the United States, 146 parishes, and 250,000 members. The Polish language is used throughout in both the worship and the educational program in parish schools taught largely by pastors.

The Polish National Union, a fraternal and insurance organization, was established by the church at Scranton in 1908, set up on parish lines and as an adjunct to parish life. It consists of twelve districts divided into 257 branches and with 35,000 members, all of which are not required to be members of the church. A missionary work in Poland was begun in 1919 and at the present time has 119 parishes and a theological seminary at Krakow. A house for the aged and disabled was established at Spojnia Farm, Waymart, Pennsylvania, in 1929 by the Polish National Union. Three joint meetings of intercommunion committees have been held with the Protestant Episcopal Church, and very cordial relations exist between the two communions.

PRESBYTERIANS

Presbyterianism has two firm and deep roots; one goes back to the Greek word *presbuteros* (elder) and has to do with the system of church government of ancient and apostolic times; the other goes back to John Calvin and the Protestant Reformation, and has to do with the form of government used by all people calling themselves Presbyterian and holding the faith of the Reformed churches.

Calvin (1509-64) was a Frenchman trained for the law; turning to theology, his keen, legalistic mind and his lust for freedom from the rigid, confining forms of Roman Catholicism drove him as a fugitive from Roman reprisal to the city of Geneva, where he quickly grasped the reins of leadership in the Reformed sector of the Reformation. Resolute and often harsh to the point of cruelty with those who opposed him, he established himself and his theological system at the heart of a "city of God" in the Swiss capital, making it according to Macaulay "the cleanest and most wholesome city in Europe."

Calvin's whole thought revolved about the concept of sovereignty: "the sovereignty of God in His universe, the sovereignty of Christ in salvation, the sovereignty of the Scriptures in faith and conduct, the sovereignty of the individual conscience in the interpretation of the Will and Word of God." His system has been summarized in five main points: divine sovereignty, human impotence, limited atonement, irresistible grace, and final perseverance. God, according to Calvinism, rules the world; man is completely dominated by and dependent upon him; man is also totally depraved and unable to save himself (the doctrine of total depravity); God chooses or elects to save some and predestines others to be lost (the doctrine of predestination); even babes may be damned and without hope (infant damnation). But both elect and damned have definite rights and duties; man has a covenant with God, which must be honored; whatever his state he must keep faith in God's grace and ultimate goodness.

Out of this Calvinism came miracles of reform; few reformers have made so many contributions as John Calvin in so many fields at once—in education, in the building of an intelligent ministry, in the liberation of the oppressed and persecuted, and in the establishment of democratic forms of government in both church and state. In his thought lay the germ which in time destroyed the divine right of kings. He gave a new dignity to man and representative government to man's parliaments and church councils; he struck the final blow at feudalism and offered a spiritual and moral tone for dawning capitalism.

Strictly speaking, John Calvin did not found Presbyterianism; he laid the foundations upon which it was reconstructed in Switzerland, Holland, France, England, Scotland, and Ireland. He inspired fellow Frenchmen out of whose ranks came the Huguenots; by 1560 there were two thousand churches of Presbyterian complexion in France. He influenced the Dutchmen who established the Dutch Reformed Church in Holland. He gave courage to British Presbyterians in their bitter struggle against Catholic Bloody Mary. To him came Scots who became Covenanters; to him came John Knox, who went home to cry, "Great God, give me Scotland, or I die." Knox and the Covenanters set Scotland afire and made it Protestant and Presbyterian.

A delegation of Scots sat in the Westminster Assembly of Divines along with 121 English ministers, 10 peers, and 20 members of the House of Commons, resolved to have "no bishop, and no king." This Westminster Assembly is a high milestone in Presbyterian history. Meeting at the call of Parliament to resolve the struggle over the compulsory use of the Anglican *Book of Common Prayer*, it sat for nearly five years (1643-48) in 1,163 sessions, produced a Large and a Shorter Catechism, a directory for the public worship of God, a form of government, and, most important of all, the Westminster Confession of Faith, which, built upon the five points of Calvinism, became the doctrinal standard of Scottish, British, and American Presbyterianism.

Dominant in the Westminster Assembly, the Presbyterians soon dominated the British government; Cromwell completed the ousting of a monarch and established a commonwealth; the commonwealth crashed, the monarchy returned, and the fires of persecution flamed again. British Presbyterians fled to America with the Puritans; an attempt to establish episcopacy in Scotland after 1662 sent many Presbyterians out of Scotland into Ireland, where economic difficulties and religious inequalities drove them on to America. The Presbyterian British, and even more the Presbyterian Scotch-Irish, became the founders of Presbyterianism in America. Beginning in 1710 and running into the middle years of the century from three to six thousand Scotch-Irish came annually into the American colonies, settling at first in New England and the middle colonies, then spreading out more widely than any other racial group ever to reach our shores.

There were Presbyterian congregations in the colonies long before the Scotch-Irish migration of 1710-50. One was worshiping in Virginia in 1611; others were worshiping in Massachusetts and Connecticut in 1630. Long Island and New York had congregations by 1640 and 1643. The oldest continuing Presbyterian church was founded by the Rev. Francis Makemie at Rehoboth, Maryland, in 1683. Makemie ranged the coast from Boston to the Carolinas, planting churches and giving them unity with each other; he united six groups into the first presbytery of churches in Philadelphia in 1706; in 1716 this first presbytery had become a synod made up of several presbyteries, which held its first meeting in 1717.

Presbyterian Church in the U.S.A.

TODAY THE largest single body of Presbyterians in the United States, this church had its beginnings in those first congregations, presbyteries, and synods set up by Makemie. The first general synod of their spiritual forefathers met in 1729 and adopted the Westminster Confession of Faith with the Large and Shorter catechisms "as being, in all essential and necessary articles, good forms of sound words, and systems of Christian doctrine." The same synod denied the civil magistrates any power whatever over the church or any right to persecute anyone for his religious faith.

Free in the new land with their Scotch-Irish fire and Convenanter background, the Presbyterians quickly set about procuring trained ministers; creeds and colleges have been their stock in trade from their earliest days. William Tennent, Sr., organized a "log college" in a cabin at Neshaminy, Pennsylvania. He started with his four sons as his first pupils, and this family school grew into the most important Presbyterian institution of higher learning in America. Out of it came Princeton and a stream of revivalistic Presbyterian preachers who played leading roles in the great awakening of the early eighteenth century. Prominent among them were William Tennent, Jr., and his brother Gilbert, who met and liked the British revivalist George Whitefield and followed him in preaching an emotional "new birth" revivalism which came into conflict with the old creedal Calvinism. The camp-meeting revival grew out of the great-awakening enthusiasm; it was born as a Presbyterian institution, continued by the Methodists when the Presbyterians had dropped it.

Presbyterian objection to emotional revivalism went deep; it split their church. Preachers took sides; those of the "old side" opposed revivalism, while those of the "new side" endorsed it, claiming that less attention should be paid to college training for the ministry and more to the recruiting of regenerated common men into the pulpit. The two sides quarreled until 1757, when they reunited; in 1758, the first year of the united synod, there were ninety-eight ministers in the Presbyterian Church in the colonies, two hundred congregations, and ten thousand members. One of the ablest of the new-side preachers was John Witherspoon, president of Princeton (founded in 1746), member of the

Continental Congress, and the only ministerial signer of the Declaration of Independence.

Witherspoon may have been instrumental in the call of the general synod upon the Presbyterian churches to "uphold and promote" the resolutions of the Continental Congress. The Scotch-Irish accepted the revolution with relish; the persecution they had experienced in England and Ulster left them as natural dissenters and solidly anti-British. Their old cry, "No bishop, and no king," was heard as far off as England; Horace Walpole remarked that "Cousin America" had run off with a Presbyterian parson.

The Presbyterians moved swiftly to strengthen their church after Yorktown, meeting in convention at Philadelphia in 1788 at the same time that the national constitutional convention was in session in the same city. The national administrative bodies of American Presbyterianism were known as the General Presbytery from 1706-16; as the General Synod from 1718-88, and as the General Assembly from 1789 to the present time. John Witherspoon was a delegate at the Presbyterian gathering; with John Dickinson he helped put into the governmental statutes of the nation and the Presbyterian Church those principles of democratic representation which make them so amazingly alike.

From 1790 to 1837 membership in the Presbyterian Church in the U.S.A. increased from 18,000 to 220,557. This growth was due to the revival which swept the country during those years and to the plan of union with the Congregationalists. Under this plan, Presbyterian and Congregational preachers and laymen moving into the new Western territory worked and built together; preachers of the two denominations preached in each other's pulpits, and members held the right of representation in both Congregational association and Presbyterian presbytery. The plan worked well on the whole, absorbing the fruits of the national revivals and giving

real impetus to missionary work both at home and abroad. Then came disagreements between Old School and New School factions within the church over matters of discipline and the expenditure of missionary money; the general assembly of 1837 expelled four New School presbyteries which promptly met in their own assembly at Auburn, New York. The Presbyterian Church in the U.S.A. was split in two between New School men who wanted to keep the plan of union and Old School men who were suspicious of "the novelties of New England [Congregational] theology."

These years promised to be an era of expansion for the Presbyterians. Marcus Whitman drove the first team and wagon over the South Pass of the Rockies into the great Northwest. After him came hosts of Presbyterian preachers and laymen, building churches, schools, colleges, seminaries. From 1812 to 1836 the Presbyterians in the United States built their first great theological seminaries: Princeton, Auburn, Allegheny, Columbia, Lane, McCormack, Union in Virginia, and Union in New York City. They also set up their own missionary and educational societies. But the era of unity suddenly became an era of schism. Even earlier than the Old School-New School division the Cumberland presbytery had broken away in 1810, following a dispute over the educational qualifications of the ministry, to form the Cumberland Presbyterian Church. And antislavery sentiment was increasing. A strong protest was made in 1818, but it was later modified. In 1846 the Old School assembly regarded slavery in the southern states as no bar to Christian communion, but the New School assembly took action in the same year, condemning it without reservation. By 1857 several southern synods had withdrawn to organize the United Synod of the Presbyterian Church, and the greater and final break came in 1861 when forty-seven southern presbyteries formed their General Assembly of the Presbyterian Church in the Confederate States of

America; in 1865 the United Synod and the Confederate churches merged into what is now known as the Presbyterian Church in the United States. The Synod of Kentucky united with it in 1869, and the Synod of Missouri in 1874.

The Old School and New School bodies, holding separate assemblies since 1837, were reunited in 1870 on the basis of the Westminster Confession; they were joined in 1906 by a large majority of the Cumberland churches and in 1920 by the Welsh Calvinistic Methodists. In 1949 there were 9 different Presbyterian denominations in the United States with a total membership of 3,426,-378; of these, 3,055,443 are found in the two major divisions: the Presbyterian Church in the United States of America and the Presbyterian Church in the United States. Five of the other groups have been seriously considering consolidation, and seven of them are working together in the Council of the Reformed Churches in the United States holding the Presbyterian system organized in 1907.

All Presbyterian bodies in the United States subscribe to the principles and theology of the Westminster Confession. Some modifications or enlargements have come as the church has developed, but the confession is its cornerstone. The Presbyterian Church in the U.S.A., proceeding from the confession, puts its main emphasis upon the sovereignty of God in Christ in the salvation of the individual, and the salvation of every individual believer is recognized as a part of the divine plan. Salvation is not a reward for either faith or good works; it is the free gift of God. Regeneration too is an act of God; man is powerless to save himself, but once saved he remains saved.

Each congregation has its local session, which acts in receiving and disciplining members and in the general spiritual welfare of the church. Congregations in limited districts are grouped in presbyteries, which examine, ordain, and install ministers, review reports from the ses-

sions and hear cases or complaints brought before them, and conduct whatever business is assigned them by the congregations. The synod supervises the presbyteries of a larger district, reviews the records of its constituent presbyteries, hears complaints and appeals from the presbyteries, organizes new presbyteries, and functions in an administrative capacity in all denominational matters lying within its jurisdiction. The highest judiciary of the church is the annual general assembly, made up of clerical and lay delegates elected by the presbyteries on a proportional basis. The general assembly settles all matters of discipline and doctrine referred to it by the lower bodies, establishes new synods, appoints boards and commissions, and reviews all appeals. Its decisions are final, except upon matters affecting the constitution of the church. The officers of the general assembly are the stated clerk as the chief executive officer of the denomination, elected for five years with the privilege of re-election, and the moderator, chosen each year to preside over the sessions of the general assembly.

The general assembly has provided for a general council and a permanent judicial commission. The general council is appointed to function between meetings of the assembly; it is composed of the moderator and two living ex-moderators, the stated clerk, four members representing the four boards of the church, one representative of the council on theological education, and fifteen "members at large." This council is an important body; it has wide powers assigned by the assembly, and it formulates much of the policy under which the boards carry on their work. The council idea is carried down through the synods and presbyteries, which elect similar bodies with comparative powers. The permanent judicial commission is composed of eight ministers and seven ruling elders, no two of which belong to the same synod; it was created in 1907 to act as a supreme judicial court. Judicial cases not affecting the doctrine or constitution of the church terminate with the synod as the final court of appeal; all others terminate with the general assembly.

Administrative direction of the work of the church is in the hands of the boards, reduced to four in 1923: the Board of National Missions, the Board of Foreign Missions, the Board of Christian Education, and the Board of Pensions. The Board of National Missions was begun by the general presbytery in 1717; the synod of 1717 set up a "fund for pious uses," which meant missionary uses. Home missions work was conducted for some time through the American Board of Commissioners for Foreign Missions organized in 1810; a series of adjustments and consolidations resulted in the formation of the present Board of National Missions in 1923. The work of the board is carried on in Alaska, the West Indies, and in all the forty-eight states; it includes aid to churches, city and rural (about 90 per cent of the churches in the United States are said to have begun with the help of national missions funds), Sunday schools in pioneer areas, schools from primary to college level, hospitals and clinics, agricultural and community projects, and so forth. The program employs more than three thousand missionaries, ordained ministers, teachers, doctors, nurses, and community workers.

The Board of Foreign Missions also worked with the American Board of Commissioners for Foreign Missions until its independent establishment under its present name by the general assembly of 1837. It is elected by the general assembly with 50 members—16 women, 16 laymen, and 18 ministers. In January of 1950 the board supported 1,140 missionaries and interchurch service representatives in 30 countries; it maintains or cooperates in the work of 43 universities, colleges, and training schools, 124 secondary schools, 1,775 schools of lower grades, 77 hospitals, and 275 dispensaries and clinics. The board annually handles nearly $6,000,000 in foreign mission funds.

The Board of Christian Education was constituted by the general assembly of 1923; it has 45 members, of whom 21 are ministers, 13 women, and 11 laymen. It provides Presbyterian youth, children, parents, and teachers with study materials and supervises the work of Westminster Foundations on 114 college campuses. Its work reaches into the 44 church-related colleges of the denomination and into its 3 Christian education training schools and 9 theological seminaries. Its publications are issued through the Westminster Press, which operates through 5 Westminster bookstores and many department stores throughout the United States. Westminster Press is one of the most efficient church publishing concerns in American Protestantism, and the Presbyterian periodicals *Today* and *Presbyterian Life* are among the finest church periodicals in the country.

The Board of Pensions administers a fund of $60,000,000, based upon a pension plan under which the ministers contribute 3 per cent of their salaries and the churches and other employee organizations contribute 8 per cent. Besides this Service Pension Plan are four other pension plans as well as relief grants and a Minister's Emergency Relief Fund. Presbyterian-affiliated homes, orphanages, and hospitals are also included among its responsibilities, and benefits are paid to the aged, widows, disabled, and needy.

On December 31, 1949, the Presbyterian Church in the U.S.A. reported 40 synods, 265 presbyteries, 9,392 ministers, 8,350 churches, and 2,391,967 members. Its steady growth was greatly accelerated through the campaign of the New Life Movement, which in a single year (1949) enabled the Presbyterian Church in the U.S.A. to show a gain of 71,133 members, its largest gain since 1921.

Presbyterian Church in the United States

THIS CHURCH was composed in 1951 of 17 southern synods with a total of 675,489 members and 3,647 churches; its separation from the Presbyterian Church in the U.S.A. has already been described. Relations between these two churches quickly became cordial once the bitternesses of the Civil War had passed. Fraternal relations were re-established in 1882, and in 1888 the two groups held a joint meeting at Philadelphia to celebrate the centenary of the adoption of the constitution of the church. In 1897 they also united to observe the 250th anniversary of the Westminster Assembly.

The original differences which separated these two bodies have been resolved, but others remain to keep them apart. The southern church is definitely conservative in theology and outlook; the northern church shows more liberal trends unwelcome to many within the southern. Beyond this there are differences in social emphases which, more than doctrine, seem to postpone any bridging of the gulf. Northern Presbyterian churches make little distinction between Negro and white membership and clergy; in the South in all denominations, it has generally been thought better for both white and Negro people to have their own churches, and the Presbyterian Church in the United States has followed the southern pattern. In 1916 the general assembly of the Presbyterian Church in the United States helped to organize four Negro presbyteries into a synod made up exclusively of Negro clergymen and members; the 1950 general assembly received overtures that the Negro presbyteries be dissolved and the congregations brought under the white presbyteries. There is now a committee for further study, which will report to the 1951 assembly.

Doctrinally this church is conservatively Calvinistic, allowing some dissent in minor details but requiring creedal allegiance of its ministers. Women are excluded from the ministry and eldership but are encouraged to enlist in other fields of Christian work. All political questions are excluded from the courts of the church. Polity follows the Presbyterian system except that ruling elders are permitted to deliver the charge at the installation of a pastor and to serve as moderators in the higher courts.

Until 1949 the administrative agencies of the church were known as executive committees; they became boards at the 1950 assembly, five in number: the Board of World Missions, the Board of Education, the Board of Church Extension, the Board of Annuities and Relief, and the Board of Women's Work. A general council was also created by this assembly to continue the work of the previous Committee on Stewardship and with other broad responsibilities, but concentrating on stewardship, public relations, research, and church finance. Various other permanent and standing committees are appointed by the assembly to work with the boards.

In the Presbyterian Church in the United States there were 17 synods, 85 presbyteries, 21,609 ministers, 3,602 churches, and 653,594 communicants scattered over 16 southern states in 1949. The church supports 4 theological seminaries—Austin, Columbia, Louisville, and Union—27 institutions of collegiate or higher rank, 10 secondary schools, 3 mission schools, and 16 orphans' homes and schools. Students' work is maintained in 30 colleges with full-time student workers and in 19 other colleges with part-time student workers. About 63 home missionary presbyteries are receiving aid for work among the Indians in Texas and Oklahoma, mountain work in the Ozarks and Appalachians, Latin-American work in Texas, and work among southern Negroes; 381 missionaries are serving abroad in Africa, Brazil, China, Japan, Korea, Mexico, Ecuador, and Portugal. There are 102,331 foreign communicants, 547 organized congregations, 2,693 outstations, 4,486 trained native workers, 1,462 mission schools attended by 58,301 students, and 14 hospitals which in 1949 treated 63,867 patients. The Board of Church Extension assists in the maintenance of 56 Negro churches and 35 Negro ministers, and the broadcasting of 2,769 individual radio programs. The Board of Annuities and Relief in 1949-50 disbursed $473,-997.12 for ministerial relief, student funds, educational, promotional, and administrative work. Twenty-seven periodicals were published by the Board of Education, which also prepared plans and materials for 3,664 Sunday schools.

Associate Presbyterian Church of North America

THIS CHURCH maintains the traditions of the secession movement of 1733 in the Church of Scotland. Missionaries from Scotland organized the Associate Presbytery in America in 1754. This presbytery merged with the Reformed Presbytery in 1782; two ministers and three ruling elders refused to accept the union and continued the organization of the Associate Presbytery of Pennsylvania; other presbyteries joined the Pennsylvania group, which in 1801 was named the Associate Synod of North America. In 1858 this associate synod and the Associate Reformed Presbyterian Church of North America consummated a union under the name United Presbyterian Church of North America. Eleven ministers refusing to enter this union continued the Associate Presbyterian Church.

This church believes in restricted Communion, expels members who join secret orders, and uses the Psalms exclusively in worship services. It follows the Westminster Confession and has an Associate Testimony of its own explaining its doctrinal position. Polity differs in no essential elements from that of other Presbyterian churches. Home missions are conducted by itinerant pastors, and foreign missionary work is supported in India. There are no colleges or other schools; there are three hundred members and eight churches.

Associate Reformed Presbyterian Church (General Synod)

THIS IS a synod of the former Associate Reformed Church, which merged in 1858 into the United Presbyterian Church; it became a general synod in 1935. It is a body of Covenanter origins and tradition. Feeling that the other three synods in the Associate Reformed Church were not in full loyalty to the old principles of the organizations, the synod of the Carolinas withdrew in 1822 to form the Associate Reformed Synod of the South. Following the creation of the United Presbyterian Church in 1858 it dropped the phrase "of the South," thereby becoming the Associate Reformed Presbyterian Church, now known as the Associate Reformed Presbyterian Church (General Synod).

The standards of the Westminster Confession are followed in this church, and the Psalms used exclusively in its worship services. Foreign missions are found in India and Mexico, and a college is located at Due West, South Carolina. There were 25,779 members in 145 churches in 1949.

Cumberland Presbyterian Church

THIS CHURCH grew out of the revival in the Cumberland country of Kentucky and Tennessee in the first ten years of the nineteenth century. The revival produced a large number of new congregations so rapidly that it was impossible to furnish them with college- and seminary-trained ministers. The Cumberland, Kentucky, presbytery ordained a number of pastors whose educational and theological qualifications were low, and as a result it was dissolved by the Synod of Kentucky of the Presbyterian Church, U.S.A., in 1806. The Cumberland presbytery was then reorganized in 1810 as an independent body. It adopted a confession of faith based on the Westminster Confession and proceeded to organize colleges, schools, and a publishing house. The desire for reunion eventually prevailed, and in 1906 the Cumberland body was reunited with the Presbyterian Church in the U.S.A., bringing back to that body about 185,212 members. A minority group, however, refused to enter the merger and separated to continue under the name of the Cumberland Presbyterian Church. The church in 1949 claimed 80,236 members and 1,035 churches, spread not only across the South but in Ohio, Indiana, Illinois, Michigan, Iowa, and California as well. The 1950 general assembly was held at Los Angeles.

The only difference in doctrine in this body lies in its rejection of eternal reprobation; it still recognizes the doctrines of the sovereignty of God and the perseverance of the saints. Some smaller groups joining the Cumberland Presbyterian Church have held Arminian doctrines, and as a consequence historians see in this church a "middle way" between Calvinism and Arminianism. The presence of the Arminian element has doubtless worked against any further union with other Presbyterian bodies.

The standard Presbyterian sessions, presbyteries, synods, and general assembly prevail in polity. Denominational boards direct work in missions, church extension, education, and so forth. Home mission fields lie in the South, West, and Southwest; foreign mission stations are located in China, Japan, Mexico, and South America. Gifts for benevolences in 1949 totaled $391,000. Bethel College at McKenzie, Tennessee, is a church-sponsored institution; a theological seminary is maintained at the same place, and a large printing and publishing plant is located at Nashville.

Colored Cumberland Presbyterian Church

THIS CHURCH was built on the twenty-thousand Negro membership of the pre–Civil War Cumberland Presbyterian Church with the full approval of the General Assembly of that Church held in 1869. The first three presbyteries were organized in Tennessee, where the first synod, the Tennessee Synod, was organized in 1871. In doctrine this church follows the Westminster Confession with four reservations: (1) there are no eternal reprobates; (2) Christ died for all mankind, not for the elect alone; (3) there is no infant damnation; and (4) the Spirit of God operates in the world coextensively with Christ's atonement in such manner "as to leave all men inexcusable." Polity is genuinely Presbyterian except that bishops are included as pastors among its officers. There were 19 presbyteries, 4 synods—Alabama, Tennessee, Kentucky, and Texas—121 churches, and 30,000 members found in all sections of the country in 1949.

Reformed Presbyterian Church in North America of

A BODY of direct Covenanter lineage; its first minister came to this country from the Reformed Presbytery of Scotland in 1752. Most of the early membership joined the union with the Associate Presbytery in 1782, but a small group remained outside the union and reorganized in Philadelphia under the name Reformed Presbytery in 1798. A synod was first constituted at Philadelphia in 1809, only to be split in 1833 into Old Light and New Light groups in a dispute over citizenship. The synod of the Reformed Presbyterian Church (Old Light) refused to allow its members to vote or participate generally in public affairs; the general synod of the Reformed Presbyterian Church (New Light) imposed no such restrictions.

The government of this church is thoroughly Presbyterian except that there is no general assembly. The Westminster Confession is the doctrinal standard. The members pledge themselves to "pray and labor for the peace and welfare of our country, and for its reformation by a constitutional recognition of God as the source of all power, of Jesus Christ as the Ruler of Nations, of the Holy Scriptures as the supreme rule, and of the true Christian religion." Until that reformation is accomplished, they refuse to vote or hold public office. They observe close Communion and use only the Psalms in worship. No instrumental music is permitted in their services, and members cannot join any secret society.

Home missionaries work among the Indians, Negroes, and Jews in America; and in Elliott and Morgan Counties in Kentucky; foreign missionaries are at work in China, Syria, Manchuria, Cyprus, and Asia Minor. There are a church college at Beaver Falls, Pennsylvania, a theological seminary at Pittsburgh, and a home for the aged; 5,585 members were reported in 74 churches in 1947.

Reformed Presbyterian Church in North America (General Synod)

THIS IS the original New Light group which was organized following the division of the Reformed Presbyterian Synod in 1833. It is similar to the preceding body except in the matter of allowing its membership to vote and hold public office; it does, however, encourage dissent from "all immoral civil institutions." It accepts the Westminster Confession, uses hymns as well as Psalms in worship, preaches the headship of Christ over all nations, advocates "public social covenanting," and holds close or restricted Communion. Polity is in accord with other Presbyterian bodies. There are 1,426 members in 11 churches.

Orthodox Presbyterian Church

THIS CHURCH was organized June 11, 1936, in protest against what were believed to be modernistic tendencies in the Presbyterian Church in the U.S.A. Led by the late Rev. J. Gresham Machen, the dissenters formed a foreign missionary society which they were ordered to disband; refusing, they were tried, convicted, and suspended from the Presbyterian Church in the U.S.A. They

organized the Presbyterian Church in America; an injunction brought against the use of that name by the parent body resulted in the change in 1939 to the name Orthodox Presbyterian Church.

The Westminster Confession and the Westminster Large and Shorter catechisms are accepted as "subordinate doctrinal standards or creedal statements." Stronger emphasis is laid upon the infallibility and inerrancy of the Bible (the books of the Bible were written by men "so guided by Him that their original manuscripts were without error in fact or doctrine"); original sin; the virgin birth, deity, and sacrificial atonement of Christ; his resurrection and ascension; his role as judge at the end of the world and the consummation of the kingdom; and salvation through the sacrifice and power of Christ for those "whom the Father purposes to save." Salvation is "not because of good works, [but] it is in order to good works."

The Presbyterian system of government is followed; a general assembly meets annually. The church constitution contains the creedal statement of the group, a form of government, book of discipline, and directory for the worship of God. Committees appointed by the general assembly conduct work in home missions and church extension, foreign missions, and Christian education. In 1949 there were 13,928 members and 72 churches.

A group split again from this church to call themselves the Bible Presbyterian Synod under the general leadership of the Rev. Carl McIntyre, who was one of those deposed by the Presbyterian Church in the U.S.A.

United Presbyterian Church of North America

THIS CHURCH was formed by the merging of the Associate Presbyterian Church and the Associate Reformed Presbyterian Church in 1858 at Pittsburgh, Pennsylvania. The doctrines, traditions, and institutions of the two bodies were preserved; government follows the Presbyterian pattern with session, presbytery, synod, and a general assembly, which meets annually.

In matters of faith this church rests upon the broad foundation of the Westminster Confession with certain modifications, one of which amends the chapter in the confession on the power of civil magistrates. A confessional statement of forty-four articles was drawn up by the United Presbyterian Church in 1925; it contained the substance of the Westminster standards and symbols, but restricted divorce to cases of marital unfaithfulness, denied infant damnation, extended sacramental privileges to all who professed faith in Christ and led Christian lives, withdrew the protest against secret or oath-bound societies, abandoned the exclusive use of the Psalms, maintained insistence upon the verbal inspiration of the Scriptures, affirmed the sufficiency and fullness of the provisions of God for the needs of a fallen race through the atonement of Christ, emphasized the renewing and sanctifying power of the Holy Spirit, and held salvation to be free to all sinners.

Boards appointed by the general assembly conduct work in missions, education, publications, pensions, and relief; the board of directors of the Women's General Missionary Society co-operates with these and reports each year to the assembly. There are six colleges and one theological seminary; a general hospital, one home for the aged, and one orphans' home are conducted by the women's association. Foreign missionary work is supported in India, Egypt, Ethiopia, and the Sudan. There were 213,810 members and 836 churches in 1949.

Protestant Episcopal Church

IT IS stated in the preface of the *Book of Common Prayer* of the Protestant Episcopal Church that "this Church is far from intending to depart from the Church of England in any essential point of doctrine, discipline or worship." Therein lies the hint of its origin: the Protestant Episcopal Church constitutes "the self-governing American branch of the Anglican Communion"; for a century and a half in this country it bore the name of the Church of England.

Its history runs back to the first missionaries who went to the British Isles from Gaul prior to the Council of Arles in A.D. 314. It is traced down through the days when Henry VIII threw off the supremacy of the pope (Henry, according to Anglican scholars, did not found the Church of England; it was a church that had always been more British than Roman); through the reign of Edward VI, when the *Book of Common Prayer* and Forty-Two Articles of Religion were written; through the period of Catholic restoration under Bloody Mary and through her successor, Protestant Elizabeth, who put the united church and state under the Protestant banner and sent Sir Francis Drake sailing to build an empire.

Drake came ashore in what is now California in 1578; his Church of England chaplain, Francis Fletcher, planted a cross and read a prayer while Drake claimed the new land for the Virgin Queen. Frobisher had reached Labrador in 1576, also with a chaplain. After them came colonists to Virginia under Sir Humphrey Gilbert and Sir Walter Raleigh; Raleigh's chaplain baptized an Indian named Manteo and a white baby named Virginia Dare before the settlement vanished. With Captain John Smith came chaplain Robert Hunt, who stretched a sail between two trees for shelter and read the service from the *Book of Common Prayer*.

In the South the transplanted Church of England quickly became the Established Church; it was at heart a tolerant and Catholic church, but the control of the crown brought an almost ruthless authority which made the church suspect in the eyes of those colonists who had come here seeking freedom from all such authority. The Virginia House of Burgesses set the salary of the Virginia clergyman at "1,500 pounds of tobacco and 16 barrels of corn." It was a British clergy supported by public tax and assessment and by contributions from the Church in England through the Society for the Propagation of the Gospel. And it was technically under the jurisdiction of the Bishop of London. In that fact lay one of its fatal weaknesses; colonial ministers had to journey to England for ordination, and few could afford it. This coupled with the rising ride of the American Revolution placed the colonial Church of England in an unenviable position.

Yet the church did well. Membership grew rapidly, William and Mary College was established in 1693, and the Church of England became the predominant church in the South. King's Chapel in Boston, the first Episcopal church in New England, was opened in 1689; in 1698 a church was established at Newport, Rhode Island, and another, called Trinity Church, in New York City. In 1702 a delegation from the Society for the Propagation of the Gospel came from England to survey the colonial church and to find about fifty clergymen at work from the Carolinas to Maine. The visitors sensed the need for American bishops to ordain American clergymen; they also sensed the increasing opposition of the American patriot to a British-governed church.

The revolution almost destroyed the colonial Church of England. Under special oath of allegiance to the king the clergy either fled to England or Canada, or remained as Loyalists in the colonies in the face of overwhelming persecution. That many of them were loyal to the American cause meant little; the Rev. William White was chaplain of the Continental Congress, and the Rev. Charles Thurston was a Continental colonel, and in the pews of the Episcopal Church sat Washington, Jefferson, Patrick

Henry, John Jay, Robert Morris, John Marshall, Charles and "Light Horse Harry" Lee, and John Randolph. But their presence could not stem the tide. The Anglican house was divided, and it fell. At the war's end there was no episcopacy, no association of the churches, not even the semblance of an establishment. Few thought of any future for this church, which suffered between Lexington and Yorktown more than any other in the colonies.

But there was a future, and a great one. In 1782 there appeared a pamphlet entitled *The Case of the Episcopal Churches in the United States Considered*, written by William White. It was a plea for unity and reorganization, and it proposed that the ministry be continued temporarily without the episcopal succession since the latter "cannot at present be obtained." In 1783 a conference of the Episcopal churches met at Annapolis, Maryland, and formally adopted the name Protestant Episcopal Church—"Protestant" to distinguish it from the Church of Rome, "Episcopal" to distinguish it from the Presbyterians and the Congregationalists. In the same year the clergy in Connecticut elected Dr. Samuel Seabury as their prospective bishop; he went to England, waited a year for consecration at the hands of English bishops. This was denied, and he then went to Scotland to be consecrated bishop in 1784. Ultimately Parliament and the Church of England cleared the way, and two other bishops-elect from New York and Pennsylvania were consecrated by the Archbishop of Canterbury in 1787. In 1789 the constitution of the Protestant Episcopal Church was adopted in Philadelphia, the *Book of Common Prayer* was revised for American use, and the Protestant Episcopal Church became an independent, self-governing body.

There were complete harmony and expansion for the next half century. There were established new churches and church institutions: Sunday schools, Bible, prayer-book, and tract societies, theological seminaries, colleges, boarding schools, guilds for men and women, and the Domestic and Foreign Missionary Society. Diocesan organizations replaced state organizations; new bishops moved into the new West; Bishops J. H. Hobart in New York, A. V. Griswold in New England, Benjamin Moore in Virginia, and Philander Chase in Ohio worked miracles in overcoming the Revolutionary prejudice against the church. Dr. W. A. Muhlenberg, one of the great Episcopalian builders, "organized the first free church of any importance in New York, introduced the male choir, sisterhoods and the fresh air movement, while his church infirmary suggested to his mind the organization of St. Luke's Hospital [in New York], the first church hospital of any Christian communion in the country." Muhlenberg was a man of wide vision; he inspired a "memorial" calling for a wider catholicity in the Protestant Episcopal Church, which resulted in the famous Lambeth Quadrilateral on Church Unity in 1888 and the movement which produced the further revision of the American *Book of Common Prayer* in 1892.

With the outbreak of the Civil War disruption again threatened the Protestant Episcopal Church, but it did not come. Among the major Protestant Episcopal churches this one alone suffered no division; New England churchmen may have been abolitionists, and a Louisiana bishop, Leonidas Polk, may have been a general under Lee, but Polk prayed for Bishop Charles Pettit McIlvaine of Ohio in public, and the Ohioan prayed for Polk, and they were still in one church. A temporary Protestant Episcopal Church in the Confederate States was organized to carry on the work in the South, but the names of the southern bishops were called in the general convention in New York in 1862; and once the war was over, the Episcopalian house was in 1865 quickly reunited.

The years following Appomattox were years of new growth; a dispute over churchmanship, rising out of the Oxford Movement in England, resulted in the separation of a group into the Reformed Episcopal Church in 1873, but otherwise Episcopalian unity held fast. New theological seminaries were established, and old ones were reorganized and strengthened; this period saw the organization of Church Congress, the Brotherhood of St. Andrew, and numerous other church agencies. The expansion continued into the next century; two world wars failed to halt it. In 1830 the Protestant Episcopal Church had 12 bishops, 20 dioceses, 600 clergymen, and 30,000 communicants; in 1930 it had 152 bishops, 105 dioceses, 6,000 clergymen, and 1,250,000 communicants.

The Episcopalian form of government closely parallels that of the Federal government. The basic unit is the parish, governed by the rector, who is called a priest; wardens, who have charge of church records and the collection of alms; and vestrymen, who have charge of all church property. There are also lay readers and deaconesses in the local congregation. Parishes are grouped geographically into seventy-four dioceses, each of which includes not less than six parishes; the dioceses, which elect the bishops, were at first identical with the states, but with the growth of the church larger dioceses became necessary, and missionary districts were added. Government in the diocese is vested in the bishop and the diocesan convention, made up of clerical and lay representatives and meeting annually. It is self-governing but appoints a standing committee as the ecclesiastical authority for all purposes declared by the general convention. Sections of states and territories not organized into dioceses are established by the house of bishops and the general convention as missionary districts, which may be elevated into dioceses or consolidated with other parts of dioceses as new dioceses. In addition to the thirteen domestic missionary districts there are twelve overseas missionary districts and five extracontinental missionary districts. Dioceses and missionary districts are grouped into eight provinces, each governed by a synod consisting of the bishops, four presbyters, and four laymen elected by each constituent diocese and missionary district. Once in three years there is a general convention composed of a house of bishops and a house of deputies with lay and clerical delegates having equal representation. The two houses sit and deliberate separately; both must approve of a measure before it can become law. The ecclesiastical head of the church is the presiding bishop elected by the general convention; he serves until the age of retirement, set at seventy.

In 1919 the general convention provided for a national council to act between sessions of the convention; it is one of the most important administrative agencies of the church, made up of thirty-two members consisting of bishops, priests, laymen, and laywomen; the presiding bishop is president, and the council facilitates the work of the church in six departments: foreign missions, domestic missions, religious education, Christian social service, finance, and promotion. There is also a division on college work and youth, and the Women's Auxiliary works in co-operation with all six of the departments.

The Episcopalian accepts two creeds, the Apostles' and the Nicene. The Articles of the Church of England, with the exception of the twenty-first and with modifications of the eighth, thirty-fifth, and thirty-sixth, are accepted as a general statement of doctrine, but adherence to them as a creed is not required. The clergy make the following declaration:

"I do believe the Holy Scriptures of the Old and New Testaments to be the Word of God, and to contain all things necessary to salvation, and I do solemnly engage to conform to the doctrine, discipline, and worship of the Protestant Episcopal Church in the United States of America."

The church expects of all its members "loyalty to the doctrine, discipline, and worship of the one holy Catholic Apostolic Church, in all the essentials, but allows great liberty in nonessentials." It allows for more variation, individuality, independent thinking, and religious liberty than most of our larger Protestant churches. Liberals and conservatives, modernists and fundamentalists, find cordial and common ground for worship in the prayer book, which next to the Bible has probably influenced more people than any other book in the English language.

There are two sacraments, baptism and the Lord's Supper, recognized as "certain sure witnesses and effectual agencies of God's love and grace." Baptism, by pouring or immersion, is necessary for regeneration for either children or adults; baptism by any church in the name of the Trinity is recognized as valid baptism; baptized children are confirmed as members by the bishop, and those not baptized in infancy or childhood must accept the rite before confirmation. Without stating or defining a holy mystery the Episcopal Church believes in the real presence of Christ in the elements of the Supper. The church also recognizes the sacramental character of confirmation, penance, orders of the ministry, matrimony, and unction.

Some Episcopalians are high churchmen with elaborate ritual and ceremony; others are low churchmen with a ritual less involved and with more of an evangelistic emphasis. There are Anglo-Catholics, stressing the catholicity of the church and perhaps more sympathetic with Roman Catholocism than the majority of the membership; they constitute about one third of the members, but the movement and the name seem to be on the wane. All, however, have a loyalty to their church which is deep and lasting; in more than three hundred years this church has known only one minor division; today it stands sixth among all denominations; it had 2,297,989 members in 7,091 churches in the United States in 1949.

Stanley I. Stuber has called this the Church of Beauty, and it is an apt description. Its prayer book is matchless in the literature of religious worship, containing the heart of the New Testament and the best of Old Testament devotions. Members have built stately cathedrals in the country, among them the Cathedral of St. John in New York City, which is the third largest cathedral in the world, and the National Cathedral at Washington, sometimes called the American Westminster Abbey. Stained-glass windows, gleaming altars, vested choirs, and a glorious ritual give the worshiper not only beauty but a deep sense of the continuity of the Christian spirit and tradition. Next to their stress on episcopacy their liturgical worship is a distinguishing feature; varying in degree according to High or Low Church inclinations, it has its roots in the liturgy of the Church of England and beyond that in the Roman mass, and includes the reading, recitation, or intonation by priest, people, and choir of the historic general confession, general thanksgiving, collects, Psalter, and prayers, all of which are written in a beauty and cadence second only to that of the King James version of the Bible.

There is, however, quite as much action as beauty in the Protestant Episcopal Church. Home missions are found in thirty-three United States dioceses and districts; special emphasis is placed upon town and country, Negro and Japanese, work, and a total of $766,279 was appropriated by national headquarters for domestic work in 1948; the figure is considerably larger when contributions from the fields themselves are added. Overseas missions are located in all American territories—Alaska, Hawaii, the Panama Canal Zone, the Virgin Islands, and Puerto Rico—and in China, Brazil, Cuba, the Dominican Republic, Haiti, India, Japan, Liberia, Mexico, and the Philippine Islands; appropriations for these fields reached $1,672,954 in 1948. The church sponsors or maintains 11 theological seminaries, 6 colleges, 1 university, 3 training schools for deaconesses, 140 secondary schools for boys and girls in the United States, Alaska, Hawaii, and the Philippines, 63 homes for the aged, 60 institutions for child care, 72 hospitals and convalescent homes, and work for seamen in 10 dioceses. A church pension fund established in 1917 raised an initial sum of $8,000,000; it was the first soundly based church pension system on such a scale in America. In 1949 pension funds totaling $122,785.23 were paid out of a fund which had reached $45,878,931.27.

The Protestant Episcopal Church has an undeserved reputation for exclusiveness and non-co-operation with other Protestant bodies; actually it has been most co-operative. The Lambeth Quadrilateral, already mentioned, was adopted by the house of bishops at the general convention of 1886 and accepted with modifications two years later. It had four points for world unity of the churches: the Scriptures as the Word of God, the Apostles' and the Nicene creeds as the rule of faith, the two sacraments of baptism and the Lord's Supper, and the episcopate as the central principle of church government. In 1910 the general convention appointed a commission to arrange for a world conference on faith and order; the first conference was held at Geneva in 1920, the second in 1927 at Lausanne, the third at Edinburgh in 1937. The church was active in the Federal Council of the Churches of Christ in America and in the World Council of Churches and is represented in the National Council of Churches.

REFORMED BODIES

*W*hen the Belgic Confession was written in 1561 as the creedal cornerstone of the Reformed churches in Belgium and Holland, "the Churches in the Netherlands which sit under the Cross" gave thanks to their God in the preface of that document, where they said, "The blood of our brethren . . . crieth out." There was real cause for crying out, for the Reformation was spreading into the Netherlands from Switzerland in the midst of the long Dutch struggle against Catholic Spain. The Dutch Reformed Church was cradled in cruelty.

Those Reformation-founded churches called Reformed, as distinguished from those called Lutheran, originated in Switzerland under Zwingli, Calvin, and Melanchthon; they were Reformed in Switzerland, Holland, and Germany; they were Presbyterian in England and Scotland, and Huguenot in France; still others in Bohemia and Hungary used national names. As they moved overseas to the American colonies, they formed into four groups of churches: two from Holland became the Reformed Church in America and the Christian Reformed Church; one from the German Palatinate became the Reformed Church in the Uinted States, now the Evangelical and Reformed Church; the fourth, coming from Hungary, became the Free Magyar Reformed Church in America. All of them were and still are Calvinistic and conservative, basing their doctrine generally upon the Heidelberg Catechism, the Belgic Confession, and the canons of the Synod of Dort and using a modified Presbyterian form of government.

Reformed Church in America

THIS CHURCH had an unorganized membership along the upper reaches of the Hudson River in the neighborhood of Fort Orange (Albany) in 1614. Members had no regularly established congregations or churches, but they were numerous enough to require the services of Reformed ministers, two of which came from Holland in 1623 as "comforters of the sick." By 1628 the Dutch in New Amsterdam had a pastor of their own in Dominie Jonas Michaelius and an organized Collegiate Church, which was to become the oldest church in the middle colonies and the oldest church in

America with an uninterrupted ministry.

When the English took New Amsterdam in 1664, Dutch churches were thriving in Albany, Kingston, Brooklyn, Manhattan, and at Bergen in New Jersey; as the immigration from Holland ceased, there were perhaps eight thousand Dutch churchmen and churchwomen in the country, holding their services in Dutch and served by either native clergymen or pastors sent from Holland. It was difficult and expensive to send nativeborn ministerial candidates to Holland for education and ordination; the question rent the Reformed Church and was finally resolved in the building of a college and seminary at New Brunswick (Queen's College, later Rutgers). It was the first theological seminary to be built in this country, and it was fathered by the famous Dominie Theodore Frelinghuysen, who also took a leading part in the revival called the Great Awakening.

A sharp controversy disputing the authority of the Classis of Amsterdam resulted in the complete independence of the Dutch churches in America; a general body and five particular bodies were created, a constitution was drawn up in 1792, and the general synod was organized in 1794. The names Dutch Reformed Church in North America and Reformed Dutch Church in the United States of America were both in use in 1792; in 1819 the church was incorporated as the Reformed Protestant Dutch Church, and in 1867 it became the Reformed Church in America.

The American Revolution had little effect upon the Reformed Church in America except to offer the Dutchmen a chance to even matters with the English. Once the war was over, Scotch, English, and Germans began joining the church, creating a problem in the use of the Dutch tongue which took years to resolve. A second Dutch immigration from the Netherlands started in the middle of the nineteenth century, bringing whole Dutch congregations with their pastors. One group, led by Dominie Albertus van Raalte, settled in western

Michigan and established the community called Holland, known today for Hope College, Western Theological Seminary, and an annual tulip festival. Van Raalte and his group became part of the Reformed Church in America in 1850. Another colony, led by Dominie Scholte, settled in Pella, Iowa, in 1847-48 and in 1856 merged with the Reformed Church in America except for a small dissenting group.

Domestic missions began in 1786; actually missionary work among the Indians had begun much earlier. Needy and destitute churches in New York, Pennsylvania and Kentucky were assisted by the domestic missionaries of the Classis of Albany for many years, and in 1806 the general synod took over administration of all missionary agencies. This church co-operated with the American Board of Commissioners for foreign missions. In 1832 the Board of Foreign Missions was created but continued to work through the American Board until 1857, from which time it has operated independently. Insisting from the start upon seven years of college and seminary training for its ministers, the church established the Education Society of the Reformed Church in America in 1828 and changed it to the Board of Education of the General Synod in 1831.

The explicit statements and principles of the Belgic Confession, the Heidelberg Catechism, and the Synod of Dort are still the doctrinal standard of the Reformed Church in America. The mild and gentle spirit of the confession with its emphasis upon salvation through Christ is a central theme: the primacy of God and his power in human life are at the heart of the preaching of the church as they are at the heart of the canons of Dort; and the Heidelberg Catechism, based as it is on the Apostles' Creed, is employed in all catechetical classes. The divine authority of the Scriptures is important here; "the final authority in the Reformed faith is the Holy Scripture, the living Word of God,

spoken to every man through the Holy Spirit of God."

Worship is semiliturgical, but it is an optional liturgy; only the forms for baptism and the Lord's Supper, the two recognized sacraments of the church, are obligatory. It is a corporate or congregational way of worship blending form and freedom and distinguishing this from other Protestant communions.

Government of the church stands midway between the episcopal and Presbyterian forms; it might be called "modified Presbyterian." The governing body in the local church is the consistory, made up of elders, deacons, and the pastor, who is always president. Elders are charged with the guidance of the spiritual life of the church, and deacons are in charge of benevolences; but they generally meet and act as one body. A number of churches in a limited area are grouped into a classis, which has immediate supervision of the churches and the ministry, and is composed of all the ministers of the area and an elder from each consistory. Classes are grouped into particular synods, of which there are five, meeting annually and made up of an equal number of ministers and elders from each classis, and supervising the planning and programing of the churches within the area. The highest court of the church is the general synod, representing the entire church, meeting once a year, and consisting of delegations of an equal number of ministers and elders from each classis. The size of the delegation, however, varies in accordance with the size of the classis. The general synod directs the missionary and educational work through its various boards. The president of the general synod, elected by the delegates, holds office for one year.

The Board of Foreign Missions directs 146 active missionaries abroad in China, south India, Japan, Arabia, Iraq, Mesopotamia, and more recently in Africa; a total of $821,482.95 was received to finance foreign missions for the year ending April 30, 1950. The Board of

Domestic Missions offers help to needy and mission churches, administers the church building fund and the Southern Normal School in Brewton, Alabama; it also directs work among Dutch immigrants in Canada and among Italians, Chinese, and Jews in the United States. The Women's Board of Domestic Missions operates missions in Indiana and Kentucky, supports other missionary projects among Japanese-Americans, Italians, Indians, migrants, and sharecroppers, and provides scholarships in the denominational colleges. Both boards share in evangelistic work in Mexico and among urban American Negroes. The Board of Education offers funds for student aid in 8 colleges and 2 theological seminaries, and plans the work for Sunday schools, catechetical classes, young people's activities, and adult groups. The Board of Pensions administers annuities, pensions, and relief funds for widows, disabled ministers, and orphans. About 310 persons received a total of $148,062 from these funds in 1949-50.

Reporting all baptized persons as members, the Reformed Church in America in 1949 listed 179,085 members in 759 churches.

Christian Reformed Church

THIS IS the second largest Reformed body in the United States, with 142,818 members and 322 churches in 1949. It began in the dissent of a number of members and two Michigan ministers of the Reformed Church in America who found themselves in disagreement with the parent church on certain matters of doctrine and discipline. A conference held at Holland, Michigan, in 1857 effected the separation of the Holland Reformed Church from the Reformed Church in America. Through a series of changes in name the Holland church became the present Christian Reformed Church.

Dissension split its ranks soon after organization; by 1863 there was only one Christian Reformed pastor for the entire body. Immigration from Holland and anti-Masonic agitation in the Reformed Church of America, however, brought several groups into merger and gave the church a new lease on life. The Christian Reformed Church today is largely an English-speaking church with a few scattered congregations of German descent clinging to the German tongue. Doctrine shows no important differences from the Reformed standards; the three historic creeds are accepted. Organization bears the usual Reformed markings, including eighteen classes which meet annually but with no intermediate or particular synods between the classes, and a general synod made up of two ministers and two elders from each classis.

Interest in missions, ministerial training, primary schools, labor unions, and tuberculosis and psychopathic hospitals distinguishes this denomination. There are domestic missions among the Navaho and Zuni Indians and among American Jews, and foreign missions in China, South America, and northern Nigeria, and there are a dozen missionary churches and stations in Canada. Calvin College and Seminary are located at Grand Rapids, Michigan, and there are a number of parochial schools in various states. There are eight homes for the aged, and a publishing house is located at Grand Rapids.

Free Magyar Reformed Church in America

THIS IS the smallest of the Reformed churches; in 1942 it had 6,126 members and 21 churches. It is a Hungarian body, formed originally in New York City in 1904 as the Hungarian Reformed Church under the care and supervision of the Reformed Church of Hungary. The Reformed Church of Hungary transferred most of these American congregations to the Reformed Church in the United States in 1922 under the Tiffin Agreement made at Tiffin, Ohio. When the Reformed Church in the United States united with the Evangelical Synod of

North America in 1934, three Hungarian congregations that had refused to accept the Tiffin Agreement, together with four other Hungarian congregations, merged to form the Free Magyar Reformed Church in America.

This church is divided into eastern and western classes, which together constitute a diocese. Both classes have a dean and a lay curator, and the diocese is headed by an archdean and a chief lay curator. The doctrine and polity of the mother church in Hungary is followed; the church recognizes the Second Helvetic Confession and the Heidelberg Catechism as "symbolic books." The diocese meets annually, and there is a constitutional meeting every three years. Local churches are found only in New York, New Jersey, Pennsylvania, Ohio, and Michigan.

Reformed Episcopal Church

THE Reformed Episcopal Church was organized in New York City in 1873 by eight clergymen and twenty laymen who formerly had been priests and members of the Protestant Episcopal Church. A long debate over the ritualism and ecclesiasticism of the Protestant Episcopal Church lay behind the separation; the immediate cause of the division lay in the participation of Bishop George David Cummins of Kentucky in a communion service held in the Fifth Avenue Presbyterian Church in New York City. In the face of criticism and in the conviction that the catholic nature and mission of the Protestant Episcopal Church were being lost Bishop Cummins withdrew to found the new denomination.

Doctrine and organization are similar to that of the parent church with several important exceptions. The Reformed Episcopal Church rejects the doctrine that the Lord's Table is an altar on which the body and blood of Christ are offered anew to the Father, that the presence of Christ in the Supper is a presence in the elements of bread and wine, and that regeneration is inseparably connected with baptism. It also denies that Christian ministers are priests in any other sense than that in which all other believers are a "royal priesthood." Clergymen ordained in other churches are not reordained on entering the ministry of the Reformed Episcopal Church, and members are admitted on letters of dismissal from other Protestant denominations.

Worship is liturgical, but not repressively or exclusively so; at the morning services on Sunday the use of the prayer book, revised to remove certain objectionable sacerdotal elements, is required. At other services its use is optional, while at any service extempore prayer may be used by the minister "as he is led by the Spirit."

Parish and synodical units prevail in the administration of the church; the triennial general council of the Reformed Episcopal Church is not like the general convention of the Protestant Episcopal Church, however, as its bishops do not constitute a separate house.

A home missionary work is conducted among the Negroes of the South, and foreign missions are maintained in India, Africa, and Anglo-Egyptian Sudan. In India and Africa there are 17 primary schools, 2 hospitals, and 1 orphanage. There are two seminaries in the United States located at Philadelphia and Summerville, South Carolina. In 1948 the church listed 8,571 members in 67 local churches.

Roman Catholic Church

ACROSS THE first thousand years of Christendom the principal church was the Roman Catholic Church; for the first fifteen hundred years, up to the time of the Protestant Reformation, the Western world was almost solidly Roman Catholic. The eleventh-century separation left the faith divided between Roman Catholic and Eastern Orthodox sectors, and the Reformation left Continental Europe and the British Isles divided between Roman Catholic, Lutheran, and Reformed Churches with the prospect of still further division as denominationalism increased.

The Roman Catholic Church dates its beginning from the moment of Christ's selection of the apostle Peter as guardian of the keys of heaven and earth and as chief of the apostles, and claims this fisherman as its first pope. It gained real authority and power when it arose as the only body strong enough to rule after the fall of the city of Rome in A.D. 410. A house of terror ravaged first by Goths, Vandals, and Franks and then by Saxons, Danes, Alemanni, Lombards, and Burgundians, Europe found its only steadying hand in the Roman Catholic Church; without the church anarchy would have been king from Britain to the Bosporus. The first mention of the term Catholic Church was made by Ignatius about A.D. 110-15, but the first real demonstrations of its authority came as it won the barbarians to its banners while it kept the flame of faith burning in its churches and the candle of wisdom alive in its monastic schools. The "City of God" of which Augustine wrote so brilliantly was in fact the Church of Rome; Augustine laid its theological and philosophical structure and gave the papacy its finest justification and defense. He left it strong enough to give crowns or deny them to Europe's kings.

The church beat back the threats of its enemies at home and from afar; it converted the barbarian, won against the Saracen, and employed the Inquisition against the heretic boring from within. It brought the hopeful interval known as the Peace of God; it also supported chivalry and feudalism, fought the Crusades, created a noble art and literature, and sent friars in gray called Franciscans as the missionaries of peace to the world and friars in black called Dominicans to instruct in the dogma of the church. It built schools and cathedrals, dominated Europe, and reached for the world with Loyola and his Jesuits. Africa, India, China, and Japan were visited by Roman Catholic missionaries.

Then came the usual temptations of wealth and power; Erasmus the Dutchman stormed against the Roman Catholics with ridicule, and Savonarola raged in sermons at Florence and was burned in the public square. Wycliffe put the Bible into the English tongue; Luther nailed his theses to the church door of Wittenberg on October 31, 1517, and the Reformation revolt broke into the open. Some scholars say that "Erasmus laid the egg and Luther hatched it."

But long before Luther, Roman Catholics had reached America. The first Roman Catholic diocese on this side of the Atlantic was established in Greenland in 1125; there were bishops in residence there until 1377. A bishop of Catholic Spain came with Columbus in 1492; missionaries came with Coronado and with the other early Spanish explorers. Most of them perished; one of them started the first permanent parish in America at St. Augustine, Florida, in 1565.

French Catholic explorers, voyageurs, and colonizers—Cartier, Joliet, Marquette, and others—were generally Roman Catholics supported by missionary groups; among them were the Recollets, Jesuits, Sulpicians, Capuchins, and the secular clergy. New France became a vicariate apostolic in 1658 with Bishop Laval at its head. The See of Quebec (1674) had spiritual jurisdiction over all the vast province of France in North America, reaching down the valley of the Mississippi to Louisiana.

In 1634 the Roman Catholics founded Maryland; later they were restricted by law in Maryland and in other colonies, and the restrictions were not removed until after the Revolution. In the face of these restrictions and in view of the fact that most of the colonial immigrants were Protestants and not Catholics, the Roman Catholic Church grew slowly. In 1696 there were only seven Catholic families in New York, and eighty years later they were still traveling to Philadelphia to receive the sacraments. In 1763 there were less than 25,000 Catholics in all the colonies; they were under the jurisdiction of the vicar apostolic of London.

Catholics in large numbers were in the Continental Army during the Revolution; among the signatures on the Articles of Confederation, the Declaration of Independence, and the Constitution are found those of Thomas Fitizsimmons, Daniel Carroll, and Charles Carroll of Carrollton, all of whom were Catholics. The Revolution brought them freedom, religious as well as political; religious equality became law with the adoption of the Constitution in 1787.

There was no immediate hierarchal superior in the United States when the war ended, and the vicar apostolic in London refused to exercise jurisdiction over the "rebels." After long investigation and delay and an appeal to Rome the Rev. John Carroll was named superior, or prefect apostolic, of the church in the thirteen original states, and the Roman Catholic Church in this country became completely independent of the Roman Catholic Church in England. At that time there were 15,800 Catholics in Maryland, 700 in Pennsylvania, 200 in Virginia, and 1,500 in New York with many others along the Mississippi, unorganized and with no priests. At the turn of the century there were 80 churches and about 150,000 Roman Catholics; by 1890 there were 6,231,417—an amazing growth due primarily to the flood tide of immigration from the Roman Catholic countries of Europe.

Baltimore became the first American diocese in 1789 and an archdiocese in 1808. Other dioceses and archdioceses were formed as the church expanded, covering the country from coast to coast. Three plenary or national councils were held at Baltimore in 1852, 1866, and 1884.

Archbishop John McCloskey became the first American cardinal in 1875, and Archbishop James Gibbons of Baltimore was elevated to the same rank in 1877, The Catholic University of America was founded at Washington, D. C., by the third plenary council in 1884. The first apostolic delegation met there in 1893.

The Civil War and two world wars failed to disturb the work of the church or to interrupt its growth; indeed the first World War produced one of the ablest hierarchal Roman Catholic agencies in the country, the National War Council, now known as the National Catholic Welfare Conference. The national and international strength of Catholicism was dramatized in the twenty-eighth International Eucharistic Congress held at Chicago in 1926 with more than a million Catholics from all parts of the world participating. There were 18,605,003 Catholics in the United States in 1926; in 1949 the Roman Catholic Church was the largest church in the United States with 26,718,343 members in 15,112 parishes or churches.

The faith and doctrine of the church are founded upon "that deposit of faith given to it by Christ and through His apostles, sustained by the Bible and by tradition," and defended by the pope when he speaks as head of the church, or ex cathedra. The statements of the supreme pontiff neither constitute nor establish any new doctrine, but are official statements that that particular doctrine was revealed by God and is contained in the *depositorium fides,* or Sacred Depository of Faith.

Three creeds—the Apostles', Nicene, and Athanasian—are recognized as containing the essential truths accepted by the church. All Catholics must reject any doctrines held to be in error by the church and must obey the authority of the church in all matters of faith. They must also subscribe to a profession of faith, which reads as follows:

One only God, in three divine Persons, distinct from, and equal to, each other—

that is to say, the Father, the Son, and the Holy Ghost.

The Catholic doctrine of the Incarnation, Passion, Death, and Resurrection of our Lord Jesus Christ; and the personal union of the two Natures, the divine and the human; the divine maternity of the Most Holy Mary, together with her most spotless virginity.

The true, real, and substantial presence of the Body and Blood, together with the Soul and Divinity of our Lord Jesus Christ, in the most holy Sacrament of the Eucharist.

The seven Sacraments instituted by Jesus Christ for the salvation of mankind; that is to say: Baptism, Confirmation, Eucharist, Penance, Extreme Unction, Orders, Matrimony.

Purgatory, the resurrection of the dead, everlasting life.

The primacy, not only of honor, but also of jurisdiction, of the Roman Pontiff, successor of St. Peter, Prince of the Apostles, Vicar of Jesus Christ; the veneration of the saints and of their images; the authority of the apostolic and ecclesiastical traditions, and of the Holy Scriptures, which we must interpret, and understand, only in the sense which our holy mother the Catholic Church has held, and does hold; and everything else that has been defined, and declared by the sacred Canons, and by the General Councils, and particularly by the Holy Council of Trent, and delivered, defined, and declared by the General Council of the Vatican, especially concerning the primacy of the Roman Pontiff, and his infallible teaching authority.

Baptism, necessary for membership in the church, is administered to both infants and adults by pouring; all baptized persons are listed as members of the church. Confirmation by the laying on of hands by a bishop and anointing with the holy chrism in the form of a cross follows baptism. The Eucharist (Lord's Supper) is served to laymen, laywomen, and children usually following a fast; the laity receive only the bread, and the body and blood of Christ are considered as actually present in the eucharistic elements. The sacrament of penance is one through which postbaptismal sins are forgiven. Extreme unction is administered to the sick who stand in danger of death. The sacrament of orders, or holy orders, is one of ordination for the bishops and priests of the church. Marriage is a sacrament which "cannot be dissolved by any human power" this rules out divorce. Members are required to attend mass on Sundays and obligatory holy days, to fast and abstain on certain appointed days, to confess at least once a year, to receive the Holy Eucharist during the Easter season, to contribute to the support of the pastors, and to observe strictly the marriage regulations of the church.

The government of the Roman Catholic Church is hierarchal and completely authoritarian; no layman may have any voice in the government; parishes cannot call their own priests, but the parish laymen are often consulted on certain phases of parish work. At the head of the government stands the pope, who is also bishop of Rome, "the Vicar of Christ on earth, and the Visible Head of the Church." His authority is supreme in all matters of faith and discipline. Next to him is the College of Cardinals, never more than seventy in number and of three orders—cardinal deacons, cardinal priests, and cardinal bishops, indicating not their jurisdictional standing but their position in the cardinalate. Generally cardinal priests are bishops or archbishops, and the cardinal deacons are priests; many of the cardinals live in Rome, acting as advisers to the pope and as heads or members of the various congregations or commissions supervising the administration of the church. When a pope dies, the cardinals elect his successor; they hold authority in the interim.

The Roman Curia is the official body of papal administrative offices through which the pope governs the church; it is composed of congregations, tribunals, and curial offices. The congregations include the Congregation of the Holy Office, Consistorial Congregation, Congregation of the Sacraments, Congrega-

ROMAN CATHOLIC CHURCH

tion of the Council, Congregation of the Affairs of Religious, Congregation of Sacred Rites, Congregation of Ceremonies, Congregation of Seminaries and Universities, Congregation for the Propagation of the Faith, Congregation for Extraordinary Ecclesiastical Affairs, and Congregation for the Oriental Church. Curia tribunals include the Sacred Penitentiary, the Sacred Roman Rota, and the Apostolic Segnatura. The offices of the curia include the Cancellaria, Dataria, Secretariate of State, and others.

In the United States the government of the church has its top representative in the apostolic delegate at Washington, and there are 4 cardinals, 15 archbishops, 99 bishops, and 25,000 priests. The archbishop is in charge of the archdiocese and has precedence in his province. There are 102 dioceses grouped into 15 provinces. Bishops are the ruling authority in the dioceses, but appeals from their decisions may be taken to the apostolic delegate and even to Rome. The diocese also has a vicar-general who acts under certain conditions as representative of the bishop; there is also a diocesan chancellor or secretary, a council of consultors, and a number of boards of examination and superintendence. The parish pastor is responsible to the bishop; he is appointed by the bishop or archbishop and holds authority to celebrate the mass and administer the sacraments with the help of such other priests as the parish may need.

Bishops are appointed from Rome, usually upon suggestions from the hierarchy in the United States; they in turn send to the Holy See at Rome every two years the names of priests fitted to become bishops and often make suggestions as to the best of the priests available. The clergy in the Roman Catholic Church are those who are tonsured; they may be members of minor orders, subdeacons, deacons, or priests. Candidates for orders studying in divinity schools—there are 104 major seminaries and 139 minor seminaries—are called seminarians; following their vows of

chastity they are ordained by the bishop as subdeacons, deacons, or priests.

Religious orders are of two kinds: monastic and religious congregations of priests, and the various brotherhoods and sisterhoods; this would not include the Franciscans or Dominicans, who are neither monastic nor religious congregations. The Catholic Directory of 1950 listed a total of 133 separate religious orders of priests, 19 religious orders of brothers, and 558 religious orders of women. Most of the members of orders take perpetual, but solemn, vows. A president or superior heads each order; he is often represented in different countries by subordinates or councils, although some orders form completely independent communities. Ordained clerical members of the orders are known as regular clergy to distinguish them from the parish priests, who are called diocesan clergy; both classes of clergy go through the same forms of ordination and induction. There are also lay members in the orders, who take vows but are not inducted or ordained into the priesthood. Lay brothers, of whom there are 7,377 in the United States, assist the ordained leaders in the work of the order. All orders are divided into provinces or communities, and their members are under the jurisdiction of the head of the province or community. Those in the sisterhoods and brotherhoods are required to take vows but are not ordained; they are engaged primarily in educational, philanthropic, or charitable work.

Three ecclesiastical councils form an important part of the Catholic system; they are known as general or ecumenical, plenary or national, and provincial councils. A general council is called by the pope or with his consent; it is composed of all the Roman Catholic bishops of the world, and its actions on matters of doctrine and discipline must be approved by the pope. Plenary councils are made up of the bishops resident in the country; their acts too must be submitted to the Holy See for confirmation and correction before promulgation; they do not define but repeat the doctrine defined by the general councils, and they apply a universal discipline determined by these councils and the Holy See through explicit statutes in each country and province; they may initiate such discipline as national circumstances demand. These councils function as legislative bodies and are known in every country in the world in which the church is represented. Below them are smaller diocesan and provincial councils which make further promulgation and application of the decrees passed by the other councils and approved by the pope.

Nationally the Roman Catholic Church in the United States is thus governed by its hierarchy, made up of 182 members, and by its priesthood, made up of 25,000 priests. Church property is controlled by a board of trustees appointed in each diocese by the bishop. The board includes a majority of priestly members and a minority of laymen; property is held under the title of the bishop or archbishop. The total work from the local parish to the highest offices and divisions is financed by pew rents, plate collections, baptismal and wedding offerings, masses, and so forth. The priest controls all moneys, retaining enough for his salary—which is determined by the diocese and is uniform throughout the diocese—and the running expenses of the parish, and putting the balance to the credit of the church.

Masses are held on Sundays from 5 A.M. to noon. High mass, with the liturgy sung in part by priest and choir and with a sermon, is held between 10 A.M. and noon; all others, called low masses—in which the mass is read and a short instruction but no sermon is given —are celebrated at various hours between 5 and 12. Vespers are sung in the afternoon and evening. Mass and liturgy, except in a few Uniat churches, are always in Latin; but sermons, instruction, and the reading of the Bible are in the language of the congregation.

With its nearly 27,000,000 members and with the most centralized govern-ment in Christendom the Roman Catholic Church has accomplished a work almost unbelievable in scope. The Holy See at Rome has representatives in 67 countries of the world; 43 are of diplomatic status, and 24 are apostolic delegations. In the Western Hemisphere there are 513 ecclesiastical jurisdictions, of which 221 are in North America; the United States has 126. The Sacred Congregation for the Propagation of the Faith has 566 missionary jurisdictions embracing over half the world's population; just prior to the Second World War the church had more than 275,000 missionaries in all foreign fields.

Missionary work in the United States is conducted under the direction of the American Board of Catholic Missions, under which the Commission for Catholic Missions for the Colored People and the Indians is at work. Approximately 365,000 American Negroes are Roman Catholics. Out of a total Negro population of about 15,000,000 there are 408 Negro Catholic churches served by 578 priests and 306 Catholic Negro elementary schools with an enrollment of 64,847 pupils and a staff of 1,600 sisters and 250 lay teachers. There are also 30 high schools, 1 ecclesiastical college and seminary, and 1 college. There are 100,000 Catholic Eskimos and Indians, of which 95,335 are living on 81 Indian reservations. They are served by 215 priests and 732 sisters, lay brothers, scholastics, and catechists in 110 Catholic mission centers, 379 churches, and 63 mission schools. The schools have 8,040 students enrolled.

In July of 1949 there were 4,123 Catholic Americans engaged in foreign missionary service outside the United States. The Society for the Propagation of the Faith is the over-all representative foreign missionary body. There are 70 religious societies engaged in missionary work and 40 other missionary societies and mission boards with their branches in the dioceses. Religious societies or orders for men—Jesuits, Franciscans, Maryknoll Fathers, and so forth—and sisterhoods—the Franciscan Sisters, Maryknoll Sisters, Sisters of Charity, and so forth—send missionaries into more than 30 countries. The Catholic population of missionary territories has increased by 10,000,000 in the last 15 years.

Education has been a primary interest of the Roman Catholic Church in the United States ever since the establishment of a classical school in St. Augustine, Florida, in 1606; the first Catholic college was established at Newton, Maryland, in 1677. Jesuits in Philadelphia founded "the mother of all parochial schools in the English-speaking colonies" in 1782, and parochial schools ever since have been the basic educational unit of the church. Today there are five classes of church schools—parochial, secondary, college, seminary, and university. Of these, parochial schools are by far the most numerous, being found in every diocese in the country. There are 7,917 elementary parochial schools with 2,477,741 students, 588 private elementary schools with 82,885 students, 1,576 diocesan and parochial high schools with 324,398 students, 806 private high schools with 195,480 students, 225 colleges and universities with 257,727 students, and 388 seminaries with an enrollment of 25,622. Elementary education is almost exclusively in the hands of religious orders of women while secondary schools and colleges have teaching staffs of religious orders of both men and women. There are 106,777 full-time teachers in Catholic schools; 7,436 are teaching priests, 3,411 are teaching brothers, 82,048 are teaching sisters, and 13,477 are lay teachers. About 5,000,000 youths are under Catholic instruction in the United States.

Roman Catholic charity and welfare work is conducted by many different organizations, religious and otherwise. The National Conference of Catholic Charities acts as a general information and co-operating body, but the bulk of the work is conducted by several religious orders of men and women devoting full time to the relief of the poor

in homes or in institutions. There are also bureaus of charities in many of the dioceses. The Society of St. Vincent de Paul is perhaps the largest and most effective group; with a membership of 30,000 it has dispensed $50,000,000 to the poor in the past 25 years. Numerous other groups and orders—such as the Little Sisters of the Poor, the Sisters of Charity, the Daughters of Charity of the Society of St. Vincent de Paul, the Sisters of Mercy, and the Third Order of Franciscans—are active among the poor in Catholic hospitals and homes for the aged. The Catholic Directory of 1950 listed 352 orphanages and asylums caring for 42,808 children, 19,462 children in foster homes, and a total of 62,271 dependent children under the direct care of the church. There are 739 general hospitals treating 4,567,934 patients annually, 110 special hospitals and sanatoria treating 54,997 annually, 367 schools for nurses, 254 homes for the aged with 22,332 inmates, and a total of 129 protective institutions. No official reports or statistics on the cost of maintenance of all this work are ever announced by the hierarchy, but it is certainly high in the millions annually.

The members of the hierarchy of the United States are also members of the National Catholic Welfare Conference, a clearinghouse of information on the activities of Catholic men and women, which works to make the teachings of the church more effective. This is not a council or a legislative body so the resolutions of the bishops in its meetings do not have the force of law. It merely facilitates discussion of all policies affecting the interests and activities of the church, and unifies, co-ordinates, and organizes the work in social welfare, education, immigrant aid, civic education, and other activities. Every bishop in the United States and its territories and possessions has a voice in the conference; it is governed by an administrative board of ten bishops elected by the hierarchy. Eight departments function under this board: executive, education, press, social action, legal, Catholic action study, youth, and lay organizations. In addition there are special episcopal committees, including committees on Catholic missions, confraternity of Christian doctrine, motion pictures, the propagation of the faith (foreign service), obscene literature, the North American college, seminaries, relief and war emergencies, the pope's peace points, and for refugees. This board is one of the most important Roman Catholic bodies in the nation.

Salvation Army

WILLIAM BOOTH, an ordained minister in the Methodist New Connection Body in England, left the pulpit of that church in 1865 to preach on the street corners of the worst slum area in his country, London's East End. He planned to make his work supplementary to that of the churches; but when the churches refused to accept his converts into their membership, Booth organized his work under the name of Christian Mission; he changed the name to the Salvation Army in 1878.

Being a Methodist the founder organized his movement at first along lines of Methodist polity with annual conferences at which reports were made and programs arranged. The nature of his work, however, demanded quick decisions and actions; to meet these emergencies an organization along military lines was perfected with Booth as "general." "Articles of War" were drawn up; converts became recruits and later cadets; following a training period cadets became lieutenants, captains, majors, and so forth. Mission halls became "citadels." Early prayer meetings became "knee drills." This was "the first international army with its heart to God and its hand to man." It rapidly became international, spreading over England, Scotland, Wales, and Ireland and reaching the United States in 1880. Today Army units are found in ninety-seven countries and territories, Evangeline Booth, the daughter of the founder, became commander of the Army in the United States in 1904.

The unit of the Army is the corps, of which there may be several in one city. Each corps is commanded by an officer whose rank ranges from lieutenant to brigadier and who is responsible to divisional headquarters. A division consists of a number of corps and is commanded by a divisional commander. Divisions are grouped into four territories—eastern, southern, central, and western—with headquarters in New York, Atlanta, Chicago, and San Francisco. Territorial work is in the charge of territorial commanders, who are co-ordinated through the national secretary at national headquarters in New York City. Each territorial headquarters is divided into departments to carry on the various phases of Army work. The national commander is chief administrative officer and official spokesman and president of the Salvation Army Corporation established under the laws of New York; there are also local corporations in fourteen other states. Property and revenues are in the custody of a board of trustees, and citizens' advisory boards assist in establishing sympathetic relations with the public.

Recruits in the corps are required to sign the Articles of War and to give free time to Army work; officers give full time. Not all Army personnel, however, are obtained through recruiting among the underprivileged or needy; some are the sons and daughters of Army officers, and many are college graduates, registered nurses and physicians, skilled and highly trained social workers, and so forth. If officership is desired, the candidate becomes a cadet, attends a training school or Army college for an intensive one-year course, and graduates a probationary lieutenant or captain. He is eligible thereafter for the ranks of senior captain, major, senior major, brigadier, lieutenant-colonel, colonel, lieutenant-commissioner, and commissioner.

The deepest motivation of all Salvation Army service is found in its religious faith, and its fundamental doctrines are stated in its Foundation Deed of 1878 in eleven cardinal affirmations. These statements document the Army's recognition of the Bible as the only rule of Christian faith and practice; one God, who is the creator and Father of all mankind; the Trinity of Father, Son, and Holy Ghost; Jesus Christ as Son of God and Son of man; sin as the great destroyer of man's soul and society; salvation as God's remedy for man's sin and man's ultimate and eternal hope made available through Christ; sanctification as the individual's present and maturing experience of a life set apart for the holy purposes of the kingdom of God; and an eternal destiny that may triumph over sin and death. The Army is evangelical before it is anything else.

Street preaching, inaugurated by the founder, is still warp and woof of the Army fabric; it is the first duty of every officer candidate and cadet. Open-air meetings are held regularly in nearly every city and town in the United States; often members march from the street corner to the accompaniment of a band—music is most important in all Army training and worship—to corps headquarters or a rented hall, where the service is continued. Proceeding on General Booth's belief that a hungry man must be fed "before his hunger can be turned Godward," the Army serves millions of meals a year. In addition to this the Army lends a helping hand to the homeless, the sick and unemployed and unemployable (in India, the East Indies, and the Celebes thousands of lepers are treated daily in Army hospitals), unmarried mothers, criminals in prison and released from prison, children, and the aged. Its primary object of the spiritual regeneration of mankind is buttressed by the most intelligent and widespread social welfare program in Christendom.

For the year ending with September 30, 1949, the Salvation Army in the United States reported 215,094 members in 1,381 corps or institutions. There were 1,378 corps and outposts, 5,084 officers and cadets, 37,511 local officers, 1,739,656 indoor and outdoor meetings held, and 58,134 junior and senior converts. There were 116 men's and women's hotels and lodges supplying 1,351,515 lodgings and serving 407,110 meals; 105 men's social service centers supplied 1,521,712 lodgings and served 5,093,218 meals; 34 maternity homes admitted 10,219 women and children; 10 general hospitals admitted 14,666 and gave a day's care to 113,011; 8 children's homes supplied 181,259 beds and served 602,660 meals; 13 Evangeline residences reported 1,021,088 room occupancies; 13 settlements and nurseries supplied lodgings for 126,510 and served 351,748 meals beside carrying on their regular settlement and nursery programs. The Army is one of the nation's largest operators of summer camps for the needy with 58 camps and an attendance for 1949 of 45,735. The Missing Persons Bureau processed 5,521 inquiries and found 1,845 missing persons. The prison work, one of the most dramatic and effective services of all, reported 17,012 hours spent in visitation, 10,798 prisoners assisted on discharge, and 1,819 prisoners paroled to the Army. Medical work separate from that of hospitals was conducted in 4 clinics and 2 dispensaries; dental cases totaled 7,921; there were 41,522 free laboratory examinations and a total of 20,525 patients treated. Four detention homes provided lodgings for 9,738 and served 28,747 meals. Some 2,300 rural units were at work.

In addition to this peacetime war on human sin and suffering the Army is notable for its courageous work in two world wars. Approximately 300 men and women officers served in World War I, and Commander Evangeline Booth was decorated with the Distinguished Service Cross by President Wilson in recognition of the Army's contributions; in World War II the Army served on 26 battle fronts with more than 3,000 war service units, rendering more than 500,000,000 individual services to the men and women of the armed forces. This service is given without respect to color, creed, or condition; it is financed through voluntary subscriptions, participation in community chests, and an annual maintenance appeal.

SCANDINAVIAN EVANGELICAL BODIES

There are two churches of Swedish, Norwegian, and Danish membership in this group: the Evangelical Mission Covenant Church of America and the Evangelical Free Church of America. Both had their beginnings in the state churches of their mother countries.

Evangelical Mission Covenant Church of America

KNOWN FOR many years as the Swedish Evangelical Mission Covenant Church of America, this is a transplantation of a free church movement in the Swedish state church to the United States in 1885. The present name was adopted in 1937. Members are deeply evangelical, accepting Lutheran teaching and faith in general but without any definite statement of faith binding upon all the churches. Polity is congregational, but the Covenant as a denomination ordains its ministers. Local churches send delegates to an annual conference and are grouped in twelve districts for work and fellowship.

Missionaries of this church are found in China and the Belgian Congo, and among the Indians and Eskimos of Alaska. North Park College and Theological Seminary is located at Chicago, and Minehaha Academy at Minneapolis. There are also 2 homes for destitute children, 2 sailors' homes, 2 hospitals, 7 homes for the aged; and there were 51,009 members in 475 churches in 1949.

Evangelical Free Church of America

THIS CHURCH is composed of two Scandinavian bodies which united in 1950: the Free Church of America and the Evangelical Free Church Association. The Evangelical Free Church of America began with a number of small congregations which refused to join the merger in 1885 of the old Ansgarii Synod and the Mission Synod into the Swedish Evangelical Mission Covenant of America. It was a body of self-governing congregations, each free to establish its own doctrine; the several churches elected delegates to an annual conference, purely advisory in character. A society of ministers and missionaries was organized in 1894 to guide the denomination generally in doctrine and practice. This church brought 12,000 members and 200 churches into the 1950 merger.

The Evangelical Free Church Association was but slightly smaller at the time of the union with 10,033 members and 51 churches. It was a Norwegian and Danish body which had grown out of the free church movement in Norway in the nineteenth century. The increase of immigration from Scandinavia resulted in the organization of a number of Norwegian and Danish Free churches that were eventually brought together in eastern and western districts that were united in Chicago in 1910, still maintaining their identity in their work. The churches in these two districts elected delegates to an annual conference which was the chief administrative body. Missionary work was conducted by four district associations, and foreign missions were supported in South Africa, South America, China, India, and Japan through the Scandinavian Missionary Alliance. This church brought two orphanages and one theological school into the merger. No noticeable changes in either polity or doctrine—still left to the individual congregations—have been brought about by the union, which gives the new Evangelical Free Church in America a total strength of 22,033 members and 251 churches.

Schwenkfelders

CASPAR SCHWENKFELD VON OSSIG (1489-1561), a Silesian nobleman, was baptized and reared in the Roman Catholic Church and experienced a spiritual awakening in 1519. Disappointed in his hope to help reform the Roman Catholic Church from within, he played a leading role in the Reformation, advocating wider reading of the Bible by laymen, urging the need of the power, guidance, and leading of the Holy Spirit, and preaching that the elements of bread and wine in the Holy Communion were symbols that did not represent the body or change into the body and blood of Christ. This interpretation of the Lord's Supper, together with his insistence upon complete separation of church and state, led him into disagreement with Luther and Lutheranism. He founded a number of spiritual brotherhoods, whose members in time came to be known as Schwenkfelders.

The body has disappeared in Europe but persists in the United States in a church of about 2,300 members in 6 local congregations. A large body of them arrived in this country in 1734; their first formal society of Schwenkfelders was organized in 1782. Their 6 churches today are all located within a radius of fifty miles of Philadelphia.

All theology, they hold, should be constructed from the Bible alone, but the Scriptures are considered as dead without the indwelling Word. Christ's divinity was progressive, his human nature becoming more and more divine without "losing its identity"; faith, regeneration, and subsequent spiritual growth work a change in human nature, but justification by faith is not to be permitted to obscure the positive regeneration imparted by Christ.

Their theology is thus Christocentric. In polity they are congregational, each church being incorporated, self-sustaining, and conducting its affairs through its district or local conference. A general conference composed of all the local churches meets twice a year to develop the larger program of education and missions. Church worship is free and nonliturgical.

The general conference sponsored the founding of the Perkiomen School for boys at Pennsburg, Pennsylvania, in 1892, and a majority of the board of trustees of that school are still members of Schwenkfelder churches. Two missionaries are supported in the Taiku Mission in Shansi, China. Since 1884 members have been engaged in preparing a critical edition of the works of their founder; fifteen volumes have been published to date.

Social Brethren

THIS IS a body organized in Illinois in 1867 by a small group of persons from various denominations, holding orthodox doctrines but disagreeing in certain matters of interpretation of Scripture, discipline, and decorum. They reported 521 members and 14 churches in 1940. Their confession of faith emphasizes the following points:

The infinite power, wisdom, and goodness of God, in whom are united three persons of one substance, power, and eternity, the Father, Son and Holy Ghost;

The authority and consistency of the Scriptures, comprising the Old and New Testaments;

Regeneration and sanctification through Jesus Christ;

Eternal salvation of the redeemed and eternal punishment for apostasy;

The ordinances of baptism and the Lord's Supper are only for true believers;

Baptism may be by sprinkling, pouring, or immersion;

Lay members of the church should have the right of suffrage and full speech, but ministers are called to preach the Gospel and not for political speeches.

Polity is a fusion of Baptist and Methodist structures and customs, and the work of the Social Brethren, aside from its efforts in mutual aid and assistance, is largely evangelical.

SPIRITUALISTS

Spiritualism is as old as man's longing to communicate with his dead; as an organized religion it began at Hydesville, New York, in 1848 with the Fox sisters. The sisters heard repeated knockings or rappings in their cottage at Hydesville and later in Rochester, and believing them to be signals from the spirit world worked out a code of communication. Their séances became famous, and interest in Spiritualism spread rapidly. However, in 1847 Andrew Jackson Davis had published a book entitled *Nature's Divine Revelations*, which stated the fundamentals and philosophy of Spiritualism; the séances of the Fox sisters only substantiated the writings of Davis.

The first Spiritualist organizations were small, scattered, and without legal sanction. Little groups gathered about the mediums, and in cities the congregations soon became large. The first attempt at national organization did not come until 1863 and lasted for only nine years. In 1893 the National Spiritualist Association was organized at Chicago; it is today the outstanding Spiritualist body in the United States. Small independent congregations are still scattered across the country, independent in polity and worship and unwilling to grant any real authority to a centralized government, but many state and sectional Spiritualist groups function under the general direction of the president and board of the N.S.A.

The movement is known popularly for its mediums, séances, clairvoyance, and so forth; Ouija boards, table tipping, and spirit rappings and conversations have attracted thousands anxious to communicate with their departed ones. But Spiritualism has genuine religious bases and connotations as well as psychic experiments. The movement has become a church, comforting and strengthening and healing thousands within and without its membership. The N.S.A. offers a Declaration of Principles, which reads as follows:

1. We believe in Infinite Intelligence.
2. We believe that the phenomena of Nature, both physical and spiritual, are the expression of Infinite Intelligence.
3. We affirm that a correct understanding of such expression and living in accordance therewith constitute true religion.
4. We affirm that the existence and personal identity of the individual continue after the change called death.
5. We affirm that communication with the so-called dead is a fact scientifically proven by the phenomena of Spiritualism.
6. We believe that the highest morality is contained in the Golden Rule. . . .
7. We affirm the moral responsibility of the individual, and that he makes his own happiness or unhappiness as he obeys or disobeys Nature's physical and spiritual laws.
8. We affirm that the doorway to reformation is never closed against any human soul, here or hereafter.

The teaching of God as love is central in Spiritualism; the Lord's Prayer is used in both public worship and private séance. Christ is recognized as a medium; the Annunciation was a message from the spirit world, the Transfiguration was an opportunity for the materialization of the spirits of Moses and Elias, and the Resurrection was evidence that all men live on in the spirit world. Man's soul is often called the "astral body"; at death the material body dissolves and the soul as the body of the spirit progresses through a series of spheres to a higher and higher existence. There are two lower spheres in which those of lower character or sinful record are purified and made ready for the higher existences. Most of the departed are to be found in the third sphere, called the Summer Land; above this are the Philosopher's Sphere, the Advanced Contemplative and Intellectual Sphere, the Love Sphere, and the Christ Sphere. All reach the higher spheres eventually; Spiritualists do not believe in heaven or hell, or that any are ever lost.

Services and séances are held in private homes, rented halls, or churches. Most Spiritualist churches have regular services with prayer, singing, music, selections read from the *Spiritualists' Manual*, a sermon or lecture, and spirit messages from the departed. The churches and ministers are supported by freewill offerings; mediums and ministers also gain support from classes and séances in which fees are charged. The attendance at church services is invariably small; one authority estimates the average congregation at 20 to 25. But membership cannot be estimated on the basis of church attendance; for every enrolled member there are at least fifteen who are not enrolled but interested in the movement and attending its services. Over 180,000 Spiritualists were reported as members of their churches by the *Christian Herald* church membership survey of 1950, but this is not comprehensive or inclusive of all using the services of the church.

Administration and government differ slightly in the various groups, but most of them have district or state associations and an annual general convention. All have mediums, and most have ministers in charge of the congregations; requirements for licensing and ordination also differ, but a determined effort is being made to raise the standards in education and character in the larger groups.

International General Assembly of Spiritualists

ORGANIZED AT Buffalo, New York, in 1936, this is a co-operative body endeavoring to establish cohesion and unity in the Spiritualist movement. It had an inclusive membership of 157,000 and 254 churches in 1949 and was organized originally as an auxiliary of the General Assembly of Spiritualists in New York to care for churches outside that state. Its present purpose is to charter new Spiritualist churches; headquarters are located at Portsmouth, Virginia.

National Spiritualist Association, Inc.

WITH 8,942 members in 265 churches, this association is influential far beyond its immediate membership, furnishing literature for the whole movement and advocating higher qualifications in mediums and ministers. It has a seminary, the Morris Pratt Institute, for the training of its ministers; a great deal of the work of the seminary is by correspondence. A national director of education directs a training course for members, licentiates, lecturers, mediums, and ordained ministers. The N.S.A. holds an annual legislative convention which elects officers triennially. This is the orthodox body of American Spiritualism.

National Christian Spiritual Alliance

THIS BODY was founded in 1913 by the Rev. G. Tabor Thompson and has its headquarters at Lake Pleasant, Massachusetts, where it was incorporated. Holding general Spiritualist doctrines, the alliance stresses subnormal and impersonal manifestations and intercommunication with the spirit world. Salvation is held to be through the development of personal character; "one reaps as he sows, yet . . . all things are working together for good and evolution obtains perpetually in all persons."

The local churches of the alliance elect their own officers and choose their own ministers; a three-day convention is held annually with delegates from all the churches electing their national officers—president, secretary, and treasurer. An official board of directors directs the missionary work of ministers and certified mediums; college training is not required of a minister, but he must have passed a course of study arranged by the alliance. Mediums may baptize, but only ministers may officiate at the ceremonies of ordination and marriage. The work of the alliance is mainly in benevolent, literary, educational, music, and scientific activities. There are 5,487 members and 267 churches.

Progressive Spiritual Church

THIS CHURCH was founded in Chicago in 1907 by the Rev. G. V. Cordingley and has its own confession of faith. It was organized "to lift spiritualism above mere psychic research, to establish it upon a sound, religious basis, and to secure its recognition among other Christian denominations." The confession of faith states the members' belief in the communion of spirits, in man's restoration to everlasting life, in God as an absolute divine Spirit, and in angels who as departed spirits communicate with the living by means of mediums. Jesus Christ is recognized as a medium controlled by the spirit of Elias and the spirit of Moses and the spirit of John the Bap-

tist. "The fingers of the hand of medium under control can write an deliver divine messages and visions. . . . A divine understanding of dreams ca be had. . . . The stars divine the path way of life of every character." Th Bible is acknowledged as the inspire Word of God, a guide to the spirit lif as well as to the phases and phenomen of Spiritualism—prophecies, spiritua palmistry, spiritual automatic writing spiritual materialization, spiritual trumpe speaking, spiritual healing by magnetize articles, and so forth. Heaven and he are believed to be conditions, not loca tions.

Four sacraments—baptism, marriage spiritual communion, and funerals—are observed. Ministers, who may be o either sex, must pass a course of instruc tion in the church seminary. Churcl officers include a supreme pastor, secre tary, treasurer, and board of trustees Local churches elect their own officer but are subject to the constitution and bylaws of the mother church. The worl of the church is largely benevolent social, literary, scientific, and psychical. There are 11,347 members and 21 churches.

Triumph the Church and Kingdom of God in Christ

FOUNDED IN 1902 by Elder E. D. Smith, this church teaches the cleansing from sin in all "justified" believers through the shed blood of Christ; entire sanctification as an instantaneous, definite work of second grace obtained through the faith of the consecrated believer; the second coming of Christ; and baptism by fire as a scriptural experience also obtainable by faith. General overseers are the chief

officers of the body; they meet quadrennially in what is called the International Religious Congress; otherwise the work of the church is carried on by state, county, and local officers.

A rather phenomenal growth is reported from two churches, both in Georgia, with 69 members in 1936 to 15,500 members and 300 churches in 1947.

Unitarians

UNITARIAN thought was prevalent in the early Christian centuries before the concept of Trinitarianism was developed; but Unitarianism as we know it today began with the Protestant Reformation

among Arminians and Socinians. The movement spread from independent thinkers and Anabaptists in Switzerland, Hungary, Transylvania, Holland, Poland, and Italy to England, where it

UNITARIANS

ound champions in such leaders as New-on, Locke, and Milton. No attempt was made to organize the movement in England until late in the eighteenth century.

American Unitarianism, however, developed independently out of New England Congregationalism. Members of the liberal wing of the Congregational Church in eastern Massachusetts asked only to join a covenant in that church and never to subscribe to a creed, were branded as Unitarian while still within the Congregational membership. The first organized church to turn to Unitarianism as a body, however, was not a Congregational church but the Episcopal King's Chapel in Boston in 1796.

In the second half of the eighteenth century many of the older and larger congregational churches moving toward Unitarianism were known as Liberal Christian churches or groups; the name Unitarian was finally accepted in 1815.

The basis for the split with Congregationalism came in 1805 with the appointment of Henry Ware as professor of theology at Harvard; it was made certain when William Ellery Channing of Boston preached his famous Baltimore sermon in 1819 and in it outlined the Unitarian view. In that sermon the liberals had their platform. A missionary and publication society known as the American Unitarian Association was formed in 1825, and with it began an activity looking forward to the formation of a separate denomination. A national conference was established in 1865.

Channing defined the true Church in these words:

By his Church our Saviour does not mean a party bearing the name of a human leader, distinguished by a form or an opinion, and on the ground of this distinction, denying the name and character of Christians to all but themselves. . . . These are the church—men made better, made holy, virtuous by his religion—men who, hoping in his promises, keep his commands.

The Unitarians proceeded from this to formulate their position. They have no creed; the constitution of the general conference says that "these churches accept the religion of Jesus, holding in accordance with his teaching that practical religion is summed up in the love to God and love to man." Cardinal points in their belief are those of the oneness of God (as opposed to Trinitarianism), the strict humanity of Jesus, the perfectibility of human character, the natural character of the Bible, and the ultimate salvation of all souls. They deny the doctrine of total depravity and believe in the divine nature of man; Trinitarianism is rejected as unscriptural, and they reject the deity of Christ but say they believe in his divinity as all men are divine as the sons of God. Salvation is by character; character is not an end but a means, and salvation lies in being saved from sin here, not from punishment hereafter. Hell and eternal punishment are held to be inconsistent with the concept of a loving and all-powerful God; to admit that God would permit eternal punishment would be to admit that he was powerless to save. Heaven is a state, not a place. Unitarians do not accept the doctrine of the infallibility of the Bible; they believe that the Bible is not a book but a library of books, all of which cannot be accepted as of equal value and importance. The widest possible freedom is encouraged in personal interpretation and belief; even students and teachers in Unitarian theological schools are not required to subscribe to any dogmatic teaching or doctrinal tests. Emphasis upon individual freedom of belief, democratic principles, and hospitality to the methods of science in seeking truth have characterized the Unitarian movement in recent years.

Organization is congregational; independent local churches are grouped in local, county, district, state, and regional conferences, and are united in the American Unitarian Association and in an international association for the purposes of fellowship, counsel, and promotion of mutual interests. The general conference in the United States meets biannually. The American Unitarian Association meets annually to elect a board of directors composed of nine regional vice-presidents and twenty-four others; it also elects a president as chief executive officer for four years and a moderator for two years. Various committees and commissions administer the united work of the denomination. There are six regional offices, including the United Conference of Icelandic Churches. Other organizations include the General Alliance of Unitarian Women, the Unitarian Sunday School Society, American Unitarian Youth, the Layman's League,

the Unitarian Temperance Society, and the Unitarian Fellowship for Social Justice. The Beacon Press as the able publishing house of the body publishes the work of religious scholars on a nondenominational basis.

There are 4 denominational colleges and seminaries and 2 preparatory schools. Foreign work is conducted through the International Association for Liberal Christianity and Religious Freedom with headquarters at Utrecht, Holland; the International Association has correspondents in 22 countries. There are 78,100 adult members in the United States and 370 churches.

UNITED BRETHREN

*T*he original and parent body of United Brethren in the United States was the Church of the United Brethren in Christ, which united with the Evangelical Church in 1946 (see Evangelical United Brethren Church, pp. 84-85). Two other Brethren groups, both of which separated from the United Brethren in Christ, are still active as independent churches; they are the Church of the United Brethren (Old Constitution) and the United Christian Church.

United Christian Church

THIS CHURCH separated in 1864 "on account of conscientious convictions" dealing chiefly with questions concerning infant baptism, the bearing of arms in war, the admission of members of secret societies to the membership of the church, and the wearing of fashionable clothes. The Rev. George W. Hoffman was one of its most influential leaders, and for years members were known as Hoffmanites.

Hesitant to create another denomination, this church had no formal organization until 1877; a confession of faith was approved that year, and the present name was adopted a year later. The confession

of faith, constitution, and discipline now in use were approved in 1920.

Orthodox and evangelistic, doctrine in this church emphasizes the inspiration of Scriptures, the Trinity, total depravity, justification, regeneration, entire sanctification, and strict Sabbath observance. Baptism (the mode of which is optional), the Lord's Supper, and foot washing are observed as ordinances. Polity is Methodistic with district, annual, and general conferences and an itinerant ministry; local preachers vote in the annual conference. Summer camp meetings and other evangelistic gatherings are popular; foreign missionaries of the church are stationed in Africa and India. There are 676 members and 14 churches.

Church of the United Brethren in Christ (Old Constitution)

THIS CHURCH was organized in 1889 in protest against changes in the constitution of the United Brethren in Christ; a minority in the general convention of that year declared the old constitution to be still in force and withdrew. A long period of dissension and lawsuits followed, but the two bodies work in harmony today.

UNIVERSALISTS

The Trinity and the deity, humanity, and atonement of Christ are important in Old Constitution doctrine; scriptural living is required of members, who are forbidden the use of alcoholic drinks, membership in secret societies, and participation in war. Baptism and the Lord's Supper are two ordinances of the church.

Quarterly, annual, and general conferences are held; the general conference meets quadrennially and is composed only of ministers, district superintendents (presiding elders), and bishops. Both men and women are eligible to the ministry and are ordained only once, as elders. Missionary societies administer a work in evangelism and church aid in the United States, and on foreign missionary fields in Sierra Leone, West Africa, and Canton, China. A college is located at Huntington, Indiana, and a school at Canton. There were 18,167 members in 316 churches in 1949.

United Holy Church of America

ORIGINATING AT Method, North Carolina, in a meeting held by the Rev. Isaac Cheshier in 1886, this body was successively called the Holy Church of North Carolina, the Holy Church of North Carolina and Virginia, and finally in 1918 the United Holy Church of America. Its purpose officially is to establish and maintain "holy convocations, assemblies, conventions, conferences, public worship, missionary and school work, orphan homes, manual and trades training, ... also religious resorts, with permanent and temporary dwellings."

Articles of faith contain statements of belief in the Trinity; the record of God's revelation of himself in the Bible, redemption through Christ's life, death, resurrection, and ascension; justification; instantaneous sanctification following justification; the baptism of the Holy Spirit; divine healing; Sabbath observance; and the ultimate reign of Christ over the earth. Church officers include a president, vice-president, secretary, corresponding secretary, treasurer, and auditor. A nine-member board of trustees manages the general enterprises of the church. About 25,000 members and 275 churches were reported in 1947.

Universalists

IN COMMON with the Unitarians, Universalists find evidence of their thinking and theology in the early Christians; Clement and Origen in the second- and third-century schools of Alexandria taught the universal salvation of man under a God of love and justice. As a church, however, their origin is American, stemming from the work of George de Benneville, John Murray, and Hosea Ballou.

De Benneville, the English-educated son of French Huguenot émigrés, studied medicine in Germany, came under the influence of the early Brethren and Friends of God, arrived in Olney, Pennsylvania, in 1741, and preached his gospel of universal salvation as he practiced medicine among the settlers and the Indians. Murray, a Wesleyan evangelist excommunicated from the Whitefield Tabernacle in London for advocating Universalist teachings, arrived in New Jersey in 1770, served as a chaplain in Washington's army, and preached up and down the Atlantic coast. His doctrine was an ameliorated Calvinism, advocating the salvation of all men through Christ; he organized a parish at Gloucester, Massachusetts, in 1779, which became the mother church of the denomination.

The scattered and poorly organized Universalists met at Philadelphia in 1790 to draft a declaration of faith and plan of church government. Governmental structure was to be strictly congregational; the doctrinal sections of the declaration stated belief in the Scriptures as containing "a revelation of the perfections and the will of God and the rule of faith and practice," faith in one God and in Christ as a mediator who had redeemed all men by his blood and in the Holy Ghost and the obligation of the moral law as the rule of life. War was condemned; and statements approving the settlement of disputes outside the courts, the abolition of slavery and the education of the Negro, testimony by affirmation rather than by oath, and free public education were approved. The Philadelphia Declaration was adopted by a group of New England Universalists in 1794; at the same meeting Hosea Ballou, a schoolteacher and itinerant preacher in Vermont, was ordained to the Universalist ministry.

Ballou gave the Universalists their first consistent and complete philosophy in his book *Treatise on Atonement.* He rejected the theories of total depravity, endless punishment in Hell, the Trinity, and the miracles. Man was potentially good, said Ballou, and capable of perfectibility; God, being a God of infinite love, recognized man's heavenly nature and extraction and loved him as his own offspring. The meaning of atonement he found not in bloody sacrifice to appease the divine wrath but in the heroic sacrifice of Jesus, who was not God but a Son of the eternal and universal God revealing the love of God and anxious to win all men to that love. It was an open Unitarian-Universalist statement of theology which deeply influenced American Universalism. Ballou made another lasting contribution with his insistence that the base of Christian fellowship lay not in creeds but in mutual good faith and good will; from this principle came two consistent aspects of modern Universalism: a broad, liberal latitudinarianism in theology and a universal concern for all people.

Early statements of faith reflected the conflict with Trinitarian thought while seeking a unitarian or universal expression; a statement of the five principles of Universalism, summing up and simplifying their thought, was drawn up in 1899 as follows:

We believe in: the Universal Fatherhood of God; the spiritual authority and leadership of His Son, Jesus Christ; the trustworthiness of the Bible as containing a revelation from God; the certainty of just retribution for sin; the final harmony of all souls with God.

The final statement of faith, adopted at the general convention at Washington, D. C., in 1935 and still acknowledged as the official covenant of the church, reads as follows:

The bond of fellowship in this convention shall be a common purpose to do the will of God as Jesus revealed it, and to co-operate in establishing the Kingdom for which he lived and died.

To that end we avow our faith in God as eternal and all-conquering love, in the spiritual leadership of Jesus, in the supreme worth of every human personality, in the authority of truth known or to be known, and in the power of men of good will and sacrificial spirit to overcome all evil and progressively establish the Kingdom of God.

Neither this nor any other statement shall be imposed as a creedal test, provided that the faith thus indicated be professed.

The organization of the church is described as "congregational in principle and democratic in operation." The basic unit is the local church; local churches are grouped in state conventions, and the entire fellowship is under the general supervision of the national organization.

Historically marked by their interest in applying the scientific method in religion and by their efforts to apply Christian principles in the social realm, the Universalists have been in the forefront of the fight for temperance, humane treatment for prisoners and ex-prisoners, civil rights, the abolition of slavery, and in relations between labor and capital. The Universalist Service Committee today operates projects in the fields of relief for war victims, rehabilitation, and so forth. Postwar work has been done in Holland and Hungary and is currently carried on in Germany under the auspices of the International Refuge Organization and in co-operation with the Unitarian Service Committee.

The National Association of Universalist Women maintains two summer camps for diabetic children, three homes for the aged, a kindergarten in Tokyo, and a rural-life service project in China;

the church supports a center for Negro children at Suffolk, Virginia.

Universalists have founded four colleges—Tufts, St. Lawrence, Lombard, and Buchtel; there are theological seminaries at Tufts and St. Lawrence. Seven centers for summer training of laymen and laywomen are supported. There were 62,927 members and 426 churches in 1949.

Vedanta Society

THE MEMBERS of the Vedanta Society are followers of the Vedas, the scriptures of the Indo-Aryans, taking their name from an old Indian philosophy which claims to explain the nature and end of all wisdom, to harmonize the findings of modern science, and to offer a scientific and philosophical basis for religion. It was first expounded in America by Swami Vivekananda at the Parliament of Religion at the World's Fair in

1893. The society was formally organized by Swami Abhedananda in 1898 and now has branch societies or centers in several American cities.

Six trustees and three other officials constitute an executive board for the society. Swamis in the movement receive no salaries and give much of their instruction by correspondence from headquarters in New York. There are 1,021 members in 11 societies.

Volunteers of America

THE Volunteers of America is a religious and philanthropic organization founded in 1896 by the late Ballington and Maude Booth and incorporated in the same year under the laws of the state of New York; about 23,500 members were reported in 1949, but this figure hardly tells the whole story of services rendered to hundreds of thousands of people in the principal cities of the United States.

Religious services are offered in missions, Volunteer churches, Sunday schools, Christian companionship leagues, prisons, and on the streets; the organization has its own rituals for baptism, the Lord's Supper, and marriage. Doctrine is of course evangelical, with strong emphasis upon the the saving grace of God, the Trinity, the atonement of Christ, regeneration through the Holy Spirit, the necessity of repentance and conversion, immortality, and future rewards and punishment. The Volunteers reported a total of 1,701 known conversions in 1949.

In philanthropic work there are departments of family welfare, salvage, health camps, day nurseries, hospices for working girls, maternity homes, homes for mothers and children, adoptive placements, clubs and homes for the aged, rehabilitation workshops, family counseling centers, men's industrial homes, and boys' and girls' clubs. There is an excellent prison department, assisting discharged and paroled prisoners, men and women in prison and their families; 300,-000 prisoners are enrolled in the Volunteer Prison League.

Operation of the Volunteers is based on a semimilitary plan modeled on that of the United States Army. All officers bear military titles and wear uniforms. The chief governing body is called the Grand Field Council and is composed of those officers bearing the rank of major or above. There is a board of nine members known as the National Executive Board, which functions when the Grand Field Council is not in session.

The incorporation has a directorate of nine who are responsible financial officers and who act as trustees and custodians of all property. Military regulations do not apply in the selection of these top officers; they are chosen by democratic election. The commander-in-chief is elected for five years and is also president of the corporate body. There are six administrative areas known as eastern, central, southern, Midwestern, Northwestern, and western areas; national officers and staff are located in New York City.

The Volunteer statistical report for 1949 showed a total of more than 2,000,-000 people receiving material assistance through its various departments, exclusive of religious services; 2,728,867 meals and 500,124 lodgings were furnished. 2,906 children were under the care of the organization; 8,756 elderly persons participated in the Sunset Club program; 21,488 interviews were held in prisons; 143,336 prisoners attended Volunteer religious services; and 1,202 released prisoners were paroled in the custody of the Volunteers; 14,958 persons were employed in the industrial department. Over 10,000,000 articles of clothing, furniture, and so forth, were distributed free or at nominal cost, and positions were found for 14,496 unemployed. The organization is maintained through the voluntary contributions of the public.

CHURCH MEMBERSHIP IN THE
UNITED STATES

*M*embership seems to have various connotations and to have different bases of reckoning among the churches. It should be kept clear that some—the Roman Catholic, Eastern Orthodox, and Protestant Episcopal churches, for instance—report as members all who have been baptized while most Protestant churches report only those thirteen years of age or over.

Most of these statistics are from the *Christian Herald's* annual "Report on Church Membership in the U.S.A.," published in the July, 1950, issue and reproduced here with the permission of the editors.

NAME	MEMBERSHIP	NO. OF CHURCHES
ADVENTISTS		
Seventh-Day Adventists	229,945	2,671
Advent Christian Church	31,413	470
Primitive Advent Christian Church	416	15
Church of God (Abrahamic Faith)	....	..
Church of God (Oregon, Ill.)	5,295	79
Life and Advent Union	207	4
African Orthodox Church	5,200	32
African Orthodox Church of New York	....	..
Amana Society	794	7
American Ethical Union	3,500	8
American Rescue Workers	800	..
Apostolic Overcoming Holy Church of God	8,000	200
Armenian Orthodox Church in America	18,787	..
Assemblies of God, General Council	275,000	5,950
Assyrian Jacobite Apostolic Church	1,400	4
Bahá'is	5,232	137
BAPTISTS		
American Baptist Convention	1,583,360	7,124
Southern Baptist Convention	6,761,265	27,285
Negro Baptists	....	..
National Baptist Convention of the U.S.A., Inc.	4,385,206	24,953
National Baptist Convention of America	2,594,521	10,596
American Baptist Association	313,817	2,460
Christian Unity Baptist Association	497	11
Colored Primitive Baptists	43,897	1,009
Duck River and Kindred Associations of Baptists	9,562	91
Freewill Baptists	255,127	3,467
General Baptists	39,600	580
General Six-Principle Baptists	269	3
Independent Baptist Church of America	129	8

185

NAME	MEMBERSHIP	NO. OF CHURCHES
National Baptist Evangelical Life and Soul-Saving Assembly of the U.S.A.	56,934	235
Primitive Baptists	69,157	1,726
Regular Baptists	17,186	266
General Association of Regular Baptist Churches (North)	85,000	521
Separate Baptists	6,490	90
Seventh-Day Baptists	6,283	63
Seventh-Day Baptists (German, 1728)	125	2
Two-Seed-in-the-Spirit Predestinarian Baptists	201	16
United American Freewill Baptist Church (Colored)	75,000	350
United Baptists	27,000	277

BRETHREN (Dunkers)

Church of the Brethren (Conservative Dunkers)	185,088	1,025
Brethren Church (Progressive Dunkers) ....about	33,500	..
Old German Baptist Brethren (Old Order Dunkers)	3,254	53
Church of God (New Dunkers)	526	8
Plymouth Brethren	25,806	664
River Brethren	7,500	..
Brethren in Christ	5,319	98
Old Order or Yorker Brethren	291	7
United Zion's Children	1,240	24
Buddhist Churches of America	70,000	46
Catholic Apostolic Church	2,577	7
Christadelphians	2,755	109
Christian and Missionary Alliance	45,348	879
Christian Nation Church	112	5
Christian Union	15,400	220
Christ's Sanctified Holy Church (Colored)	884	27
Church of Christ (Holiness), U.S.A.	7,685	170
Church of Christ, Scientist	(See Note)	2,250

CHURCH OF GOD

Church of God (Anderson, Ind.)	105,022	1,893
(Original) Church of God	5,000	58
Church of God (Stanberry, Mo.)	45,000	1,250
Church of God and Saints of Christ	34,610	193
Church of God in Christ	340,530	3,000
Church of the East and of the Assyrians	3,000	10
Church of the Nazarene	220,042	3,370
Churches of Christ	814,200	11,760
Churches of Christ in Christian Union in Ohio	4,797	142
Churches of God, Holiness	5,872	35
Churches of God in North America (General Eldership)	33,831	373

CHURCHES OF THE LIVING GOD

Church of the Living God (Christian Workers for Fellowship)	120	6
Church of the Living God, the Pillar and Ground of the Truth	3,185	85

CHURCH MEMBERSHIP

NAME	MEMBERSHIP	No. of Churches
CHURCHES OF THE NEW JERUSALEM		
General Convention of the New Jerusalem in the U.S.A.	4,621	52
General Church of the New Jerusalem	1,496	10
Congregational Christian Churches	1,184,661	5,715
Congregational Holiness Church	3,399	103
Disciples of Christ	1,738,605	7,771
Divine Science College and Church	(Statistics not available)	
EASTERN ORTHODOX CHURCHES		
Albanian Orthodox Church	3,137	13
American Holy Orthodox Catholic Apostolic Eastern Church	2,000	7
Apostolic Episcopal Church		
Eastern Province	7,010	38
Western Province	876	8
Bulgarian Orthodox Church	150	1
Greek Orthodox Church (Hellenic)	300,000	286
Holy Orthodox Church in America (Eastern Catholic and Apostolic)	1,300	14
Romanian Orthodox Church	390	1
Russian Orthodox Church	300,000	300
Serbian Orthodox Church	80,000	50
Syrian Antiochian Orthodox Church	20,300	76
Ukrainian Orthodox Church of America	39,500	44
Erieside Church on the Boulevard	140	1
Evangelical Congregational Church	27,093	163
Evangelical and Reformed Church	714,583	2,784
Evangelical United Brethren Church	711,537	4,460
EVANGELISTIC ASSOCIATIONS		
Apostolic Christian (Nazarean)	1,663	31
Apostolic Christian Church of America	6,550	
Apostolic Faith Mission	2,228	17
Christian Congregation	5,272	47
Church of Daniel's Band	131	3
Church of God (Apostolic)	3,085	49
Church of God as Organized by Christ	2,192	14
Hephzibah Faith Missionary Association	700	20
Metropolitan Church Association	961	14
Missionary Bands of the World	200	6
Missionary Church Association	5,000	58
Pillar of Fire	5,100	61
Faith Tabernacle	200	1
Federated Churches	88,411	508
Fire Baptized Holiness Church of God of the Americas	6,000	300
Free Christian Zion Church of Christ	2,478	37
FRIENDS		
Society of Friends (Five Years Meeting)	68,343	472
Religious Society of Friends (General Conference)	19,016	155
Religious Society of Friends (Conservative)	1,014	11
Primitive Friends	10	1
House of David	350	1

NAME	MEMBERSHIP	NO. OF CHURCHES
Church of Illumination	5,000	7
Independent Churches	40,275	384
Independent Fundamental Churches of America	65,000	650
International Church of the Foursquare Gospel	66,611	502
Italian Christian Church of North America	23,000	196
Jehovah's Witnesses	300,000	3,056
Jewish Congregations	5,000,000	4,500
Kodesh Church of Immanuel	1,200	7

LATTER-DAY SAINTS, or Mormons

Church of Jesus Christ of Latter-Day Saints	980,347	2,066
Reorganized Church of Jesus Christ of Latter-Day Saints	144,094	641
Church of Christ (Temple Lot)	2,179	56
Church of Jesus Christ (Bickertonites)	1,600	29
Church of Jesus Christ (Cutlerites)	24	2
Church of Jesus Christ (Strangites)	123	4
Liberal Catholic Church	2,000	13
Lithuanian National Reformed Church	3,325	6

LUTHERANS

American Lutheran Conference

American Lutheran Church	714,556	2,010
Augustana Evangelical Lutheran Church	439,231	1,126
Evangelical Lutheran Church	757,352	2,720
Lutheran Free Church	54,608	339
United Evangelical Lutheran Church	46,442	180

Evangelical Synodical Conference of North America

Lutheran Church (Missouri Synod)	1,569,364	4,212
Joint Synod of Wisconsin and Other States	297,922	833
Slovak Evangelical Lutheran Church	21,000	66

Norwegian Synod of the American Evangelical Lutheran

Church	9,587	66
Negro Mission of the Synodical Conference	15,001	107
United Lutheran Church in America	1,950,569	4,150
Church of the Lutheran Brethren in America	3,088	35
Evangelical Lutheran Church in America (Eielsen Synod)	1,350	12
Finnish Apostolic Lutheran Church of America	14,511	65
Finnish Evangelical Lutheran Church (Suomi Synod)	29,001	172
Finnish Evangelical Lutheran National Church of America	6,559	65
Icelandic Evangelical Lutheran Synod of North America	1,386	16
Danish Evangelical Lutheran Church in America	19,048	80
Protestant Conference (Lutheran)	3,253	22
Independent Lutheran Congregations	7,645	17
Mayan Temple	3,312	13

MENNONITES

Mennonite Church	56,746	434
General Conference of the Mennonite Church of North America	45,200	230
Church of God in Christ (Mennonite)	3,000	30
Evangelical Mennonite Church	1,830	18
Evangelical Mennonite Brethren	1,500	10
Conservative Amish Mennonite Church	3,679	24

CHURCH MEMBERSHIP

NAME	MEMBERSHIP	NO. OF CHURCHES
Hutterian Brethren	1,255	15
Krimmer Mennonite Brethren Conference	1,408	9
United Missionary Church	10,776	..
Mennonite Brethren Church of North America	18,410	145
Mennonite Klein Gemeinde (Little Congregation)	275	2
Old Order Amish Mennonite Church	14,364	156
Old Order Mennonite Church (Wisler)	3,304	30
Reformed Mennonite Church	1,000	27
Stauffer Mennonite Church	161	2

METHODISTS

African Methodist Episcopal Church	1,066,301	7,408
African Methodist Episcopal Zion Church	520,175	2,096
African Union Methodist Protestant Church	2,504	41
Apostolic Methodist Church	31	2
Colored Methodist Episcopal Church	381,000	4,300
Congregational Methodist Church	11,187	160
Congregational Methodist Church of America, Inc.	5,857	131
Free Methodist Church of North America	49,104	1,194
Holiness Methodist Church	780	8
Independent African Methodist Episcopal Church	1,000	12
The Methodist Church	8,792,569	40,472
New Congregational Methodist Church	1,449	25
Primitive Methodist Church	11,963	88
Reformed Methodist Church	326	13
Reformed Methodist Union Episcopal Church	1,025	22
Reformed Zion Union Apostolic Church	20,000	52
Southern Methodist Church	5,325	42
Union American Methodist Episcopal Church	9,369	71
Wesleyan Methodist Church of America	34,202	893

MORAVIANS

Moravian Church in America (Unitas Fratrum)	46,327	149
Bohemian and Moravian Brethren	208	2
Evangelical Unity of Bohemian-Moravian Brethren	5,000	32
National David Spiritual Temple of Christ Church Union, Inc., U.S.A.	40,565	56
New Apostolic Church of North America	6,888	73

OLD CATHOLIC CHURCHES

American Catholic Church	4,023	29
American Catholic Church, Archdiocese of New York	8,435	20
North American Old Roman Catholic Church	78,000	29
Old Catholic Church in America	6,274	28

PENTECOSTAL BODIES

Pentecostal Holiness Church	30,154	826
Pentecostal Fire-Baptized Holiness Church	1,444	74
Church of God in Christ (Pentecostal)	210	9
International Pentecostal Assemblies	6,333	98
Pentecostal Assemblies of the World	5,713	87
Pentecostal Church of God of America	60,000	580

United Pentecostal Church, Inc.	19,136	1,075
Calvary Pentecostal Church, Inc.	20,000	35
Pilgrim Holiness Church	40,661	1,075
Polish National Catholic Church	250,000	146

PRESBYTERIANS

Presbyterian Church in the U.S.A.	2,391,967	8,350
Presbyterian Church in the United States	675,489	3,647
Associate Presbyterian Church of North America	300	8
Associate Reformed Presbyterian Church (General Synod)	25,779	145
Cumberland Presbyterian Church	80,236	1,035
Colored Cumberland Presbyterian Church	30,000	121
Reformed Presbyterian Church in North America	5,585	74
Reformed Presbyterian Church in North America (General Synod)	1,426	11
Orthodox Presbyterian Church	13,928	72
United Presbyterian Church of North America	213,810	836
Protestant Episcopal Church	2,297,989	7,091

REFORMED BODIES

Reformed Church in America	179,085	759
Christian Reformed Church	142,818	322
Free Magyar Reformed Church in America	6,126	21
Reformed Episcopal Church	8,571	67
Roman Catholic Church	26,718,343	15,112
Salvation Army	215,094	1,381

SCANDINAVIAN EVANGELICAL BODIES

Evangelical Mission Covenant Church of America	51,009	475
Evangelical Free Church of America	12,000	200
Schwenkfelders	2,300	6
Social Brethren	521	14

SPIRITUALISTS

International General Assembly of Spiritualists	157,000	254
National Spiritualist Association, Inc.....................	8,942	265
National Christian Spiritual Alliance	5,487	267
Progressive Spiritual Church	11,347	21
Triumph the Church and Kingdom of God in Christ	15,500	300
Unitarians	78,100	370

UNITED BRETHREN

United Christian Church	676	14
Church of the United Brethren in Christ (Old Constitution)	18,167	316
United Holy Church of America	25,000	275
Universalists	62,927	426
Vedanta Society	1,021	11
Volunteers of America	23,500	93

TOTALS

234 bodies	82,069,872	278,442

Note: In the above figures the membership of the Church of Christ, Scientist, is not included. The impossibility of getting near an accurate figure is due to a prohibition in this church's *Manual* forbidding "the numbering of people and the reporting of such statistics for publication."

GLOSSARY OF TERMS

The definitions here depend largely upon four sources: *The Dictionary of Religion and Ethics*, by Matthews and Smith (Macmillan); *Funk and Wagnalls College Standard Dictionary*; *Webster's Dictionary* (Merriam); and the new *Comprehensive Desk Dictionary*, by Thorndike and Barnhart (Doubleday).

ABSOLUTION: The remission of guilt and penalty for sin, by a priest, following confession.

ADOPTION: A legal term appropriated by theology, originating in Paul and signifying the act by which the privileges of a child of God are conferred upon the believer in Christ.

ADVENTIST: A believer in the incarnation of God in Christ, at the time of Christ's birth, or in the Second Coming or Advent.

AFFUSION: The pouring or sprinkling of water in baptism.

ANNUNCIATION: The announcement by the angel Gabriel to the Virgin Mary that she was to be the mother of Christ.

ANOINTING: The act of consecrating by the application of oil, used in consecrating sacred objects or persons, as preparation for death or in completing the efficacy of baptism.

ANTINOMIANISM: The doctrine that the Gospel or the Christian faith does away with the old moral law, so that the Christian is not bound by it.

APOSTOLIC: Of or pertaining to an apostle, or according to the belief or practices of the apostles.

APOSTOLIC SUCCESSION: The doctrine of an unbroken line of succession in the episcopacy from the apostles to the present time, maintained in Greek, Roman, and Anglican churches.

ARMINIAN: The follower of Arminius (1560-1609), a Dutch Protestant theologian. Arminius denied Calvin's doctrine of unconditional predestination, limited atonement, and irresistible grace, and stood for universal salvation for all.

ATHANASIAN: The belief of Athanasius (293-373), who was a defender of the orthodox view of the divinity of Christ. He opposed and won over Arius at the Council of Nicea; Arius held that Christ was created by but was essentially different from the Father.

ATONEMENT: The reconciliation of the sinner with God through the sufferings of Jesus Christ.

AUTOCEPHALOUS: Ecclesiastically self-controlling, or having jurisdiction as an independent head. "Autocephali" was a term applied to bishops in early Christian times who recognized no ecclesiastical superior.

AUTONOMOUS: Self-governing, or independent.

BAN, THE: A sentence which amounts to excommunication or outlawry by the church upon those guilty of an act or speech forbidden by the church.

BAPTISM: The ceremonial application of water to a person, by either sprinkling, immersion, or affusion, as a sign of the washing away of sin and of admission into the church, as commanded by Christ in Matthew 28:19. "Spirit" baptism, in some sects, is a baptism by the Holy Ghost, not with water.

CALVINISTS: Those holding the faith of John Calvin (1509-64). (For a summary of the five points of Calvinism, see page 148.)

CATHOLICOS: An Oriental primate or head of a sect. "Catholikos" was a term assumed

191

by the spiritual head of the Armenian Church and later applied to several prelates under him.

CELIBACY: The state of being unmarried.

CHASTITY: The state of refraining from sexual relations in order to obtain religious or moral purity.

CHRISM: An ungent, usually olive oil or balm, used in the Greek and Roman Catholic churches for anointing at baptism, confirmation, ordination, and consecration services, and sometimes for extreme unction. Chrismation is the act of anointing.

CHRISTOCENTRIC: With Christ as the center.

CLASSIS: In some Reformed churches a court made up of ministers and ruling elders, with a status between a consistory and a synod, corresponding to the presbytery in Presbyterian churches. It may also mean the district it represents.

COMMUNION: The Lord's Supper. "Open" communion is a sacrament open to all Christians; "close" communion is closed to all except those of a particular faith or belief. The word is also used occasionally as a synonym for denomination.

CONFESSION: A statement of the religious beliefs of a religious body, or an admission of sin upon conversion.

CONFIRMATION: The initiatory rite by which persons are inducted into the church, or the approval of authorities by which the election of bishops is ratified by the church.

CONGREGATIONAL: The church polity which makes the authority of the local congregation supreme within its own area.

CONSECRATE: To set apart as sacred certain persons, animals, places, objects, or times.

CONSUBSTANTIATION: The theory of the substantial presence of Christ in the elements of the Lord's Supper; applied to Lutheran doctrine, it is denied by the Lutherans.

CREED: A statement of belief including the fundamentals considered necessary to salvation; a creed differs from a confession in that it may be held by Christians generally and recited in public worship.

DEACON: A minor church officer; its origin is often identified with the appointment of the seven in Acts 6:1-6.

DIOCESE: The territory of a church under the jurisdiction of a bishop.

DOCTRINE: That which is taught as the belief of a church.

ECCLESIASTICAL: Pertaining to the church or the clergy.

ECUMENICAL OR OECUMENICAL: General; universal; representing the whole Christian Church.

ELECTION: Selection of an individual by God for salvation.

EPISCOPAL: Having to do with bishops, or governed by bishops.

EUCHARIST: Holy Communion; the Lord's Supper.

EVANGELICAL: A word used to denote primary loyalty to the gospel of Christ, in contrast to ecclesiastical or rationalistic types of Christianity; spiritual-mindedness and zeal for Christian living, as distinguished from ritualism, and so on.

EXTREME UNCTION: See Unction.

FASTING: Going without food, or certain foods, for a specified period.

FOOT WASHING: The practice of washing the feet of fellow church members, sometimes as a ceremonial cleansing from defilement preparatory to worship, sometimes as an ordinance, by Mennonites, Dunkards, the Church of God, and so on.

FREE WILL: Man's power to choose between good and evil without compulsion or necessity.

FUNDAMENTALIST: One who believes in the infallibility of the Bible as inspired by God, and that it should be accepted literally, as distinguished from the modernist, who interprets the Bible in accordance with more modern scholarship or scientific knowledge.

GIFT OF TONGUES: Ecstatic speech induced by religious excitement or emotion.

GLOSSARY OF TERMS

GRACE: The gift of God to man of the divine favor and inner power necessary to salvation.

HIERARCHY: Government by priests or prelates, as in the Roman Catholic Church.

HOLINESS: A state of moral and spiritual purity and sinlessness, or designating persons set apart for religious service.

IMMACULATE CONCEPTION, THE: The dogma that the Virgin Mary was conceived free of original sin.

IMMERSION: Baptism by complete submersion in water.

IMPANATION: The doctrine that the body and blood of Christ are present in one substance in the bread and wine of the Eucharist after consecration, but without transubstantiation; held to be heretical by the Roman Catholic Church.

IMMORTALITY: Life after death; life imperishable.

INFALLIBILITY: The authority of the Scriptures as incapable of error; or a term applied to the Pope of Rome.

INSPIRATION, VERBAL: Signifying the supernatural influence upon the writers of the Scriptures by which divine authority was given their work and which places the Bible beyond error.

JUSTIFICATION: Freeing, or being freed, from the guilt or penalty of sin, and restored to divine favor.

JUDGMENT, JUDGMENT DAY: The act of judging by God on the last "Judgment Day," when rewards and punishments are to be declared.

KISS OF PEACE, OR HOLY KISS: A religious greeting or ceremony; a kiss of welcome.

LITURGY, LITURGICAL: A liturgy is a prescribed form or collection of forms for public worship; in "liturgical" churches rite and ceremony are more prominent than the emphasis upon preaching or evangelism.

LAYING ON OF HANDS: A rite of consecration.

LOVE FEAST: A common devotional meal partaken of by the early Christians, culminating in the Eucharist; sometimes called *agape*.

MASS, THE: The central worship service of the Roman Catholic Church, consisting of prayers and ceremonies; sometimes the Holy Eucharist as a sacrifice.

MODERNIST: *See* Fundamentalist.

MEDIUM: A person through whom supposed messages from the spirit world are sent, as in Spiritualism.

MONOPHYSITISM: The doctrine that Christ had but one composite divine-human nature.

NESTORIAN: Member of a Christian sect named after Nestorius, a fifth-century Syrian patriarch of Constantinople condemned as a heretic; still found in Turkey and Persia.

NICENE: Pertaining to Nicaea, where the Nicene Creed was adopted at the famous Council of 325, settling the controversy concerning the persons of the Trinity; properly called the Niceno-Constantinopolitan Creed.

ORDERS, HOLY: The clerical office, or the spiritual power distinguishing the ecclesiastical hierarchy from the laity.

ORDINANCE: A religious rite or ceremony not considered as a sacrament.

ORTHODOXY: Belief in doctrine considered correct and sound, or holding the commonly accepted faith.

PACIFISM: Opposition to all military ideals, preparedness, war, and so on.

PATRIARCH: A bishop of highest rank, standing above metropolitans and ruling patriarchates.

POLITY: A particular form or system of government.

PENANCE: An ecclesiastical punishment inflicted for sin, or a sacrament of the Christian Church.

PENTECOSTAL: The religious experience of conversion based upon the descent of the Holy Ghost upon the apostles at the Jewish Pentecost.

HANDBOOK OF DENOMINATIONS

PERFECTION: The complete realization of moral or spiritual possibilities in personal experience.

PLENARY: Full, complete; a "plenary council" is attended by all its qualified members.

PREDESTINARIAN: A believer in predestinarianism—that all events are predetermined by God, and that each person's eternal destiny is fixed by divine decree.

PREMILLENARIANISM: Belief that the personal visible return of Christ will precede his reign for a thousand years on earth; postmillenarians believe that the return will come at the end of the Millenium.

PRESBYTERY: A church court or assembly having the ecclesiastical or spiritual rule and oversight of a district, or the district itself.

REGENERATION: A new birth, re-creation, a radical renewal of life, or conversion.

REMISSION OF SIN: Pardon, or forgiveness, for sin.

REPENTANCE: Turning from a sinful to a godly life.

REPROBATION: Eternal condemnation, the fate of those not included in God's election.

SABBATARIAN: One who believes that the seventh day should be observed as the Christian Sabbath.

SACERDOTAL: A term denoting a religious system in which everything is valued in relation to the ministrations of the priestly order.

SACRAMENT: A religious rite composed of two elements, a physical sign and a spiritual good.

SALVATION: The rescue of man from evil or guilt by God's power, that he may obtain blessedness.

SANCTIFICATION: The work of the Holy Spirit by which the believer is set free from sin and exalted to holiness of life.

SECOND COMING: The second advent of Jesus; see Premillenarianism.

SEE: The local seat from which a bishop, archbishop, or the Pope exercises jurisdiction.

SYNOD: An ecclesiastical council, either of regular standing or appointed as needed; in Presbyterian churches a body between the presbyteries and the General Assembly.

TOTAL DEPRAVITY: The equivalent of original sin, every human faculty having an innate evil taint.

TONSURED: The shaved head of a person admitted to a monastic order, or to holy orders.

TONGUES, GIFT OF: An ecstatic utterance induced by religious excitement.

TRANSFIGURATION: Change in form or appearance, such as the transfiguration of Jesus (Mark 9:2-10).

TRANSMUTATION: The change from one nature, substance, or form to another.

TRINE IMMERSION: A form of baptism in which the candidate is immersed three successive times, in the name of the Father, Son, and Holy Ghost.

TRINITARIAN: A believer in the Trinty—that there is a union of Father, Son, and Holy Ghost in one divine nature.

UNCTION: A ceremonial anointing with oil, as in Extreme Unction in case of death or imminent death.

UNIAT: Persons or churches acknowledging the supremacy of the Pope, but maintaining their own liturgies or rites.

UNITARIAN: The theology which insists upon the unity of God, denying the doctrine of the Trinity.

INDEX

Ab, Feast of, 103
Abdu'l-Bahá, 24, 25
Act of Toleration, 64
Act of Uniformity, 64
Adler, Felix, 21
Advance, 67
Advanced Contemplative and Intellectual Sphere (Spiritualist), 177
Advent Christian Association, 18
Advent Christian Church, 16, 17-18
Adventists, 15-19, 49, 56, 91, 100, 108
African Methodist Church, 131
African M. E. Church, 134, 137
African M. E. Zion Church, 107, 131, 134, 137
African Orthodox Church, 19
African Orthodox Church of New York, 19
African Union Church, 138
African Union Methodist Protestant Church, 134-35
Age to Come Adventists, 19
Albanian Orthodox Church, 74
Albright, Jacob, 84
Alemanni, The, 166
Alexander, Archbishop, 77
Alfred University, 39
Allegheny Theological Seminary, 150
Allen, Richard, 134
Alvarez, Archbishop, 142
Amana Society, the, 20
American Baptist Association, 33
American Baptist Convention, 27, 28-30, 31, 35
American Baptist Foreign Missionary Society, 28, 29
American Baptist Home Missionary Society, 28
American Baptist Missionary Society, 28
American Baptist Publication Society, 27, 28
American Baptist Theological Seminary, 31
American Board of Commissioners for Foreign Missions, 27, 65, 152, 163
American Catholic Church, 142
American Catholic Church, Archdiocese of N. Y., 142
American Ethical Culture Union, 21
American Friends Service Committee, 93
American Holy Orthodox Catholic Apostolic Eastern Church, 75

American Holy Orthodox Catholic Eastern Church, 73
American Jewish Committee, 105
American Jewish Yearbook, 104
American Joint Distribution Committee, 105
American Lutheran Church, 115, 117, 120
American Lutheran Conference, 115, 117, 118
American Millerite Association, 15
American National Baptist Convention, 32, 34
American National Educational Baptist Convention, 32
American Rescue Workers, 22
American Unitarian Association, 66, 179, 180
Amherst College, 65
Amish, 125, 126
Amish Mennonite Church, 126
Amman, Jacob, 125
Anabaptists, 26, 124, 178
Anastasy, Archbishop, 79
Ancient and Mystical Order of Po-aktun, 124
Ancient Christian Fellowship, 76
Andrew, Bishop James O., 131
Angelus Temple, 99
Anglo-Catholics, 112, 160
Ansgarii Synod, 174
Anti-Defamation League, B'nai B'rith, 105
Anti-mission Baptists, 36
Anti-Pedobaptists, 26
Antioch, Patriarch of, 80
Apache Indians, 120
Apostles' Creed, 19, 48, 115, 120, 131, 139, 160, 161, 163, 167
Apostolic Christian Church of America, 86
Apostolic Christian Church (Nazarean), 86
Apostolic Episcopal Church, 73, 75-76
Apostolic Faith Mission, 86
Apostolic Methodist Church, 135
Apostolic Overcoming Holy Church of God, 22
Apostolic Segnatura (Roman Catholic), 169
Ararat, Mount, 23
Arles, Council of, 157
Armageddon, 100
Armenian Orthodox Church in America, 22
Arminian Baptists, 35
Arminians, 78

INDEX

Buddha, 24, 47
Buddhist Churches of America, 47-48
Buddhist Mission of North America, 48
Bulgarian Orthodox Church, 76
Bulgarian Orthodox Mission, 76
Burgundians, 166
Burkhart, Roy, 98
Burning Bush, 88
Burrus, K. H., 60, 61

Caesar Bardas, 72
California Yearly Meeting, 97
Calvary Pentecostal Church, Inc., 145
Calvin College and Seminary, 164
Calvin, John, 26, 114, 147, 148, 162
Campbell, Alexander, 60, 67, 69
Campbell, Thomas, 69
Campbellites, 67
Cancellaria, The, 169
Canterbury, Archbishop of, 158
Capuchins, 166
Carey, William, 26
Carfora, Archbishop C. H., 113, 142
Carroll, Charles, 167
Carroll, Daniel, 167
Carroll, John, 167
Cartier, 166
Case of the Episcopal Churches in the U. S. Considered, 158
Cathedral of St. John, N. Y. C., 161
Catholic Apostolic Church, 48, 141
Catholic Directory, 171
Catholic University of America, 167
Central Conference of American Rabbis, 104
Central Conference of the Mennonite Church of N. A., 126
Central Mennonite Conference, 126
Ceylon and India General Mission, 51
Chalcedon, Council of, 58, 73
Channing, William Ellery, 179
Charles the Great, 72
Chase, Bishop Philander, 159
Cheshier, the Rev. Isaac, 181
Chesser, H. L., 54, 55
Chicago Tract Society, 51
Children of Light, 92
Children of Truth, 92
Christ Missionary and Industrial College, 52
Christadelphians, 48
Christian Advocate, The, 133
Christian Alliance, 49
Christian Association of Washington, Pa., 69
Christian Catholic Apostolic Church in Zion, 50
Christian Church, 67-68
Christian Congregation, 87
Christian Endeavor Society, 66-67
Christian Faith Band, 87

Christian Herald, The, 177, 185
Christian Indicator, 87
Christian and Missionary Alliance, 49-50
Christian Nation Church, 50
Christian Reformed Church, 162, 164
Christian Science *Sentinel, Journal, Quarterly, Monitor*, 54
Christian Spiritual Voice, 140
Christian Union, 50
Christian Union Churches, 60
Christian Unity Baptist Association, 33-34
Christian, William, 62
Christians. *See* Disciples of Christ
Christmas Conference (Methodist), 130
Christ's Sanctified Holy Church (Colored), 51-52
Chrysostom, St. John, 77
Church Abroad, 79
Church of the Blessed Hope, 19
Church of the Brethren (Conservative Dunkers), 41-42, 43
Church of Christ (Holiness) U.S.A., 52
Church of Christ (Scientist), 52-54, 91
Church of Christ (Temple Lot), 111
Church to Come, 19
Church Congress (Protestant Episcopal), 159
Church Congress (Romanian Orthodox), 77
Church of Daniel's Band, 87
Church of the East and of the Assyrians, 58
Church of England, 85, 92, 129, 130, 131, 139, 157, 158, 160
Church Equality Baptists, 33
Church of God, 54-57, 61
Church of God (Abrahamic Faith), 18
Church of God (Anderson, Ind.), 55-56
Church of God (Apostolic), 87
Church of God in Christ, 57-58
Church of God in Christ (Mennonite), 126
Church of God (New Dunkers), 41, 43-44
Church of God (Oregon, Ill.), 18
Church of God as Organized by Christ, 87-88
Church of God (Pentecostal), 144
Church of God and Saints in Christ, 57
Church of God (Seventh-day), 56
Church of God (Tomlinson groups), 54-55, 143
Church of Illumination, 97-98
Church of Jesus Christ (Bickertonites), 111
Church of Jesus Christ (Cutlerites), 111
Church of Jesus Christ of Latter-day Saints, 110
Church of Jesus Christ (Strangites), 111-12
Church of the Living God, Christian Workers for Fellowship, 62
Church of the Living God, General Assembly, 62

197

INDEX

199

INDEX

INDEX

INDEX

Religious Society of Friends of Philadelphia and Vicinity, 196
Reorganized Church of Jesus Christ of Latter-day Saints, 110-11
Republican Methodists, 67, 131
Restitution Church, 19
Restitutionists, 19
Review and Herald Publishing Association, 16
Revolution, American, 65, 93, 158, 162, 166, 167
Rhenish Missionary Society, the, 82
Rhodes, S. W., 16
Rieger, Johann Bartholomew, 82
Rigdon, Sidney, 111
River Brethren, 41, 46-47
Roberts, the Rev. B. T., 135
Robinson, John, 64
Roman Catholic Church, 72, 73, 75, 79, 102, 112, 113, 138, 141, 142, 143, 146, 148, 158, 165-72, 175
Roman Curia, 168
Romanian Orthodox Church, 77
Romanian Orthodox Episcopate (Diocese) of America, 77-78
Rosh Hashana, 103
Russell, Charles Taze, 100
Russellites, 100
Russian Orthodox Church, 78-79
Rutgers (Queens) College, 162
Rutherford, Judge J. F., 100

Sacred Congregation for the Propagation of the Faith, 170
Sacred Depository of Faith, 167
Sacred Penitentiary, 169
Sacred Roman Rota, 169
Sahak, St., 23
St. Basil's Academy, 77
St. David Orthodox Christian Spiritual Seminary, 140
St. Lawrence College, 183
St. Luke's Hospital (N.Y.C.), 159
St. Sava's Serbian Monastery, 79
St. Sophia, Council of, 72
Salem College, 39
Salomon Korteniemi Lutheran Society, 122
Salvation Army, 172-74
Salvation Army Corporation, 172
Santamaria, John, 100
Santamaria, Rocco, 100
Saracens, 166
Savonarola, 166
Saxons, 166
Scandinavian Augustana Synod of North America, 117
Scandinavian Evangelical Bodies, 174
Scandinavian Missionary Alliance, 174

Schlatter, Michael, 84
Schmalkald Articles, 113, 115, 120
Scholte, Dominie, 163
Schwartz, Bishop, 141
Schwenkfelders, 175
Schwenkfeld von Ossig, Caspar, 175
Science and Health with Key to the Scriptures, 52, 54
Seabury, Dr. Samuel, 158
Secession (Presbyterian) Church, Ireland, 69
Semple, Robert, 99
Separate Baptists, 27, 34, 38, 40
Separatists, 26, 64
Serbian Orthodox Church, 79
Serbian Patriarchate of Yugoslavia, 79
Serious Call (William Law), 129
Seven Keys, The, 57
Seventh-Day Adventists, 16-17
Seventh-Day Adventists, General Conference of, 17
Seventh-Day Baptists, 16, 38-39
Seventh-Day Baptists (German, 1728), 39, 41
Shabuoth (Feast of Weeks), 103
Sheerith Israel, 102
Shoghi Rabbini, 25
Short, David William, 140
Simons, Menno, 26, 124
Simpson, A. B., 49
Sisters of Charity, 171
Sisters of Mercy, 171
Slovak Evangelical Lutheran Church, 120
Slovak Evangelical Synod of America, 119
Smith, Captain John, 157
Smith, Elder E. D., 178
Smith, Hyrum, 108, 109
Smith, Joseph, 107, 108, 110, 111
Smith, Jr., Joseph, 110
Smyth, John, 26
Social Brethren, 175-76
Society of Friends (Five Years Meeting), 95-96
Society for the Propagation of the Faith, 170
Society for the Propagation of the Gospel, 129, 158
Society of St. Vincent de Paul, 171
Socinians, 178
Söderblom, Bishop Nathan, 116
Soule, Bishop Joshua, 132
Southcott, Johanna, 97
Southern Baptist Convention, 27, 28, 29, 30-31, 37
Southern Baptist Theological Seminary, 31
Southern Methodist Church, 137
Southern Methodist Layman, 137
Southwestern Baptist Theological Seminary, 31
Spiritualists, 91, 176-77

HANDBOOK OF DENOMINATIONS

Spiritualist's Manual, 77
Spurling, the Rev. R., 56
Stauffer, Jacob, 128
Stauffer Mennonite Church, 128
Stinson, Benoni, 35
Stone, Barton W., 67, 70, 87
Strangites, 111-12
Strawbridge, Robert, 130
Strong, James J., 111
Stuber, Stanley I., 160
Stuyvesant, Peter, 102
Sukkoth (Feast of Tabernacles), 103
Sulpicians, 166
Summer Land, the, 177
Suomi Synod, 115, 122-23
Supreme Ecclesiastical Council, 75
Swami Abhedananda, 183
Swami Vivekananda, 183
Swedenborg, Emanuel, 62-63
Swedenborg Society in America, 63
Swedenborgian Foundation, 63
Swedenborgians, 62-63
Swedish Evangelical Mission Covenant Church of America, 174
Swedish Free Baptists, 36
Swiss Brethren, 124
Synagogue Council of America, 104
Synod of Dort, 162, 163
Synod of South and North Holland, 82
Synodical Conference (Lutheran), 115, 116, 119, 120, 121, 123
Syrian Antiochian Orthodox Archdiocese of New York and all North America, 80
Syrian Antiochian Orthodox Church, 80
Syrian Church of Antioch, 142
Syro-Jacobite Church of Malabar, 142

Tabernacle Pentecostal Church, 143
Taike (China) Mission, 175
Talmud, 102, 105
Tammuz, Fast of, 103
Taufers, the, 40, 124
Tebeth, Fast of, 103
Tennent, Jr., William, 149
Tennent, William, 149
Thaddeus (apostle), 22
Theosophical Society, 112
Thirty-Nine Articles of Religion, 85, 131, 139
Thomas, John, 48
Thompson, the Rev. G. Tabor, 177
Thurston, the Rev. Charles, 158
Tiffin Agreement, the, 164, 165
Tikhon, Patriarch, 77
Today, 152
Toleration Act (1689), 92
Tomlinson, A. J., 54, 55
Tomlinson, Homer A., 55
Tomlinson, Milton A., 55

Torah, 102, 105, 106
Tosks, 75
Treatise on the Atonement (Ballou), 182
Treatise on Christian Perfection (William Law), 129
Trinity Church (N.Y.C.), 158
Triumph the Church and Kingdom of God in Christ, 178
Truth About the Pharisees, 102
Tufts College, 183
Tunkers, 40
Two-Seed-in-the-Spirit Predestinarian Baptists, 39

Ukrainian Orthodox Church of America, 80
Uniat Churches, 78-79
Union of American Hebrew Congregations, 104
Union American M. E. Church, 131, 138
Union Church of Africans, 138
Union of Orthodox Jewish Congregations in America, 104
Union of Orthodox Rabbis of the U.S.A. and Canada, 104
Union Theological Seminary, N.Y.C., 150
Union Theological Seminary, Richmond, Va., 150
Unitarians, 49, 66, 91, 178-80, 181
Unitas Fratrum (Moravians), 138, 139
United American Freewill Baptist Church (Colored), 40
United Baptist Churches for Christ in Virginia, 38
United Baptists, 34, 37, 40
United Brethren, 180
United Brethren in Christ, 84, 180
United Christian Church, 180
United Conference of Icelandic Churches, 180
United Evangelical Church, 84
United Evangelical Lutheran Church in America, 115, 117, 119, 123
United Evangelical Synod of the East, 82
United Holy Church of America, 181
United Jewish Appeal, 105
United Lutheran Church in America, 115, 116, 117, 121, 123
United Missionary Church (Mennonite), 127
United Norwegian Church, 118
United Palestine Appeal, 105
United Pentecostal Church, Inc., 144, 145
United Presbyterian Church of N.A., 154, 156-57
United Service for New Americans, 105
United Synagogue of America, 104
United Synod of the Presbyterian Church, 150, 151

INDEX

United Synod of the South (Lutheran), 115, 117, 121

United Zion's Children, 41, 46, 47

Universalists, 91, 181-83

University of Judaism, 105

Van Raalte, Dominie Albertus, 162-63

Vandals, the, 166

Vattra (Albanian Federation), 75

Vedanta Society, 183

Vedas, the, 183

Vilatte, Archbishop Joseph Rene, 19, 142

Virginia House of Burgesses, 158

Vitaly, Archbishop, 79

Vladimir the Great, 78, 80

Voliva, Wilbur Glen, 50

Volunteer Prison League, 183

Volunteers of America, 183

Walpole, Horace, 150

Ware, Henry, 179

Warren Association of Rhode Island, 28

Washington, George, 158

Watch Tower Bible and Tract Society, 100

Watch Tower Bible and Tract Society of N.Y., 100

Watch Tower Bible and Tract Society of Pa., 100

Weaver Mennonites, 128

Webb, Captain Thomas, 130

Weiss, George Michael, 82

Welsh Calvinistic Methodists, 151

Welsh Tract, 34

Wentz, Abdel R., 113

Wesley Chapel, N.Y.C., 130

Wesley, Charles, 129

Wesley, John, 56, 58, 129, 130, 131, 139

Wesleyan Methodist Church of America, 138

Wesleyan Methodist Connection, 130, 136

Western News Review, 62

Western Theological Seminary, 163

Western Yearly Meeting, 97

Westminster Assembly of Divines, 148, 153

Westminster Confession, 139, 140, 148, 149, 151, 154, 155, 156, 157

Westminster Large and Shorter Catechisms, 148, 149, 156

Weyeneth, Benedict, 86

Wheeler, Frederick, 16

White, Mrs. Alma, 89

White, Bishop William, 134, 158

White, Ellen Harmon, Mrs., 16, 18, 56

White, James, 16

White, Mrs. Martha, 86

Whitefield, George, 26, 38, 65, 129, 131, 139, 149

Whitefield Tabernacle (London), 181

Whitman, Marcus, 150

Whittier, John, 93

Wiebe, Jacob A., 127

Wilburites, 93, 96

William and Mary College, 158

Williams College, 65

Williams, Roger, 26, 64

Wilmington (Ohio) Yearly Meeting, 97

Wilson, President, 173

Winebrenner, John, 61

Wisler, Bishop Jacob, 128

Witherspoon, John, 149-50

Woolman, John, 93

World Council of Churches, 67, 116, 161

World's Crisis, The, 18

Wycliffe, John, 166

Yale University, 65

Yeshiva University, 105

Yiddish Scientific Institute, 105

Yom Kippur, 103

Young, Brigham, 108, 109, 110

Zinzendorf, Count, 138, 139

Zion City, Ill., 50

Zion Latter-Day Saints, 111

Zion Union Apostolic Church, 137

Zionism, 105, 106

Zoroaster, 24

Zuni Indians, 164

Zwingli, Ulrich, 114, 124, 162

207

S